TERRY BROOKS

DARK WRAITH of SHANNARA

Illustrated by Edwin David
Adapted by Robert Place Napton

orbit

www.orbitbooks.net

ORBIT

First published in the United States in 2008 by Del Rey Books,
an imprint of The Random House Publishing Group
First published in Great Britain in 2008 by Orbit
Reprinted 2008

Adapter: Robert Place Napton
Inker: Dennis Crisostomo
Toner: Brian Buccellato
Lettering: Dana Hayward

A CIP catalogue record for this book
is available from the British Library.

ISBN 978-1-84149-638-2

Printed and bound in Great Britain by
MPG Books Ltd, Bodmin, Cornwall

Orbit
An imprint of
Little, Brown Book Group
100 Victoria Embankment
London EC4Y 0DY

An Hachette Livre UK Company
www.hachettelivre.co.uk

www.orbitbooks.net

contents

prologue

The Great Wars have come and gone, and a world much like our own has succumbed to an armageddon of its own making.

A thousand years have passed. Now science—once thought to hold all the secrets of the universe—has been replaced by a new power with an arcane name . . . magic.

Using this power, new races of Druids, Men, Dwarfs, Trolls, Gnomes, and Elves have struggled to bring a lasting order to the new world. New heroes have emerged to meet the challenge, and new legends have been born.

In the tale known as The Sword of Shannara, the Warlock Lord—once a wise Druid named Brona—succumbed to the dark magic of a dread tome known as the Ildatch and sought mastery over the other races. The Druid Allanon, protector of the Four Lands, conscripted Shea Ohmsford, descendant of the great Elven house of Shannara, to rediscover the mythic sword. After much adventure, the blade of truth was recovered, and it empowered Shea to vanquish the Warlock Lord once and for all.

In The Elfstones of Shannara, Allanon recruited Shea's grandson, Wil Ohmsford, and charged him with protecting the Elven girl Amberle on her quest to find the Bloodfire, which would save the Ellcrys tree and prevent imprisoned demons from overrunning the land. To complete his quest, Wil was forced to use the magic Elfstones—and in the process he permanently altered his own genetic makeup.

For the first time the Ohmsfords had magic in their blood, and Wil's daughter, Brin, and son, Jair, were born with the power of the wishsong. In The Wishsong of Shannara, Jair and Brin, like their father and great-grandfather before them, reluctantly embraced the Ohmsford heritage and answered the call of Allanon. The Ildatch—the very book of dark magic that had subverted the Warlock Lord—was working its twisted spell on his onetime mortal followers, transforming them into the Mord Wraiths, and only Brin and Jair could prevent the ruin of the world. The quest was a costly one, for Allanon was slain, and Jair lost many companions, including his most trusted, Weapons Master Garet Jax, in a fierce battle to save his sister, Brin, from becoming the Ildatch's dark minion. Ultimately, Brin used the wishsong to rend the Ildatch to shreds, burning it alive . . .

Though the price was high, Jair and Brin were successful. Evil was vanquished . . .

Or so they thought.

chapter 1

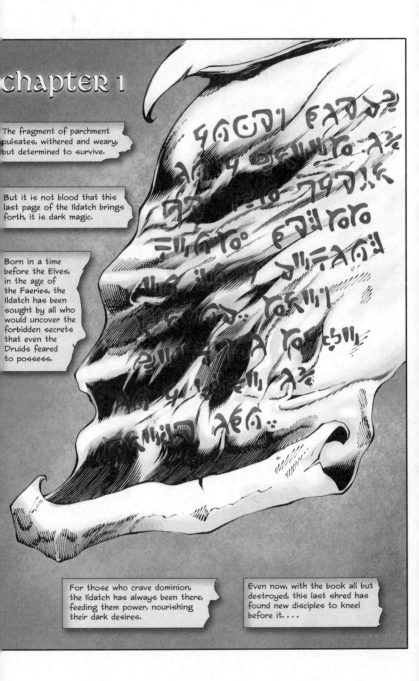

The fragment of parchment pulsates, withered and weary, but determined to survive.

But it is not blood that this last page of the Ildatch brings forth, it is dark magic.

Born in a time before the Elves, in the age of the Faeries, the Ildatch has been sought by all who would uncover the forbidden secrets that even the Druids feared to possess.

For those who crave dominion, the Ildatch has always been there, feeding them power, nourishing their dark desires.

Even now, with the book all but destroyed, this last shred has found new disciples to kneel before it. . . .

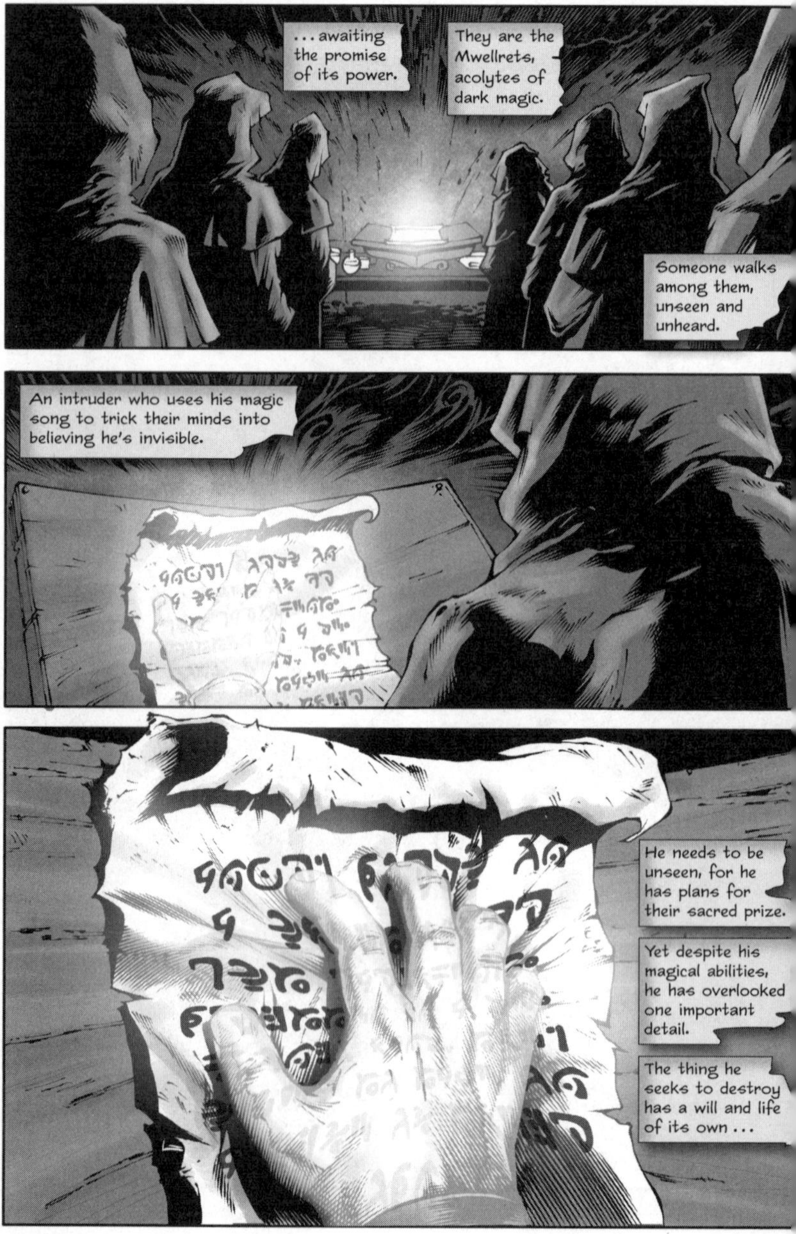

...awaiting the promise of its power.
They are the Mwellrets, acolytes of dark magic.
Someone walks among them, unseen and unheard.
An intruder who uses his magic song to trick their minds into believing he's invisible.
He needs to be unseen, for he has plans for their sacred prize.
Yet despite his magical abilities, he has overlooked one important detail.
The thing he seeks to destroy has a will and life of its own...

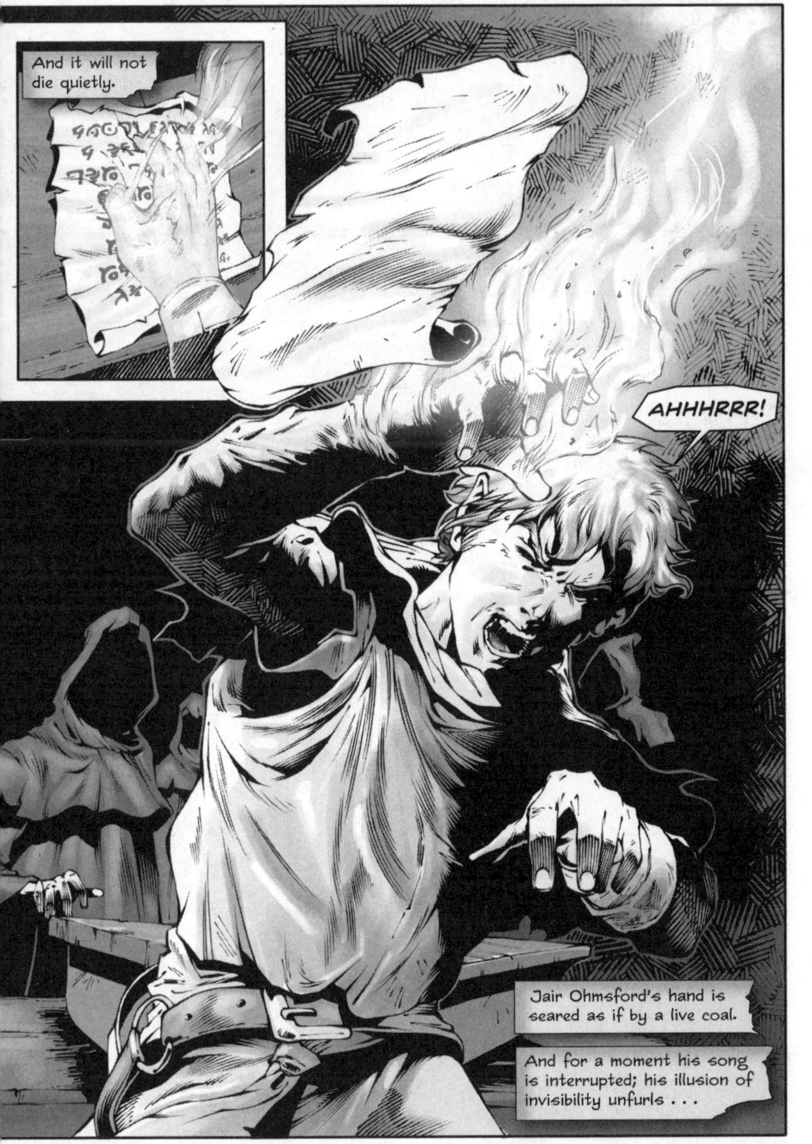
And it will not die quietly.
AHHHRRR!
Jair Ohmsford's hand is seared as if by a live coal.
And for a moment his song is interrupted; his illusion of invisibility unfurls . . .

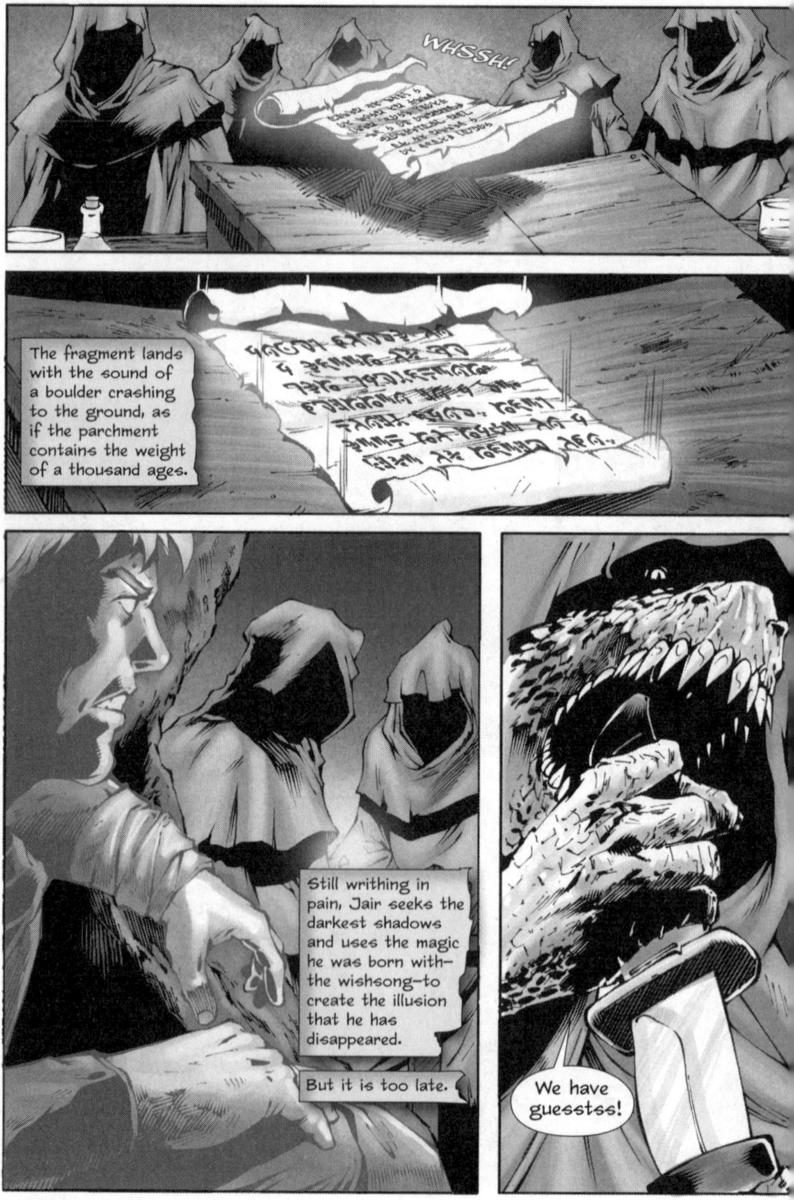
WHSSH!
The fragment lands with the sound of a boulder crashing to the ground, as if the parchment contains the weight of a thousand ages.
Still writhing in pain, Jair seeks the darkest shadows and uses the magic he was born with—the wishsong—to create the illusion that he has disappeared.
But it is too late.
We have guesstss!

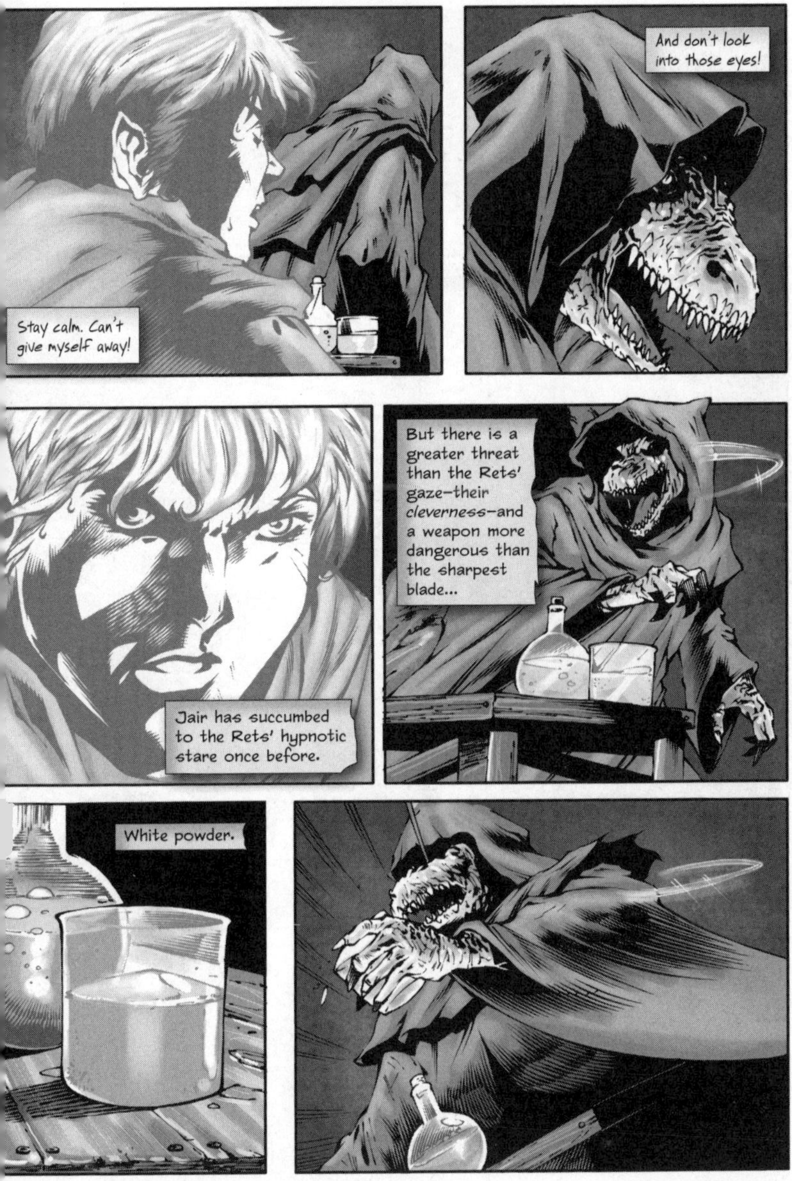
Stay calm. Can't give myself away!
And don't look into those eyes!
Jair has succumbed to the Rets' hypnotic stare once before.
But there is a greater threat than the Rets' gaze—their *cleverness*—and a weapon more dangerous than the sharpest blade...
White powder.

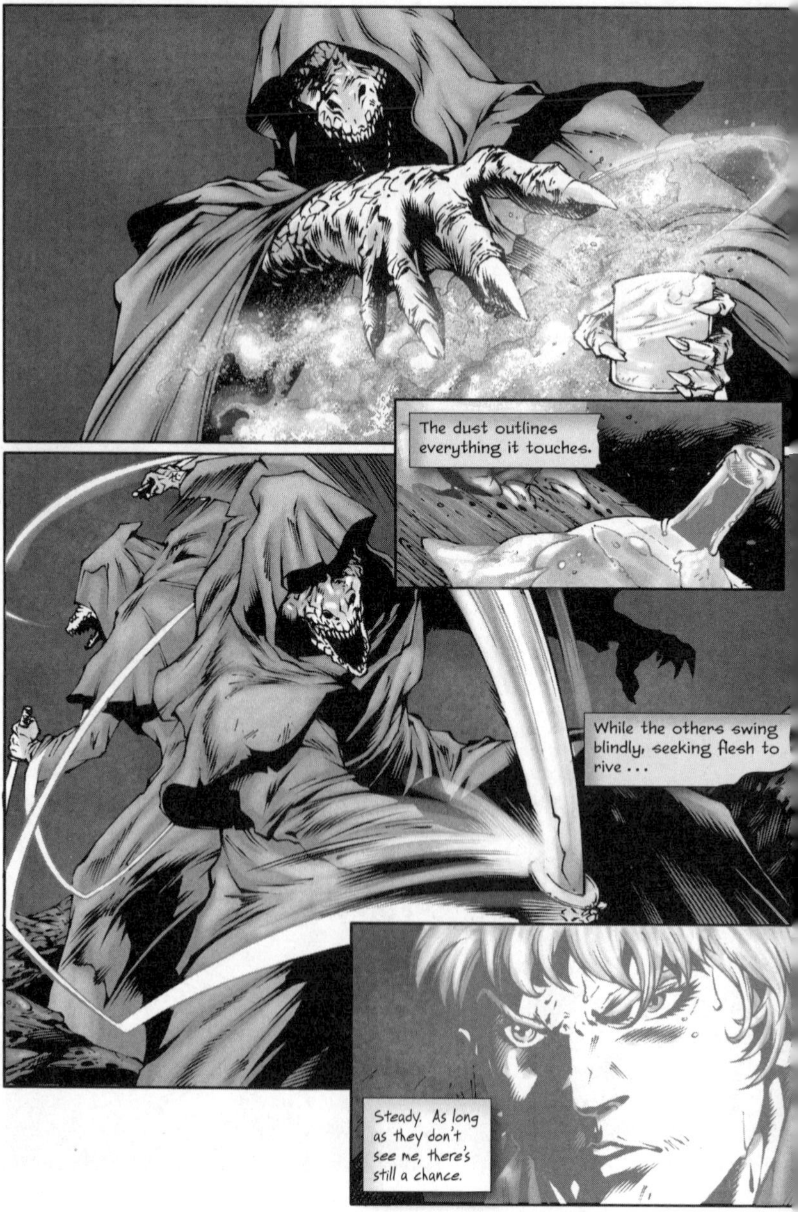
The dust outlines everything it touches.
While the others swing blindly, seeking flesh to rive . . .
Steady. As long as they don't see me, there's still a chance.

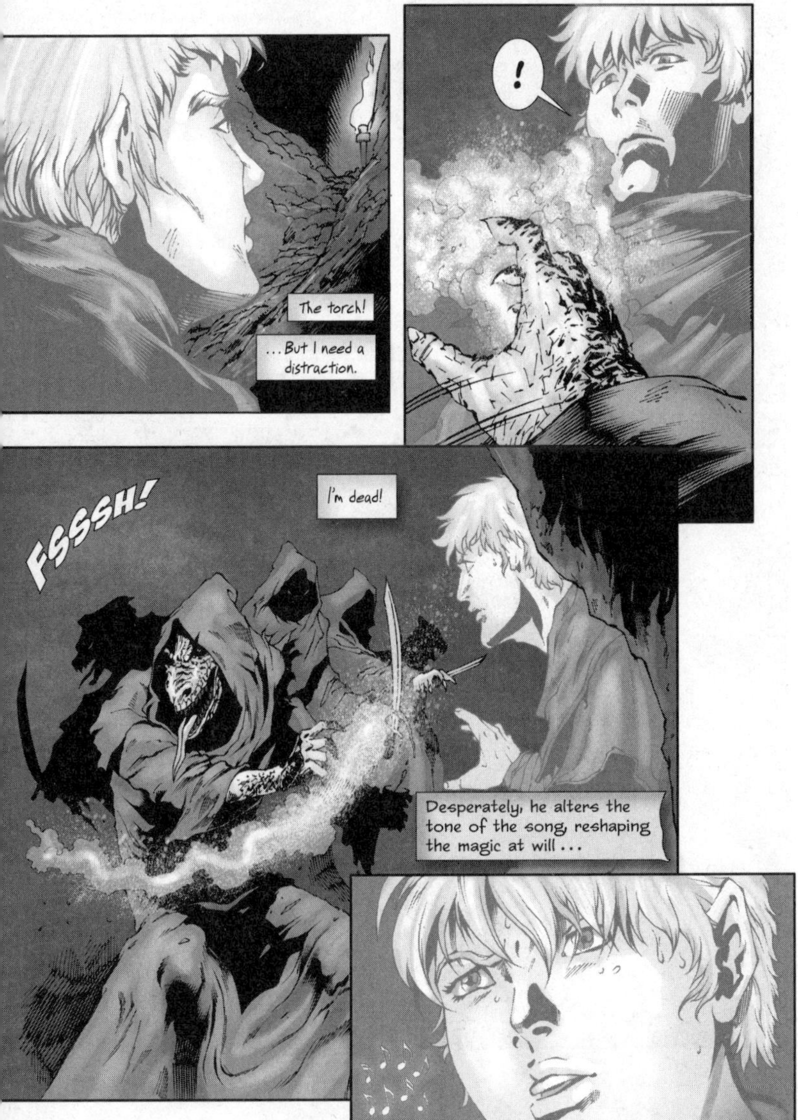
The torch!
. . . But I need a distraction.
!
I'm dead!
FSSSH!
Desperately, he alters the tone of the song, reshaping the magic at will . . .

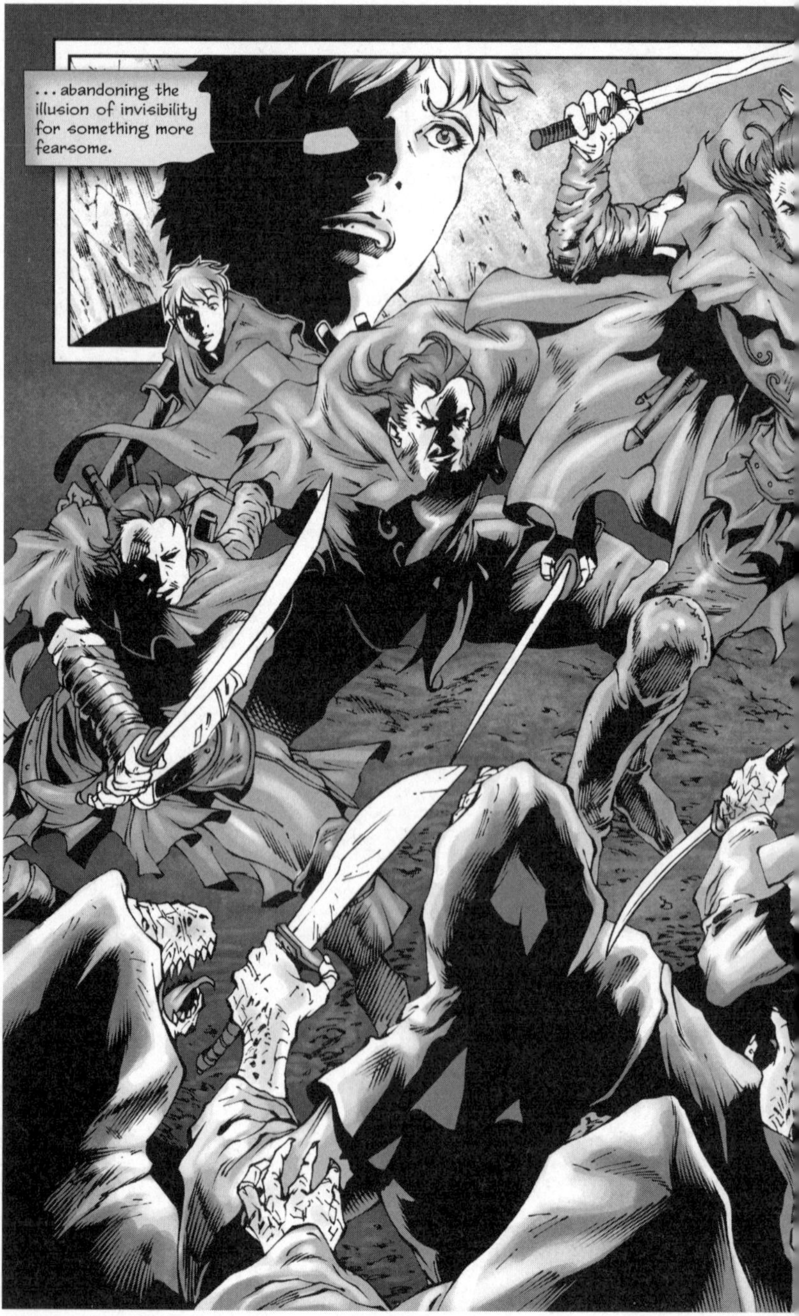
...abandoning the illusion of invisibility for something more fearsome.

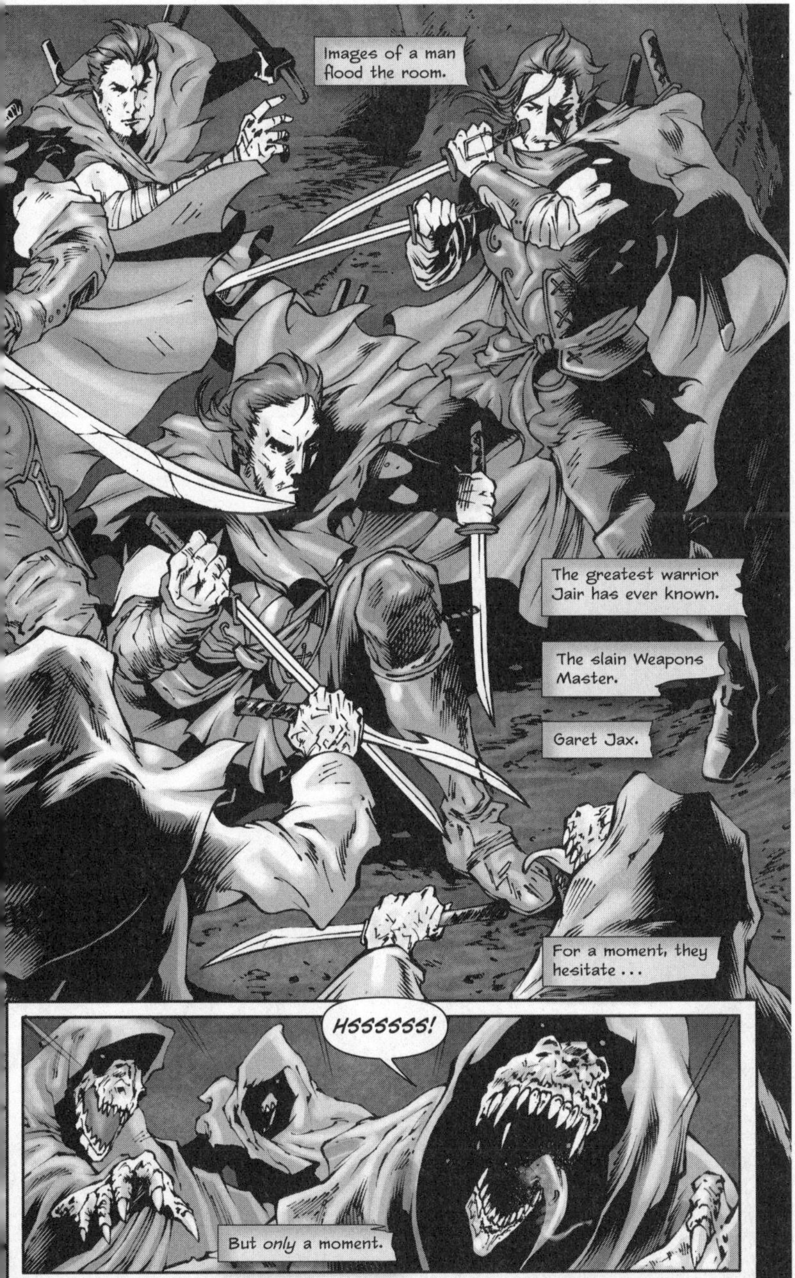
Images of a man flood the room.
The greatest warrior Jair has ever known.
The slain Weapons Master.
Garet Jax.
For a moment, they hesitate . . .
HSSSSSS!
But *only* a moment.

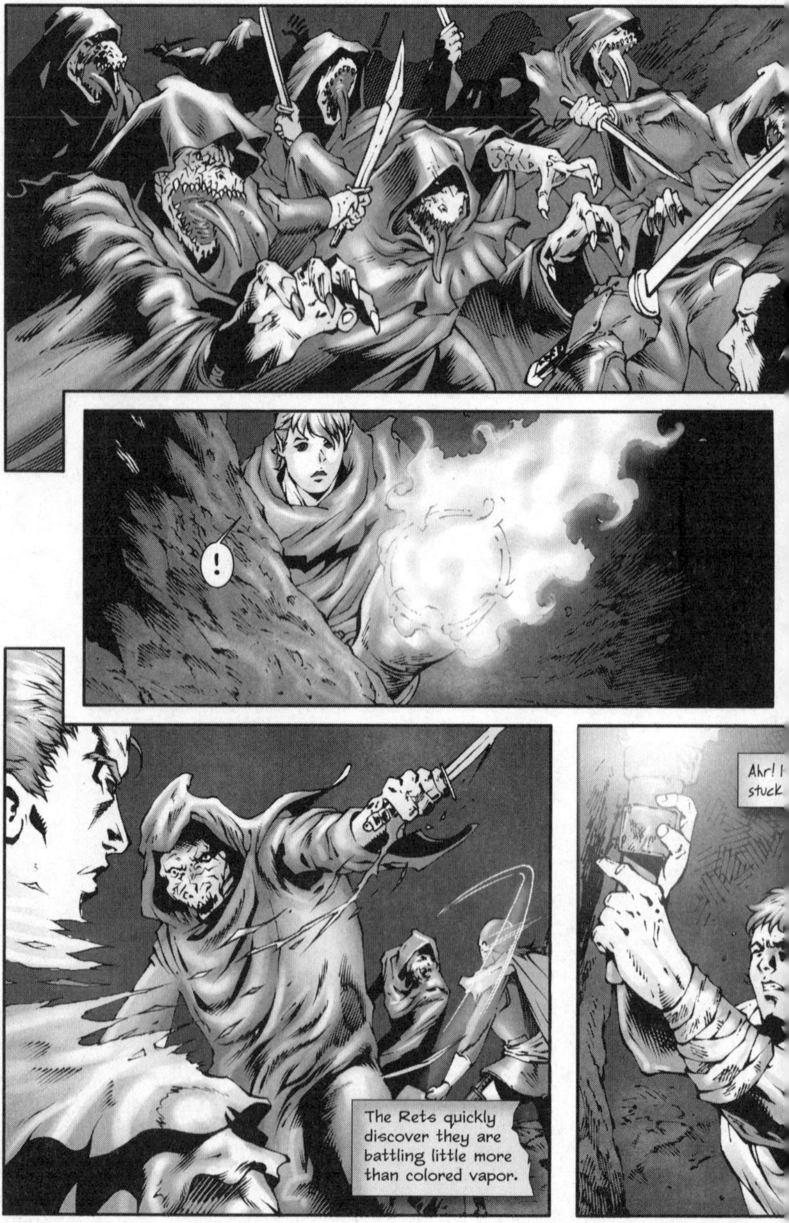
!
The Rets quickly discover they are battling little more than colored vapor.
Ahr! I
stuck

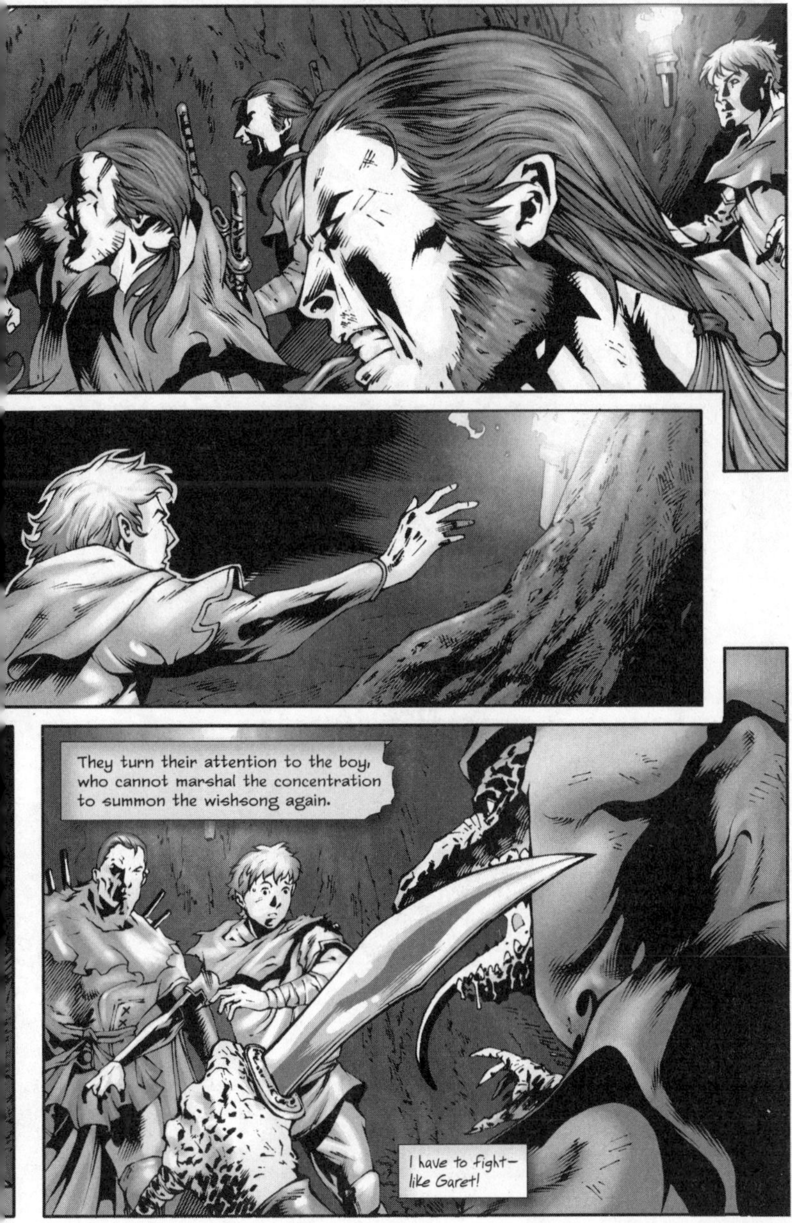
They turn their attention to the boy, who cannot marshal the concentration to summon the wishsong again.
I have to fight— like Garet!

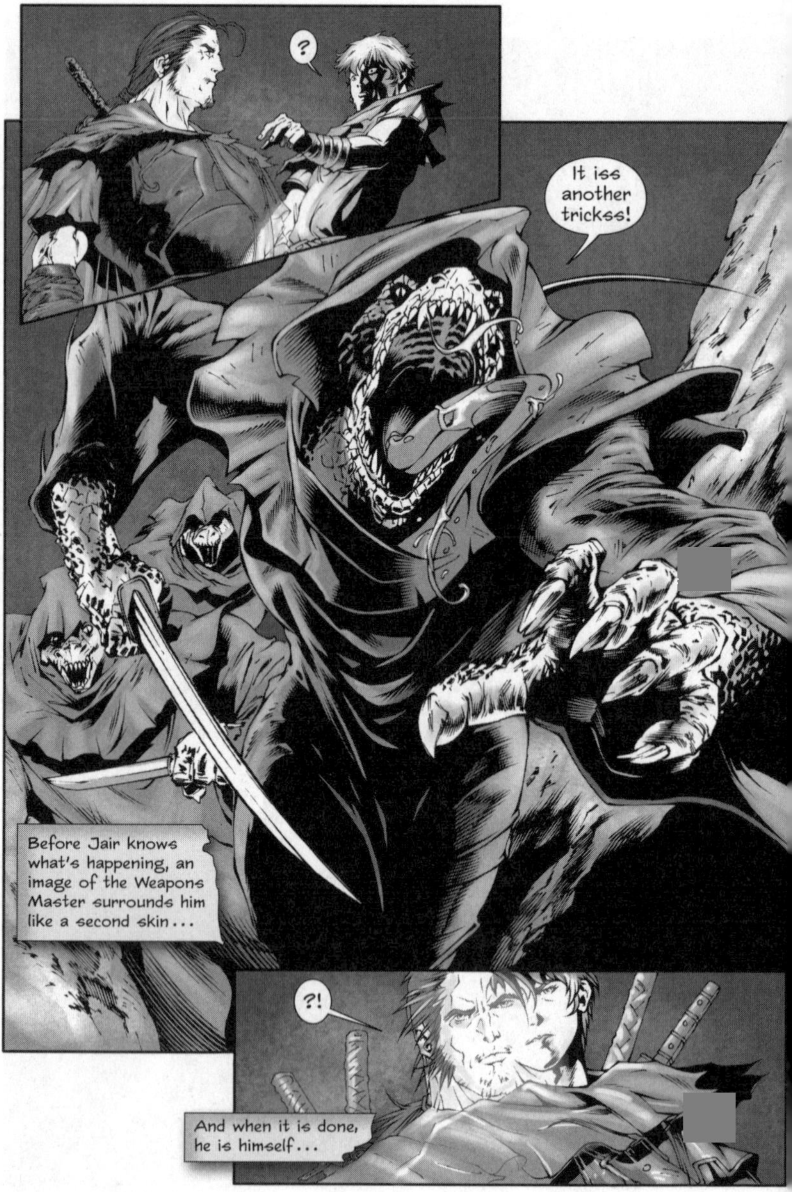
?
It iss another trickss!
Before Jair knows what's happening, an image of the Weapons Master surrounds him like a second skin...
?!
And when it is done, he is himself...

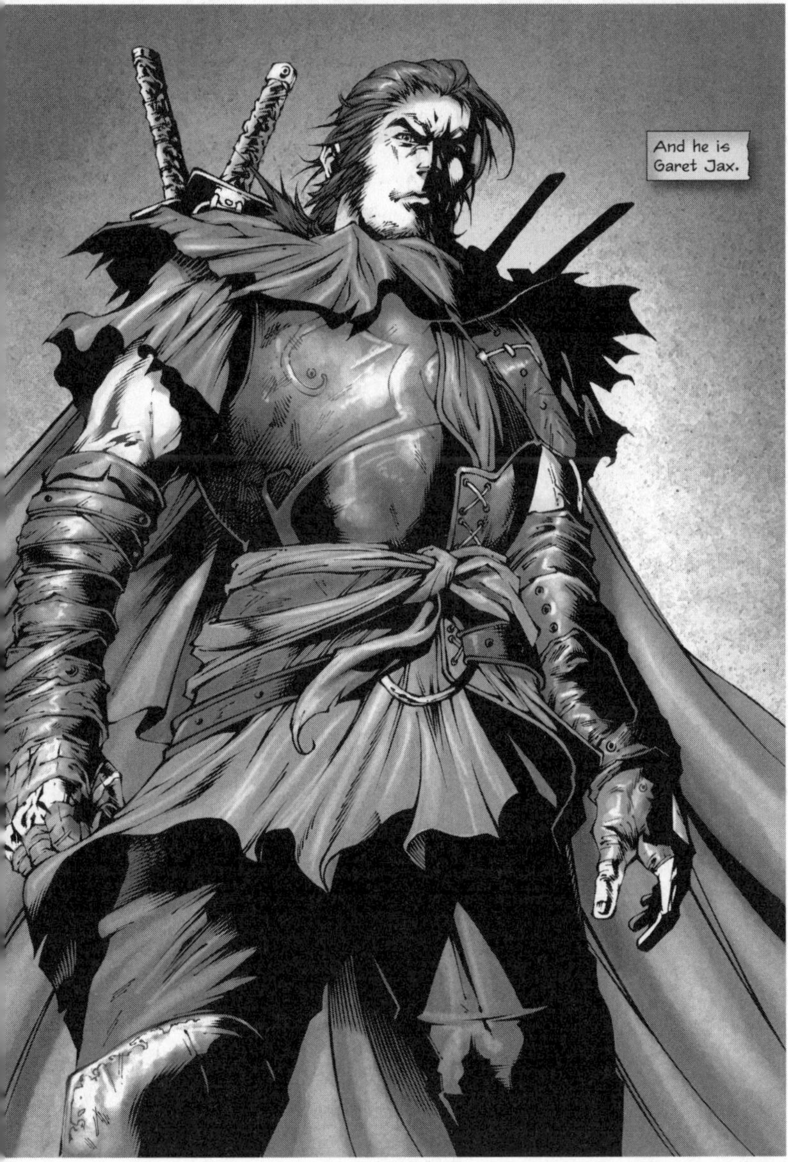
And he is
Garet Jax.

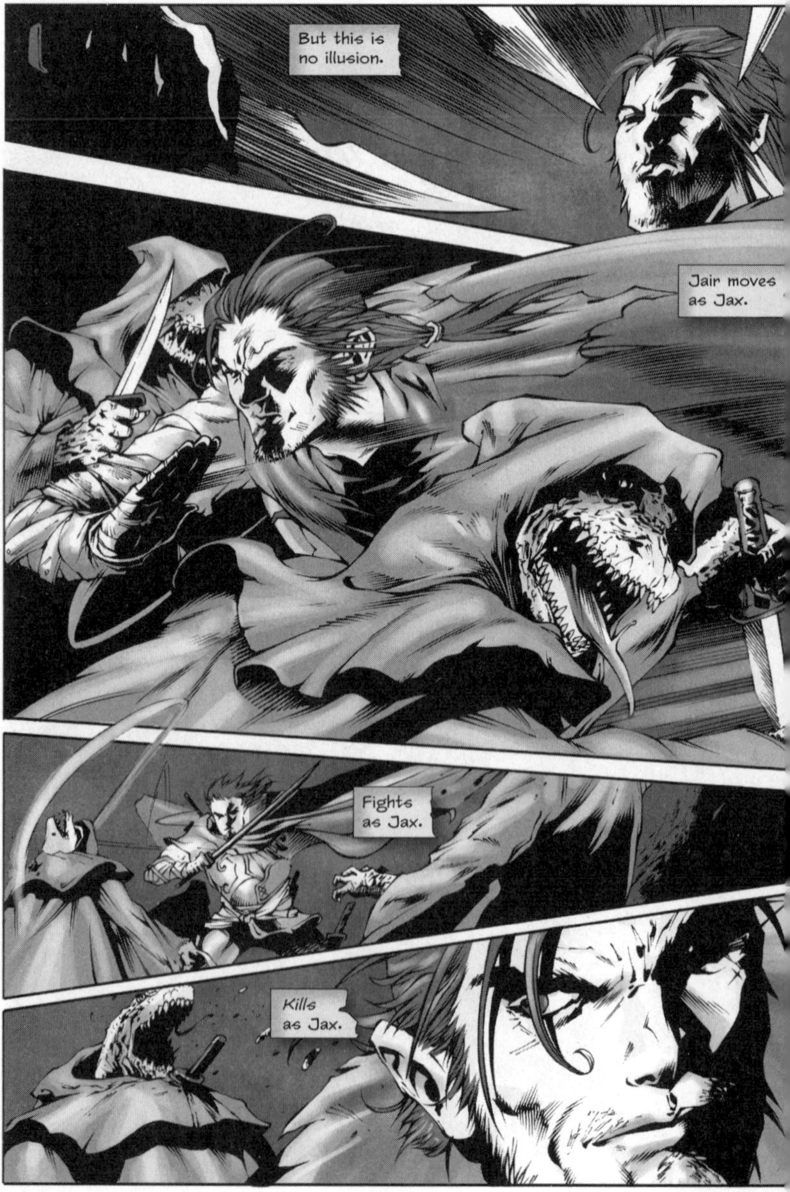
But this is no illusion.
Jair moves as Jax.
Fights as Jax.
Kills as Jax.

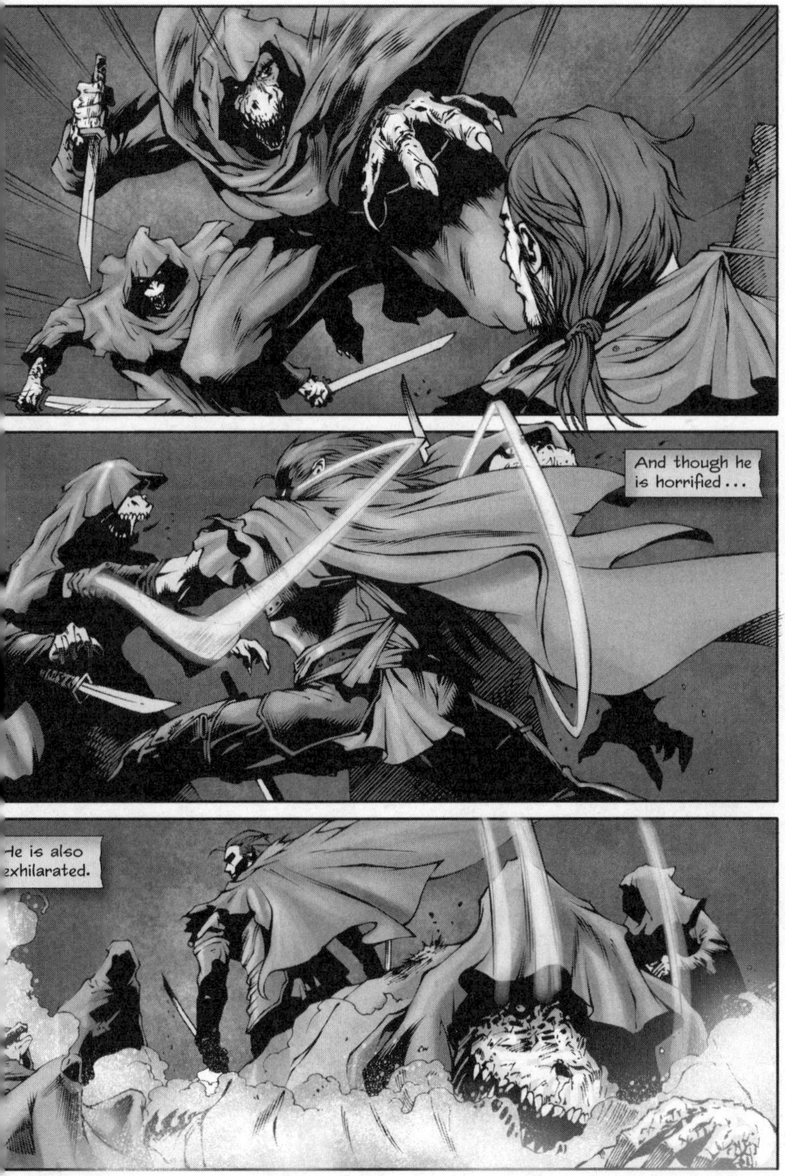
And though he is horrified...
He is also exhilarated.

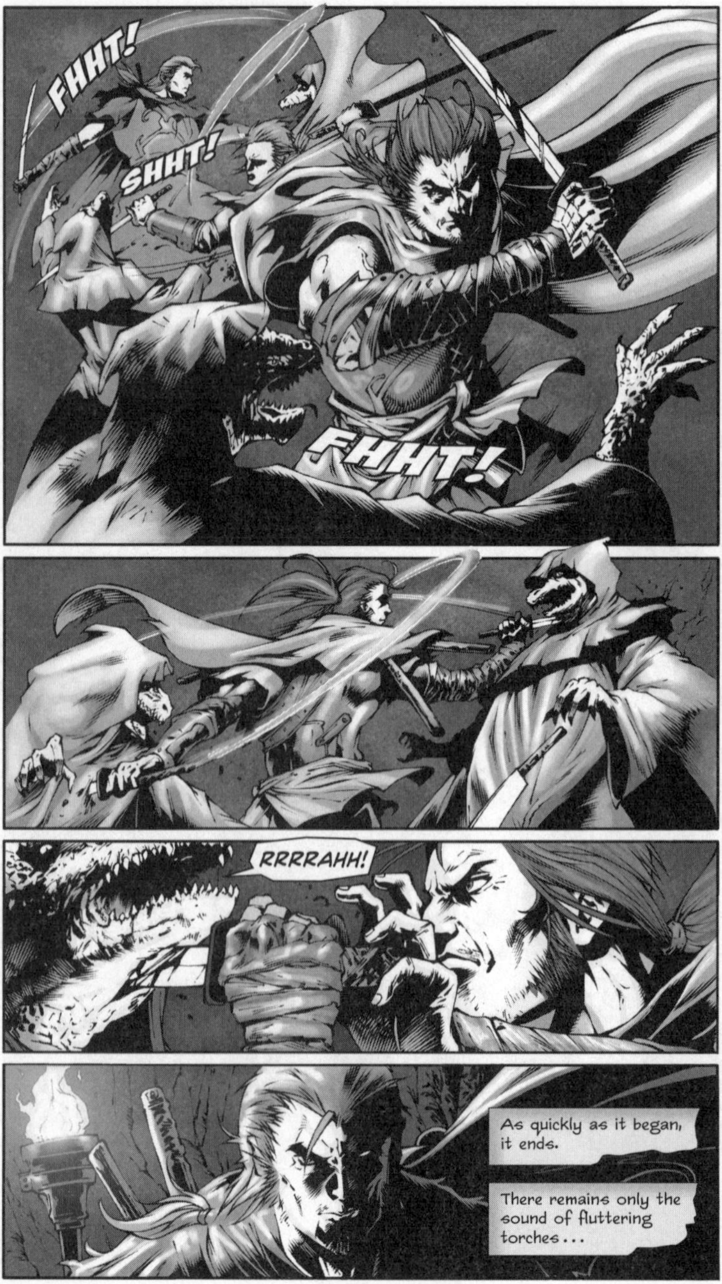
FHHT!
SHHT!
FHHT!
RRRRAHH!
As quickly as it began, it ends.
There remains only the sound of fluttering torches...

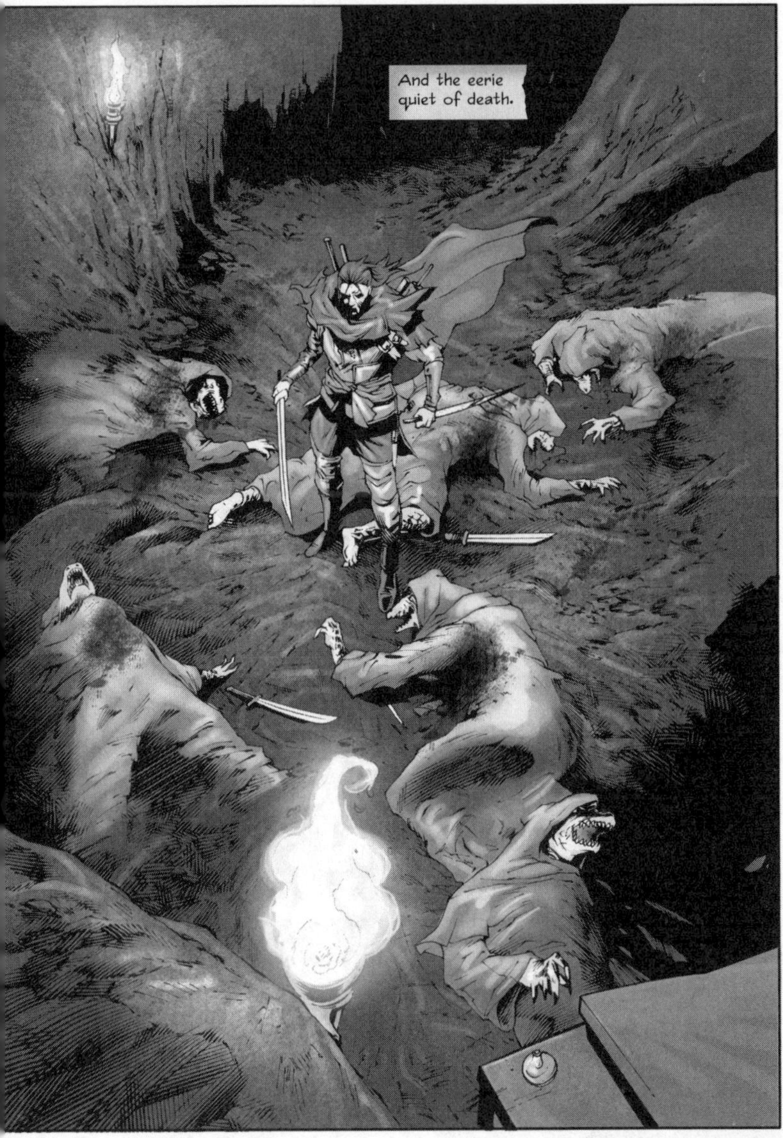
And the eerie
quiet of death.

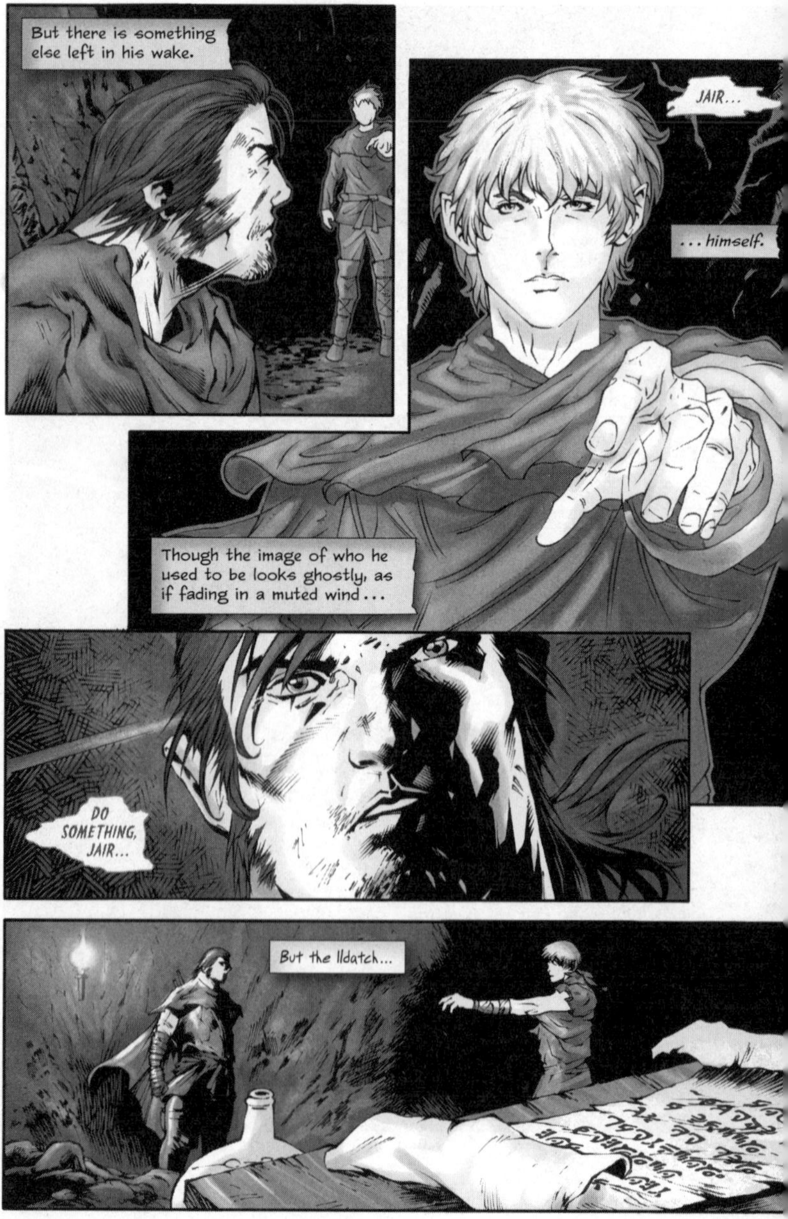

But there is something else left in his wake.
JAIR...
...himself.
Though the image of who he used to be looks ghostly, as if fading in a muted wind...
DO SOMETHING, JAIR...
But the Ildatch...

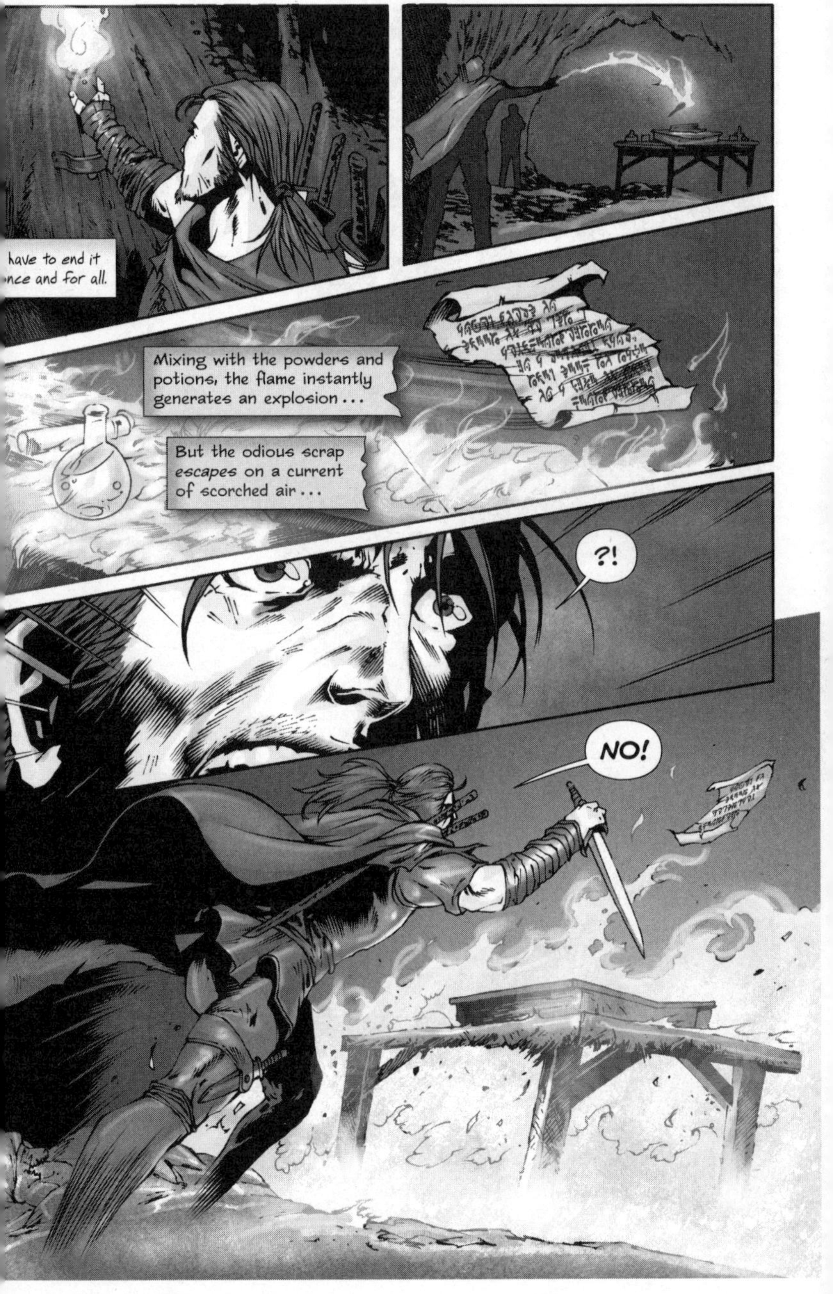
have to end it
nce and for all.
Mixing with the powders and potions, the flame instantly generates an explosion . . .
But the odious scrap *escapes* on a current of scorched air . . .
?!
NO!

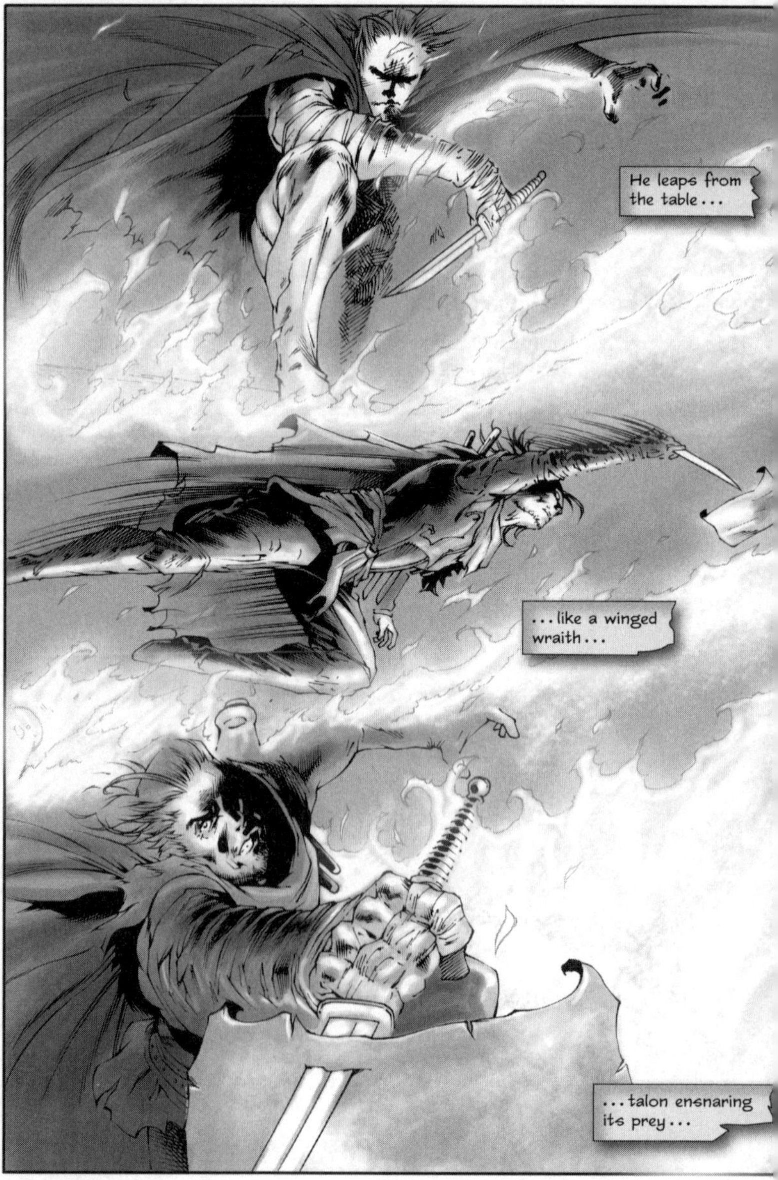
He leaps from the table...
...like a winged wraith...
...talon ensnaring its prey...

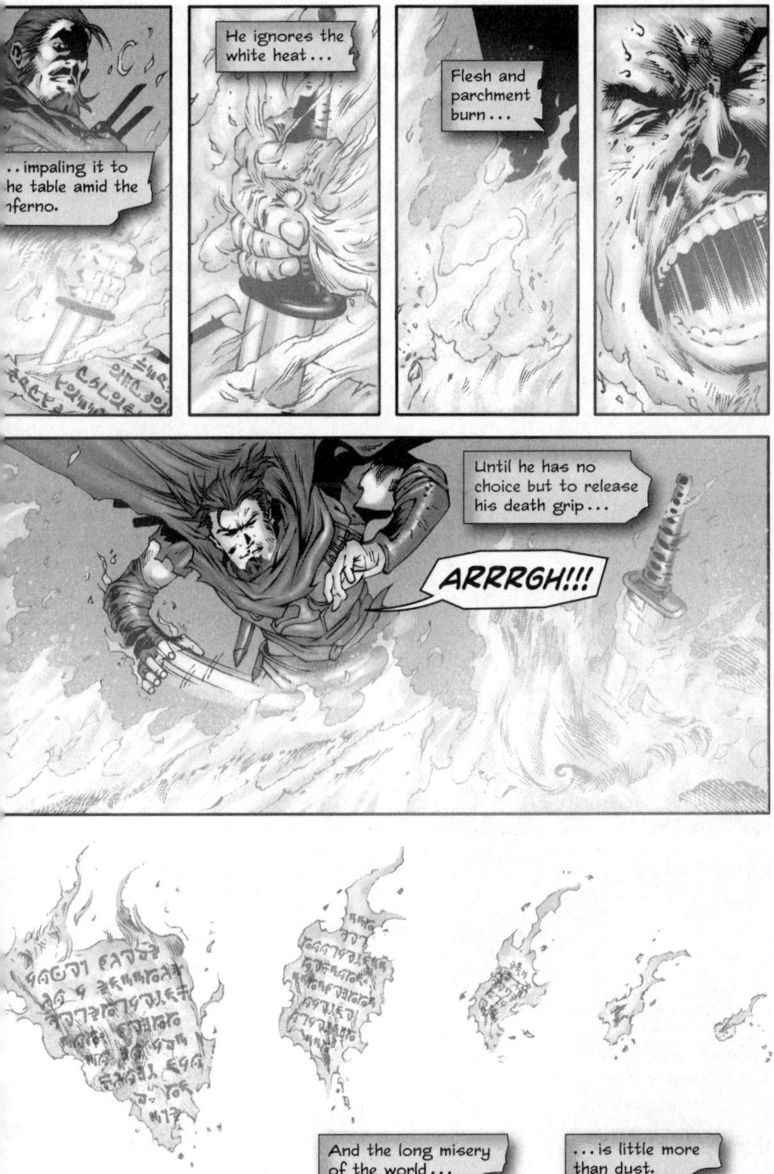
...impaling it to
he table amid the
nferno.
He ignores the
white heat...
Flesh and
parchment
burn...
Until he has no
choice but to release
his death grip...
ARRRGH!!!
And the long misery
of the world...
...is little more
than dust.

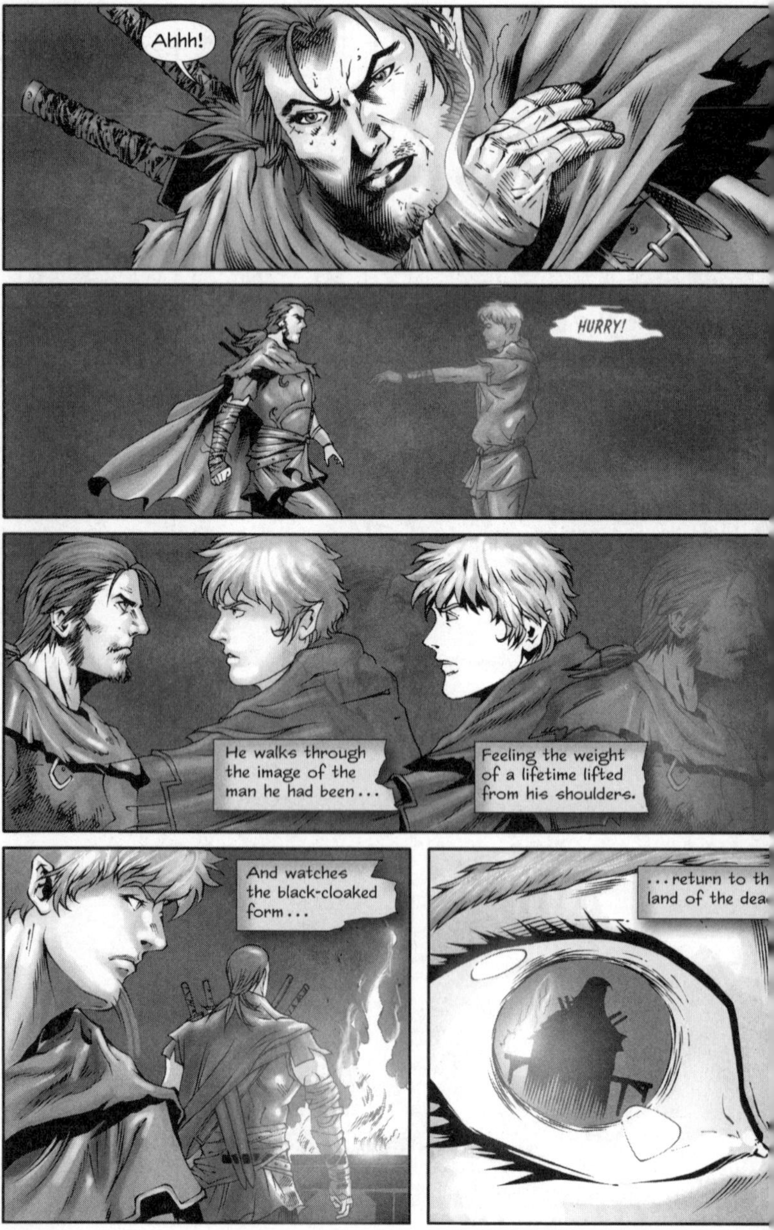
Ahhh!
HURRY!
He walks through the image of the man he had been...
Feeling the weight of a lifetime lifted from his shoulders.
And watches the black-cloaked form...
...return to th
land of the dea

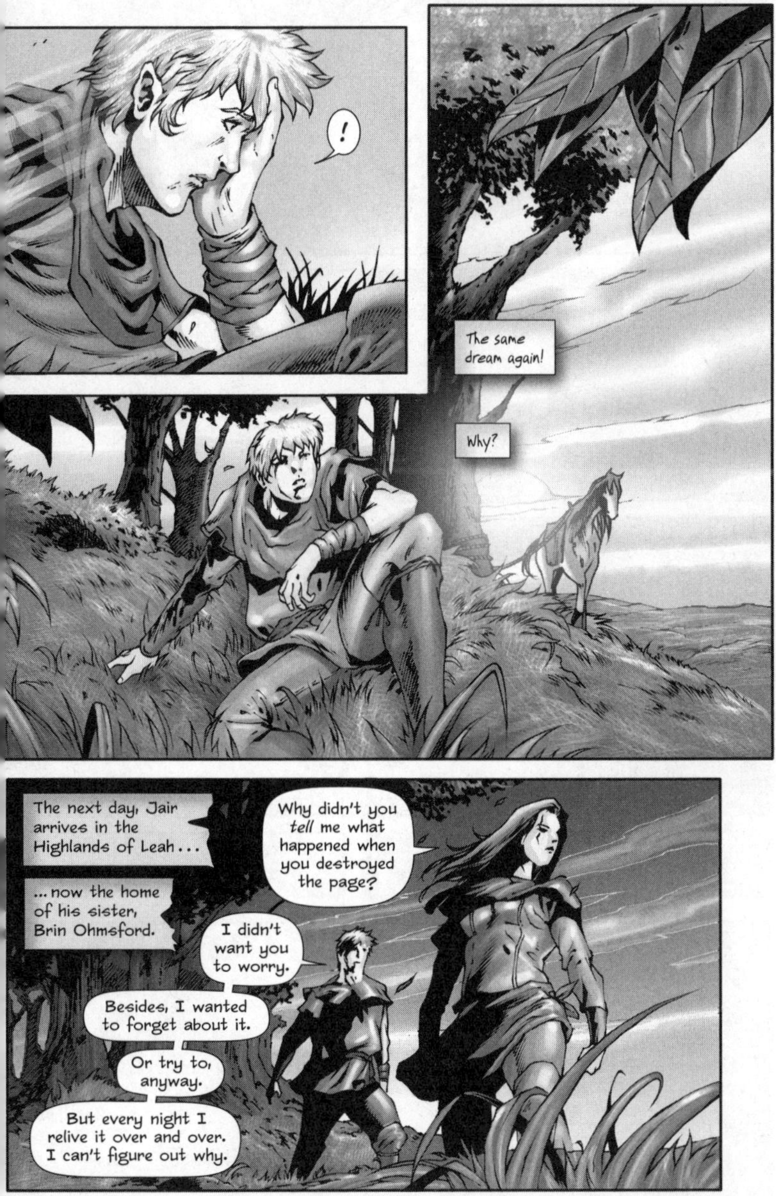
!
The same dream again!
Why?
The next day, Jair arrives in the Highlands of Leah...
...now the home of his sister, Brin Ohmsford.
Why didn't you *tell* me what happened when you destroyed the page?
I didn't want you to worry.
Besides, I wanted to forget about it.
Or try to, anyway.
But every night I relive it over and over. I can't figure out why.

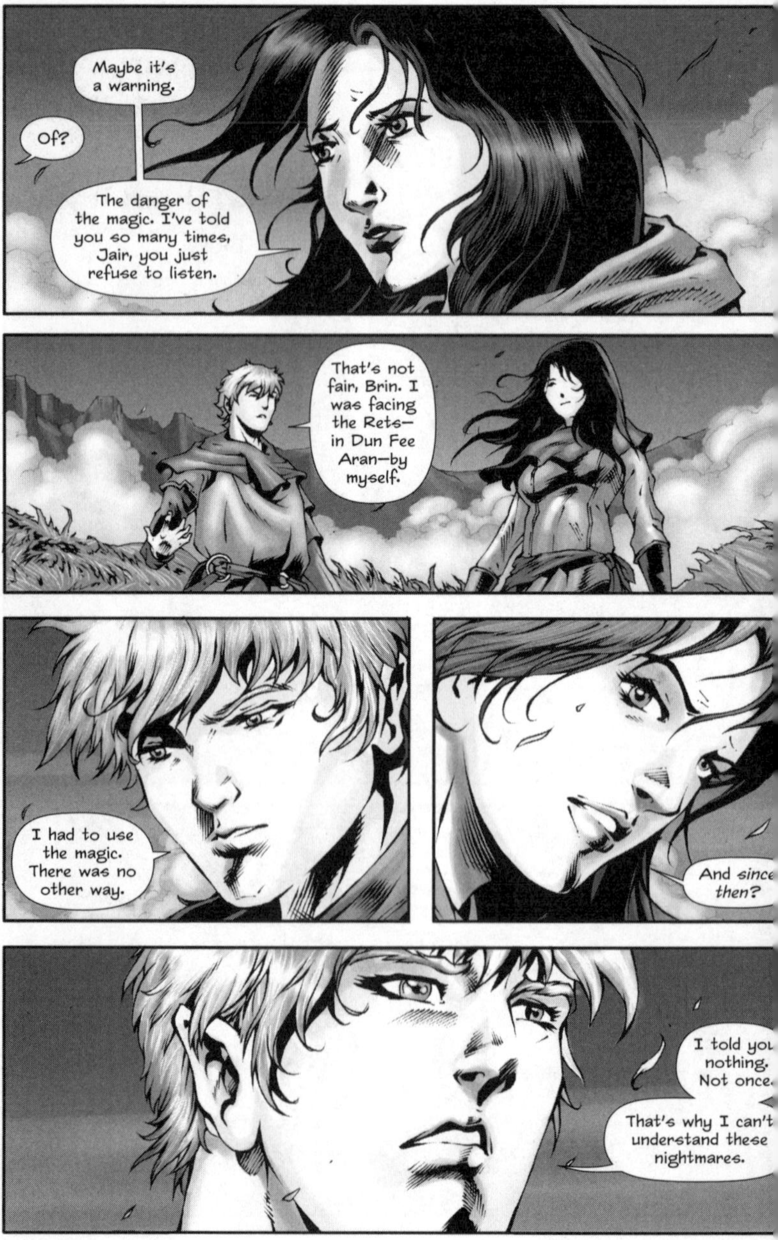
Maybe it's a warning.
Of?
The danger of the magic. I've told you so many times, Jair, you just refuse to listen.
That's not fair, Brin. I was facing the Rets—in Dun Fee Aran—by myself.
I had to use the magic. There was no other way.
And *since then?*
I told you nothing. Not once.
That's why I can't understand these nightmares.

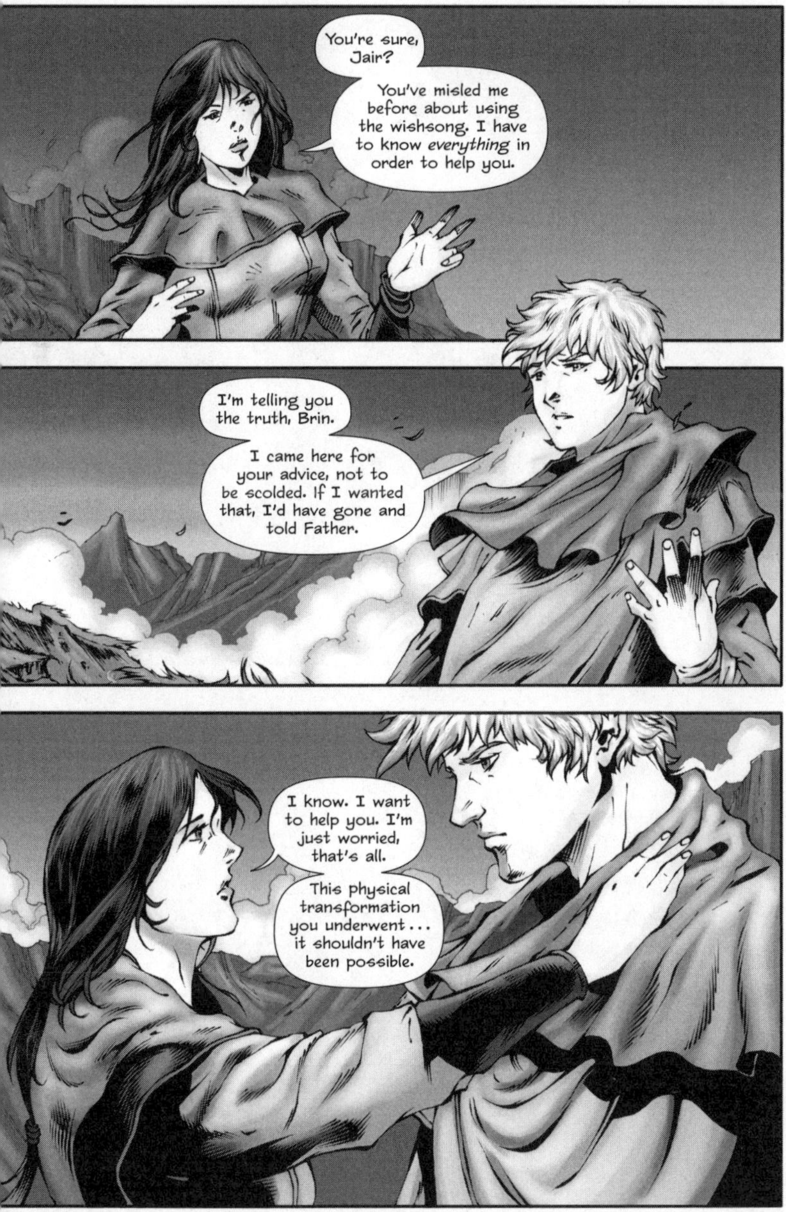
You're sure, Jair?
You've misled me before about using the wishsong. I have to know *everything* in order to help you.
I'm telling you the truth, Brin.
I came here for your advice, not to be scolded. If I wanted that, I'd have gone and told Father.
I know. I want to help you. I'm just worried, that's all.
This physical transformation you underwent . . . it shouldn't have been possible.

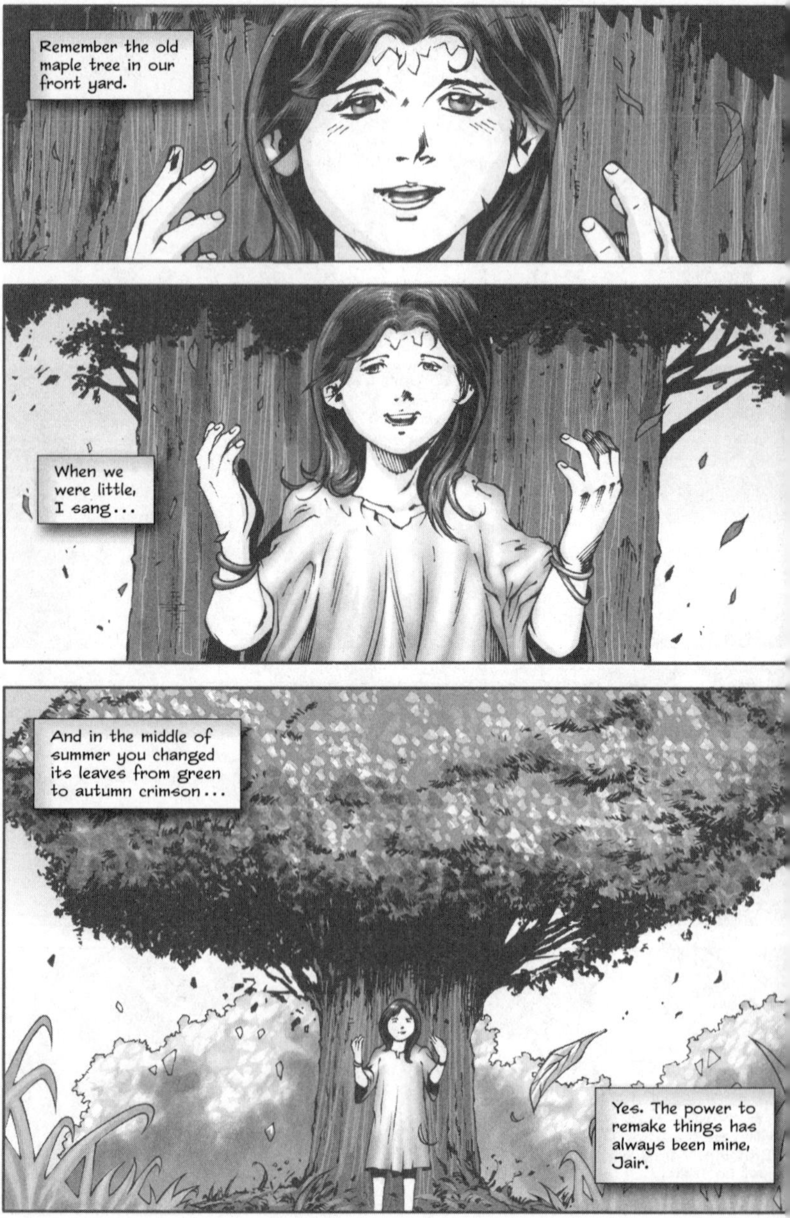
Remember the old maple tree in our front yard.
When we were little, I sang...
And in the middle of summer you changed its leaves from green to autumn crimson...
Yes. The power to remake things has always been mine, Jair.

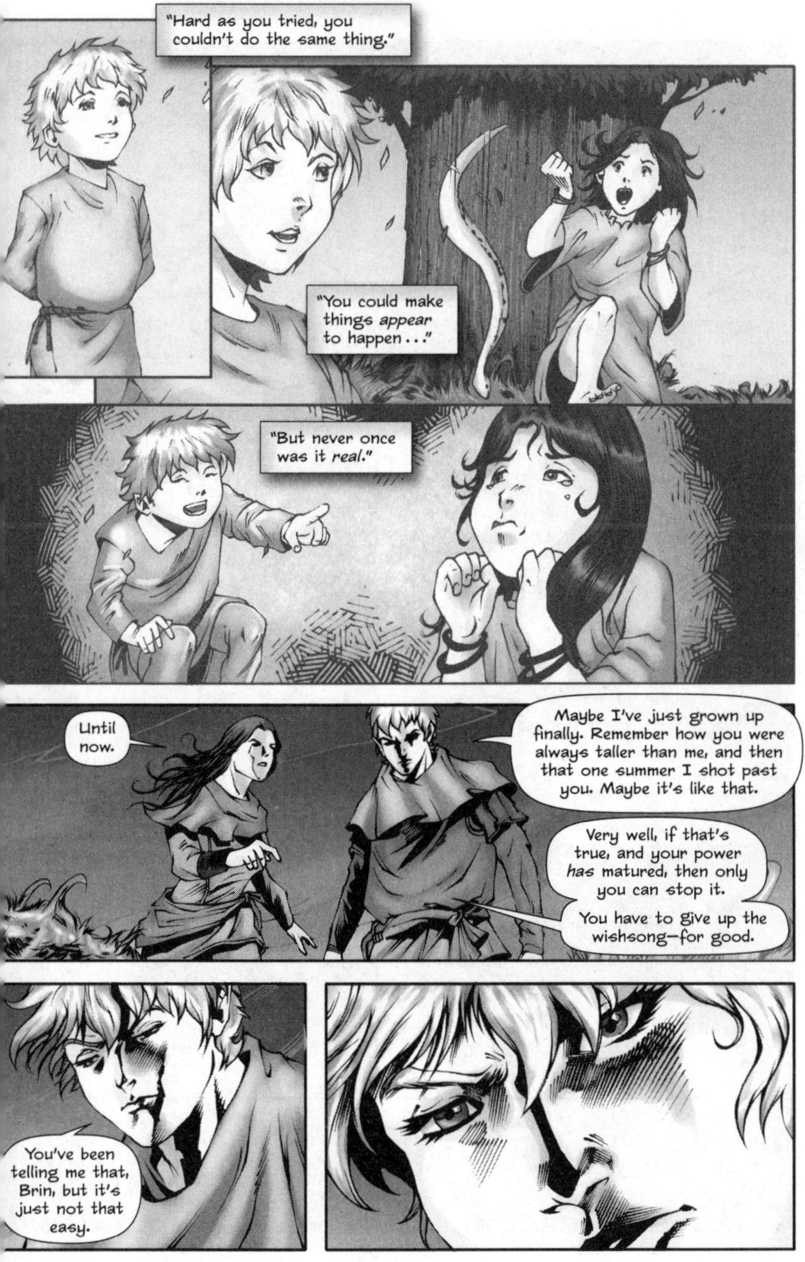
"Hard as you tried, you couldn't do the same thing."
"You could make things *appear* to happen . . ."
"But never once was it *real*."
Until now.
Maybe I've just grown up finally. Remember how you were always taller than me, and then that one summer I shot past you. Maybe it's like that.
Very well, if that's true, and your power *has* matured, then only you can stop it.
You have to give up the wishsong—for good.
You've been telling me that, Brin, but it's just not that easy.

Ha, ha, ha!

....

Three years ago, the Ildatc tried to turn n into somethin worse than th Warlock Lord

It would have succeede had it not bee for you.

Ha, heh, ha!

Come, on Jair. "Fa-ther."

You can say it! "Fa-ther."

I almost lost everything.

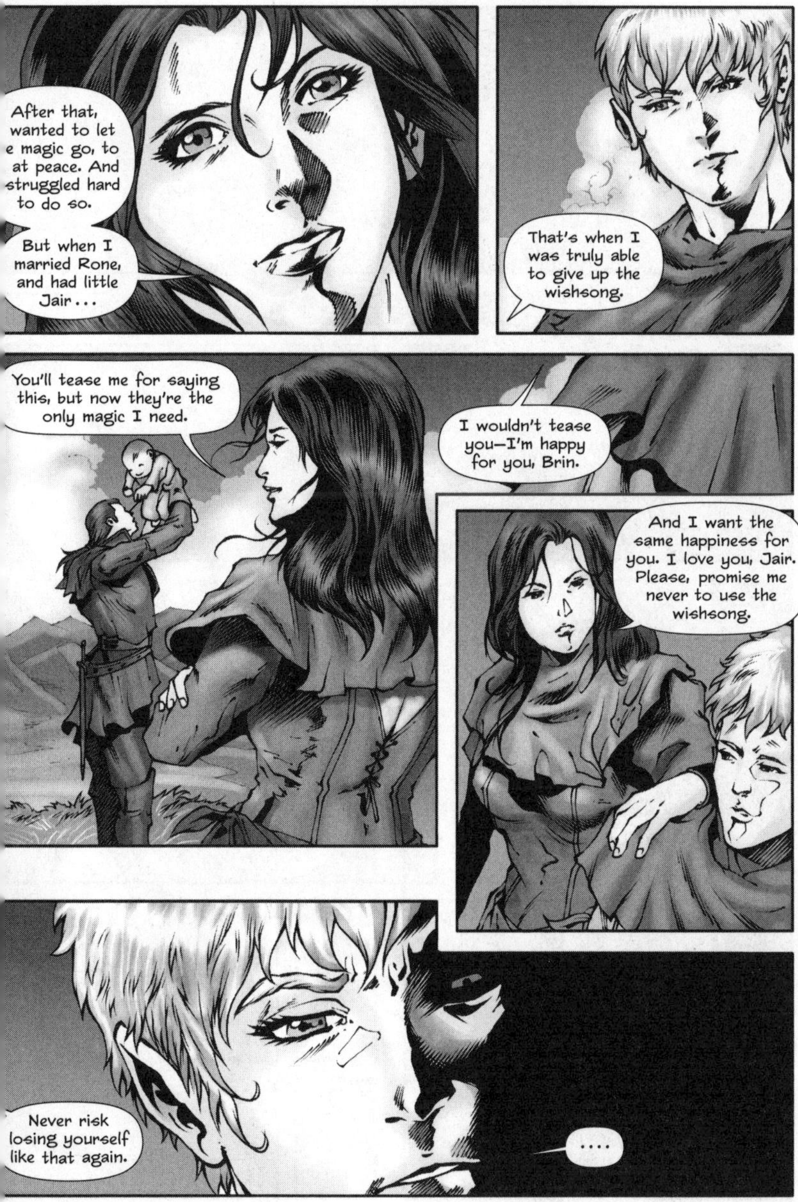
After that, wanted to let e magic go, to at peace. And struggled hard to do so.
But when I married Rone, and had little Jair...
That's when I was truly able to give up the wishsong.
You'll tease me for saying this, but now they're the only magic I need.
I wouldn't tease you—I'm happy for you, Brin.
And I want the same happiness for you. I love you, Jair. Please, promise me never to use the wishsong.
Never risk losing yourself like that again.
....

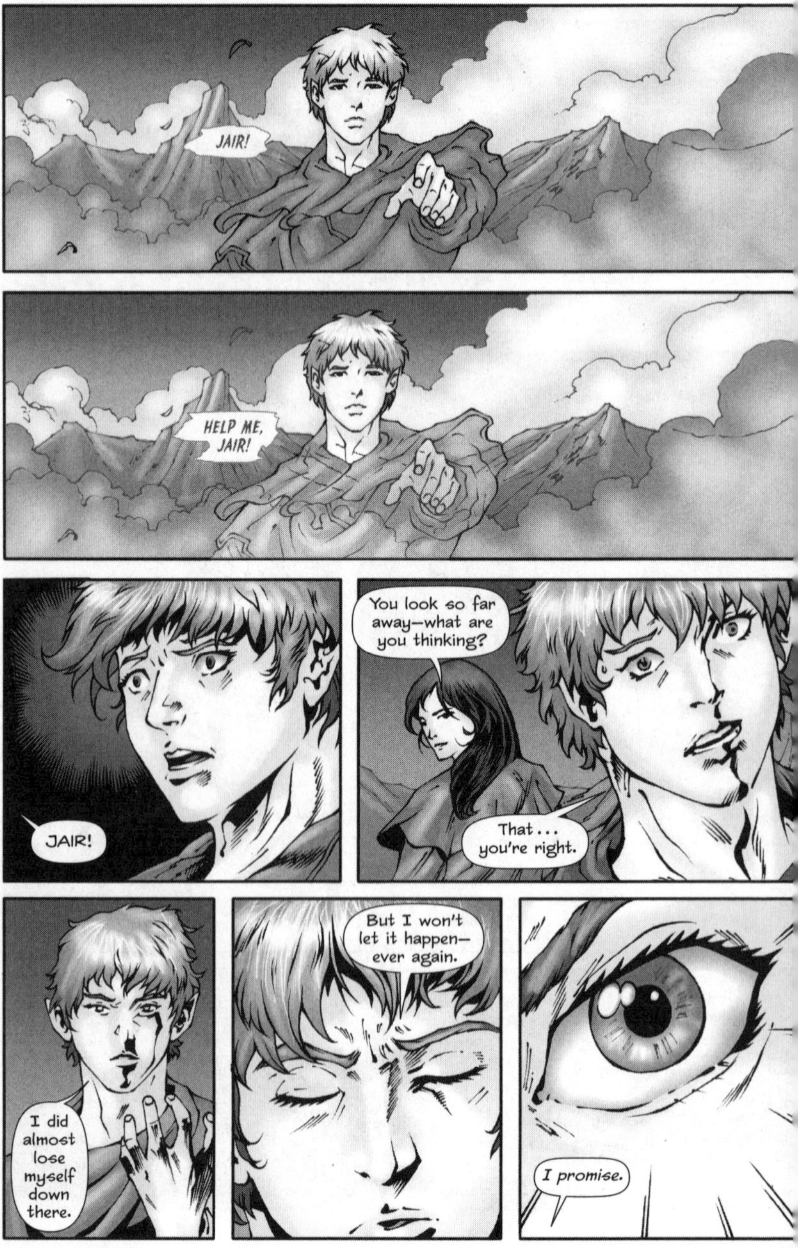
JAIR!
HELP ME, JAIR!
JAIR!
You look so far away—what are you thinking?
That . . . you're right.
I did almost lose myself down there.
But I won't let it happen—ever again.
I promise.

For cat's sake, surely you can stay for another day! You only just arrived.

Not this time, Rone. I want to get home to Shady Vale, get some sleep in my own bed.

Don't forget your promise.

I won't. Kiss little Jair good-bye for me when he wakes up. I'll see you both soon.

As he looks back, a strange sense of dread passes through Jair, and he wonders if he'll be able to make good on that promise.

Wasting no time to linger on dark thoughts, he rides westward from the Highlands, toward the Vale and home...

e rides hard and fast, asing the sun until s fading rays paint e land in twilight...

...making it as far as the Rappahalladran River...

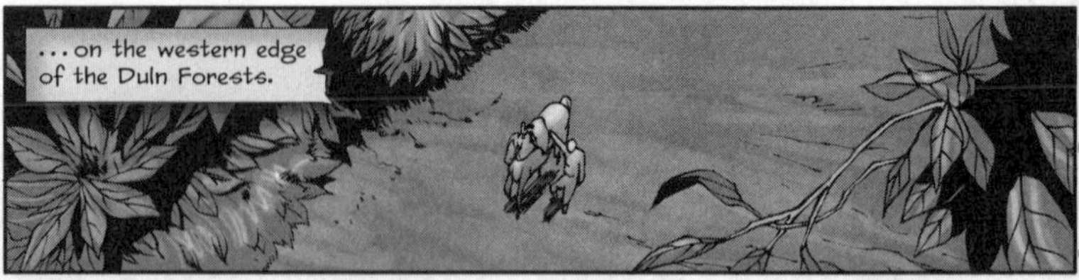
...on the western edge
of the Duln Forests.

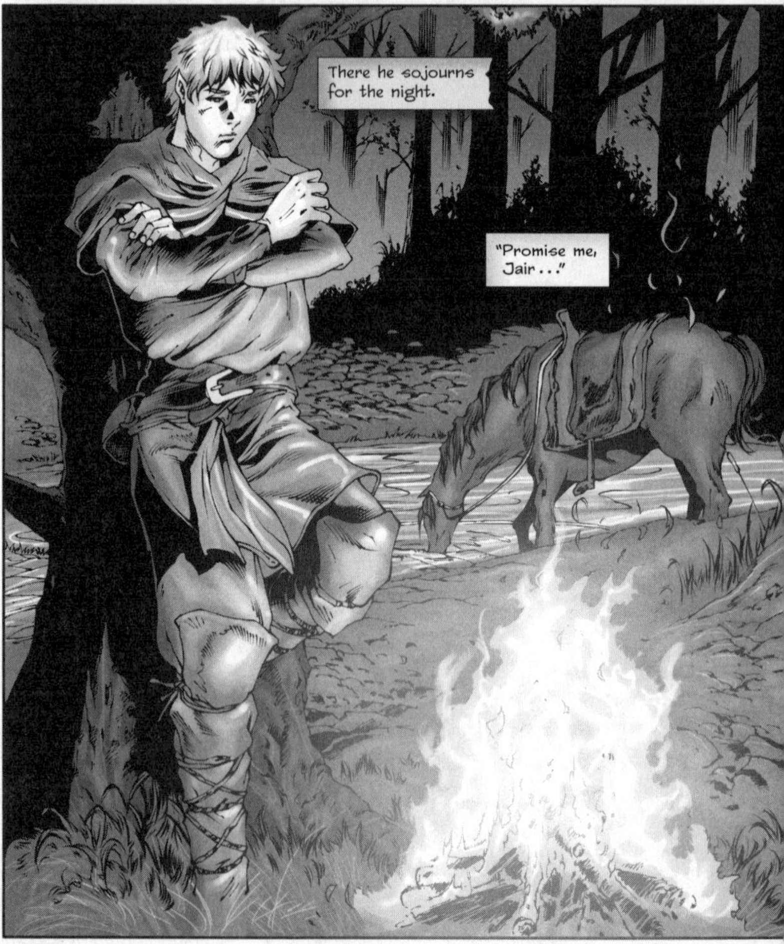
There he sojourns
for the night.
"Promise me,
Jair..."

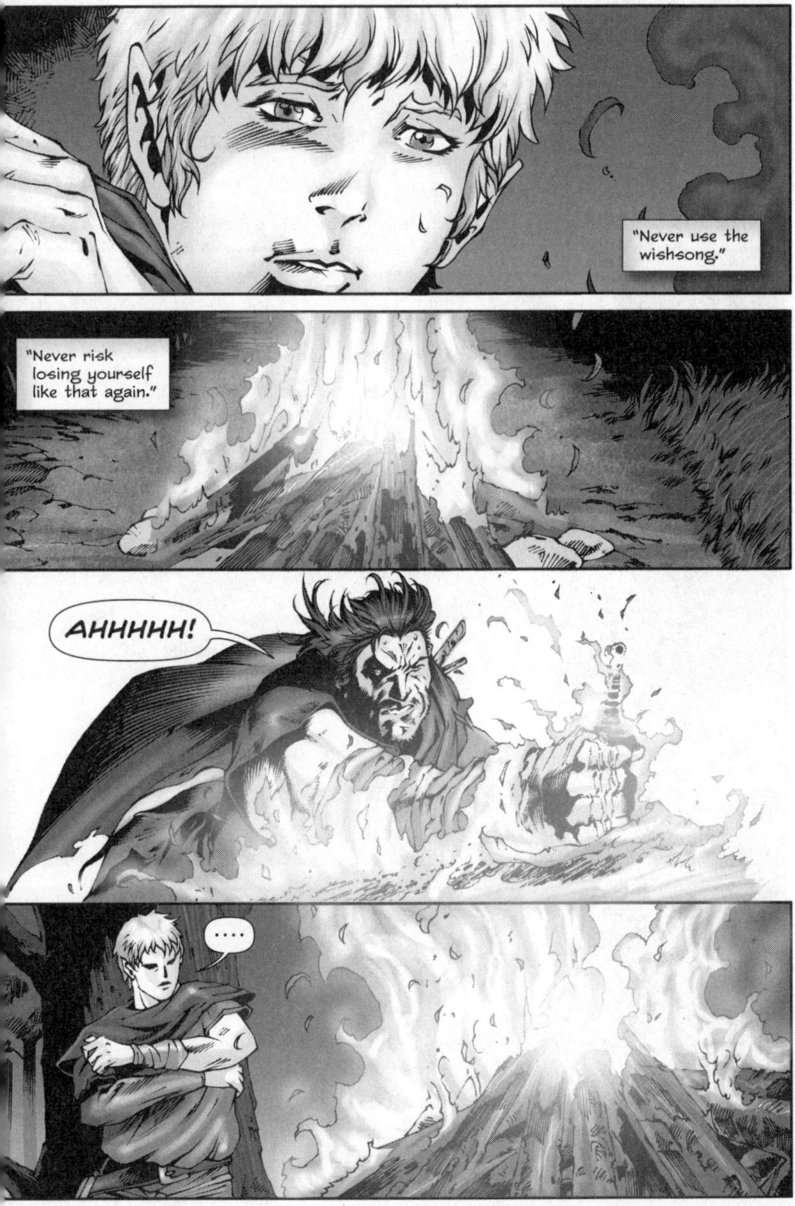
"Never use the wishsong."
"Never risk losing yourself like that again."
AHHHHH!
....

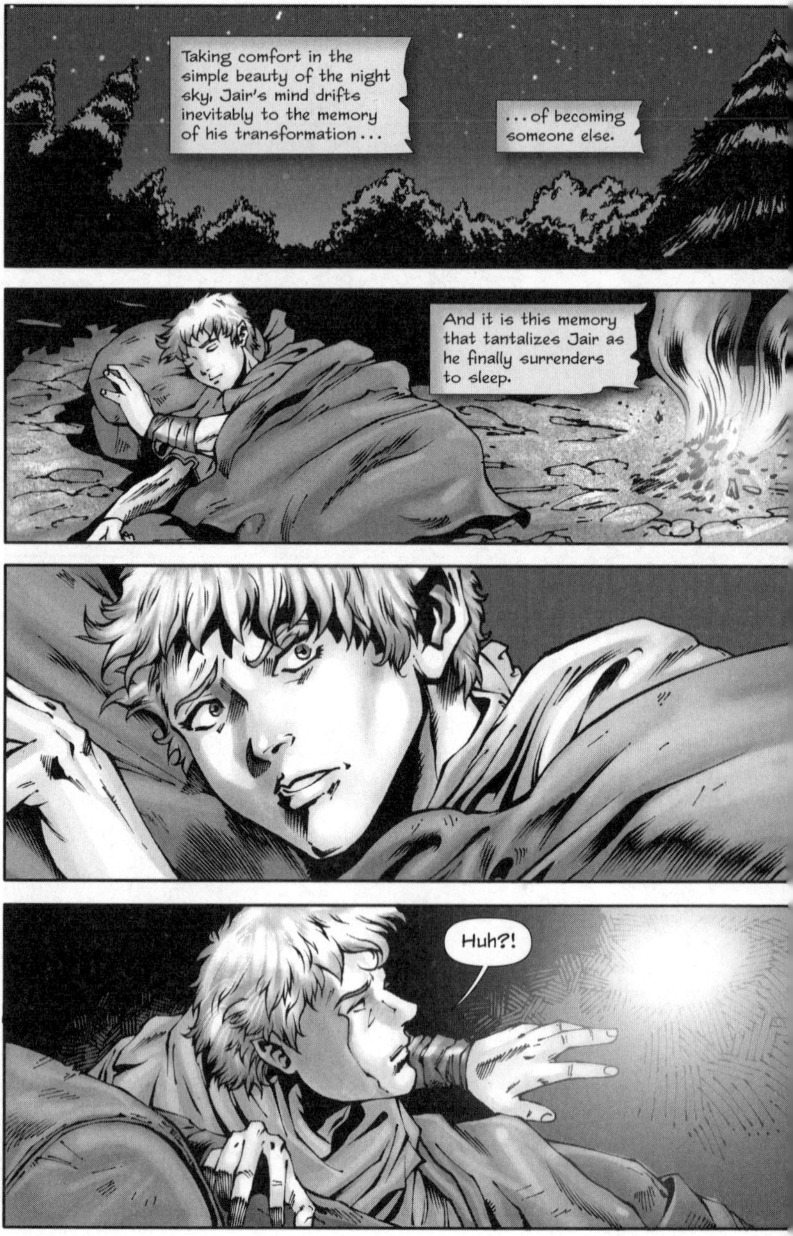
Taking comfort in the simple beauty of the night sky, Jair's mind drifts inevitably to the memory of his transformation...
...of becoming someone else.
And it is this memory that tantalizes Jair as he finally surrenders to sleep.
Huh?!

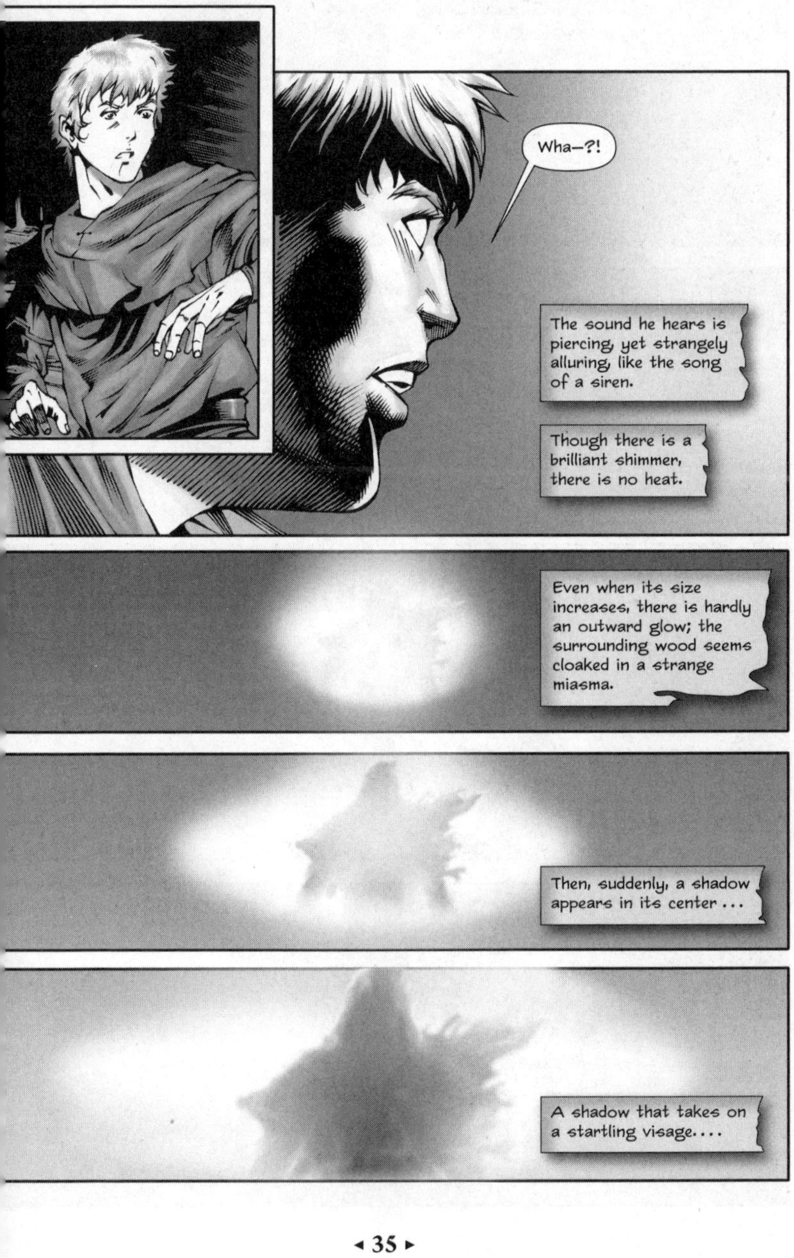
Wha—?!
The sound he hears is piercing, yet strangely alluring, like the song of a siren.
Though there is a brilliant shimmer, there is no heat.
Even when its size increases, there is hardly an outward glow; the surrounding wood seems cloaked in a strange miasma.
Then, suddenly, a shadow appears in its center . . .
A shadow that takes on a startling visage. . . .

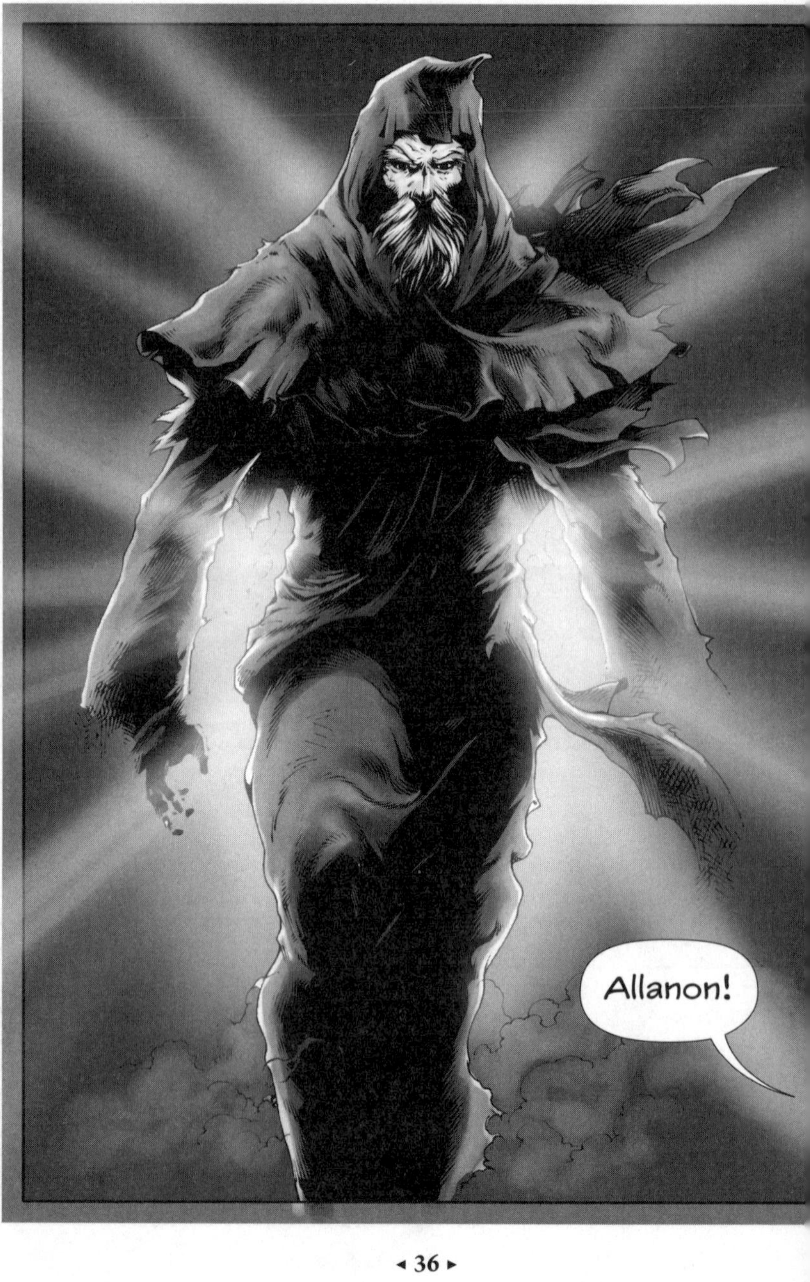
Allanon!

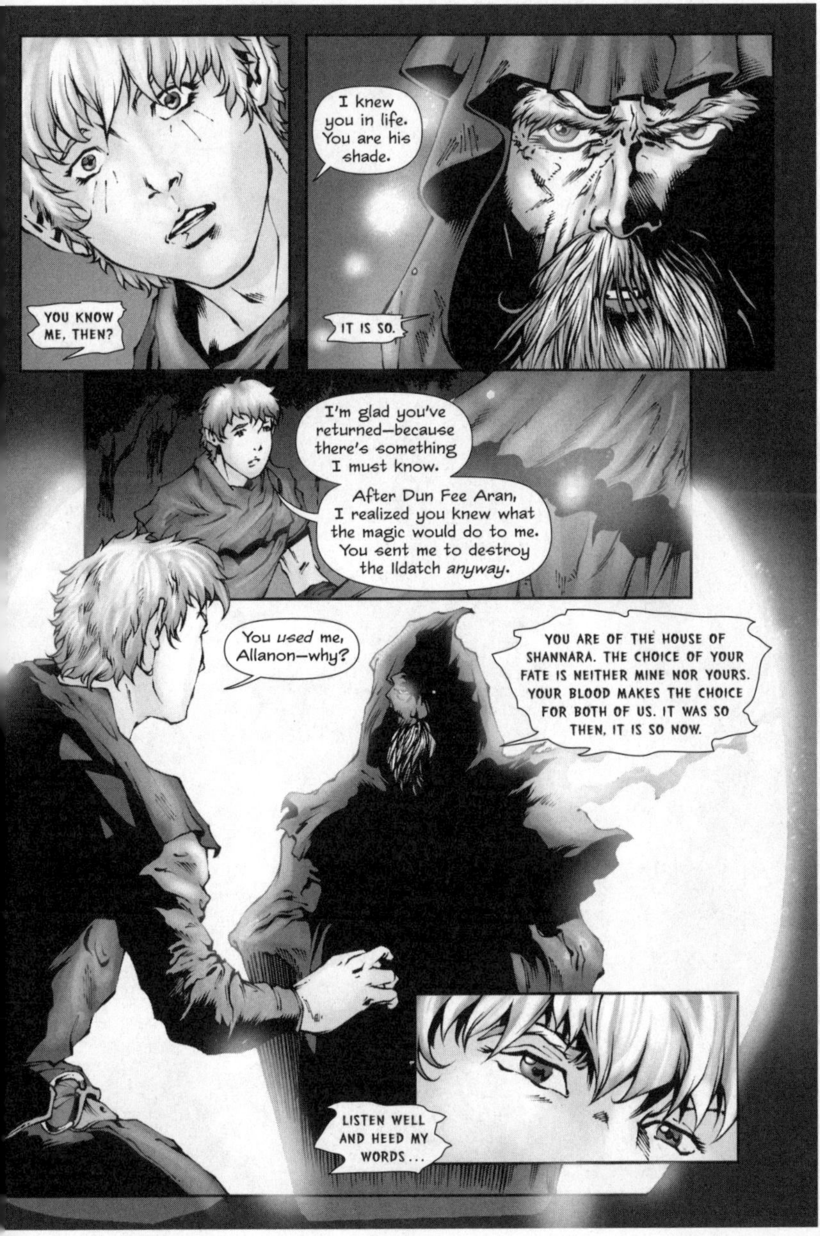
YOU KNOW ME, THEN?
I knew you in life. You are his shade.
IT IS SO.
I'm glad you've returned—because there's something I must know.
After Dun Fee Aran, I realized you knew what the magic would do to me. You sent me to destroy the Ildatch *anyway*.
You *used* me, Allanon—why?
YOU ARE OF THE HOUSE OF SHANNARA. THE CHOICE OF YOUR FATE IS NEITHER MINE NOR YOURS. YOUR BLOOD MAKES THE CHOICE FOR BOTH OF US. IT WAS SO THEN, IT IS SO NOW.
LISTEN WELL AND HEED MY WORDS . . .

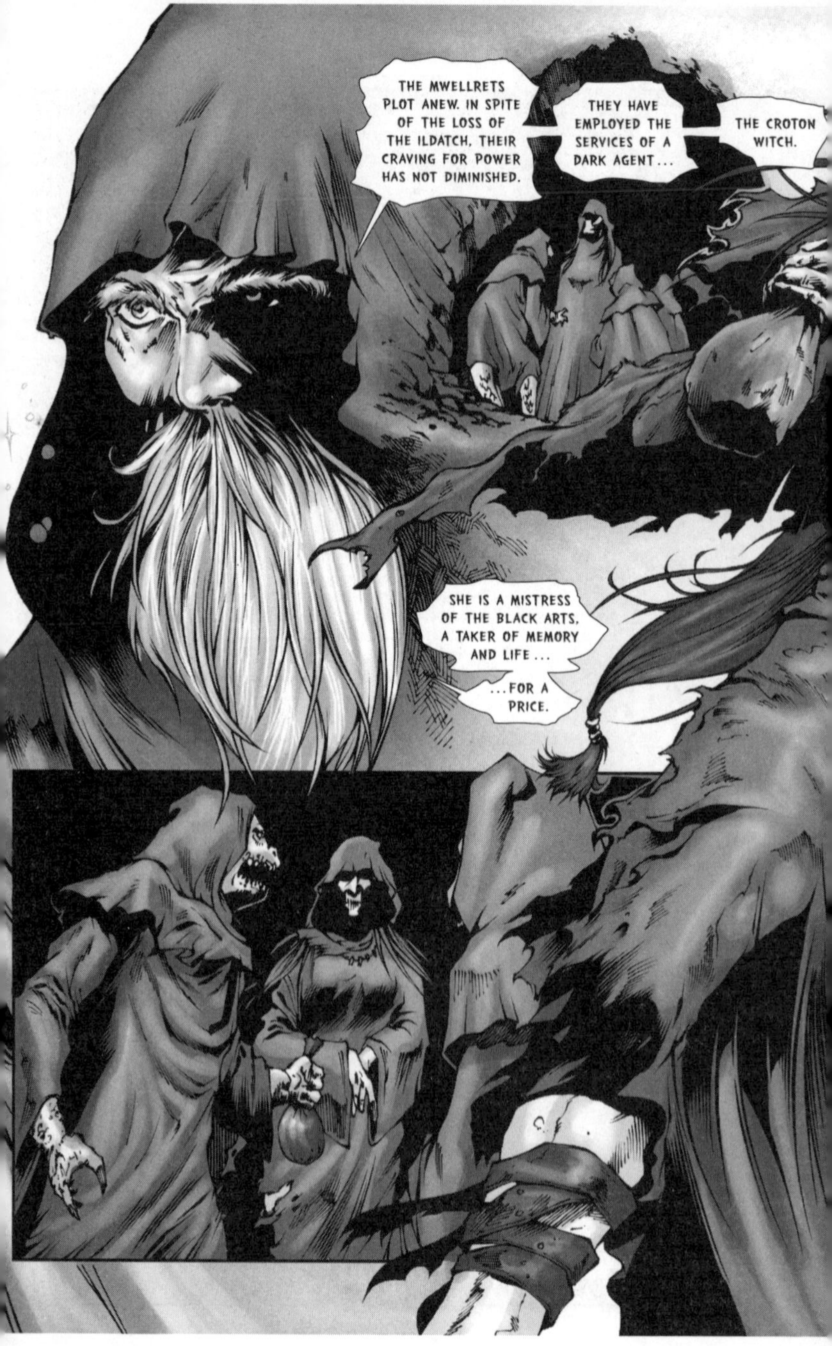

THE MWELLRETS PLOT ANEW. IN SPITE OF THE LOSS OF THE ILDATCH, THEIR CRAVING FOR POWER HAS NOT DIMINISHED.
THEY HAVE EMPLOYED THE SERVICES OF A DARK AGENT...
THE CROTON WITCH.
SHE IS A MISTRESS OF THE BLACK ARTS, A TAKER OF MEMORY AND LIFE...
...FOR A PRICE.

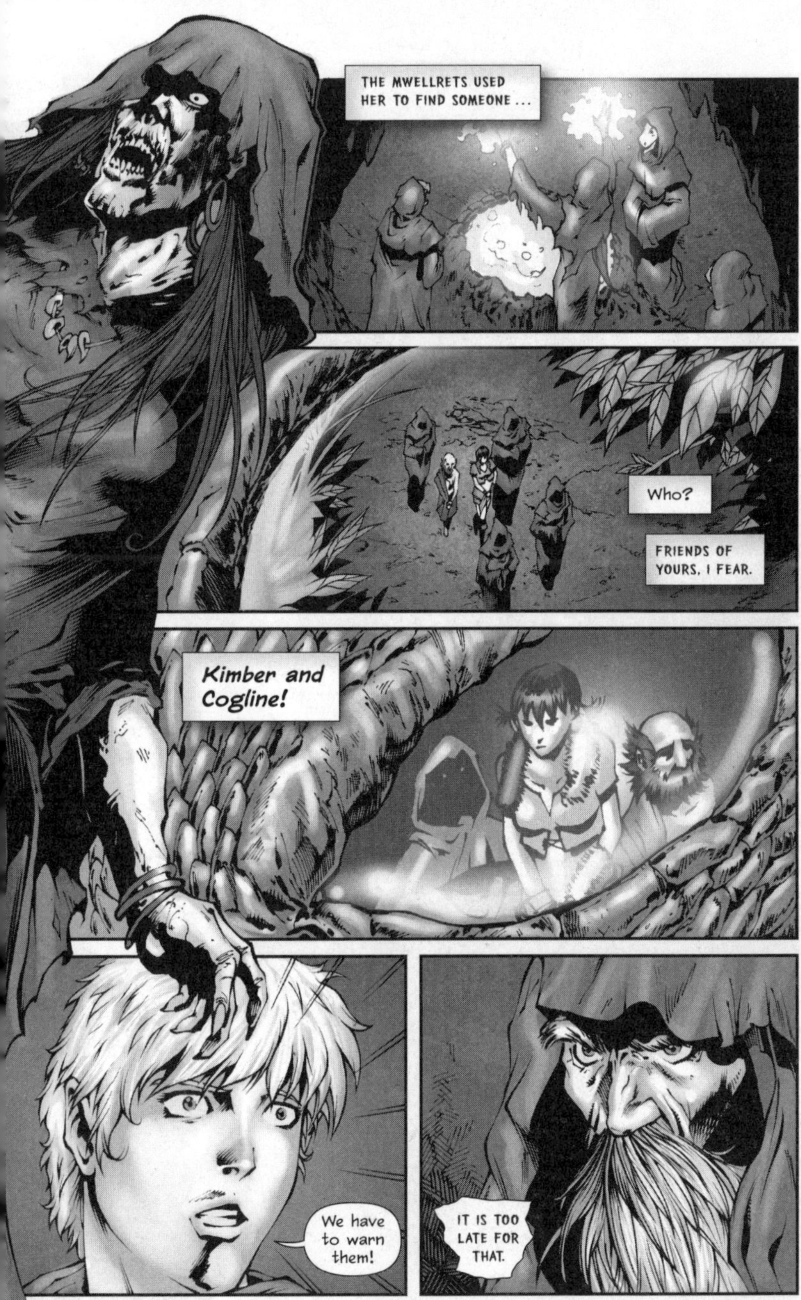
THE MWELLRETS USED HER TO FIND SOMEONE ...
Who?
FRIENDS OF YOURS, I FEAR.
Kimber and Cogline!
We have to warn them!
IT IS TOO LATE FOR THAT.

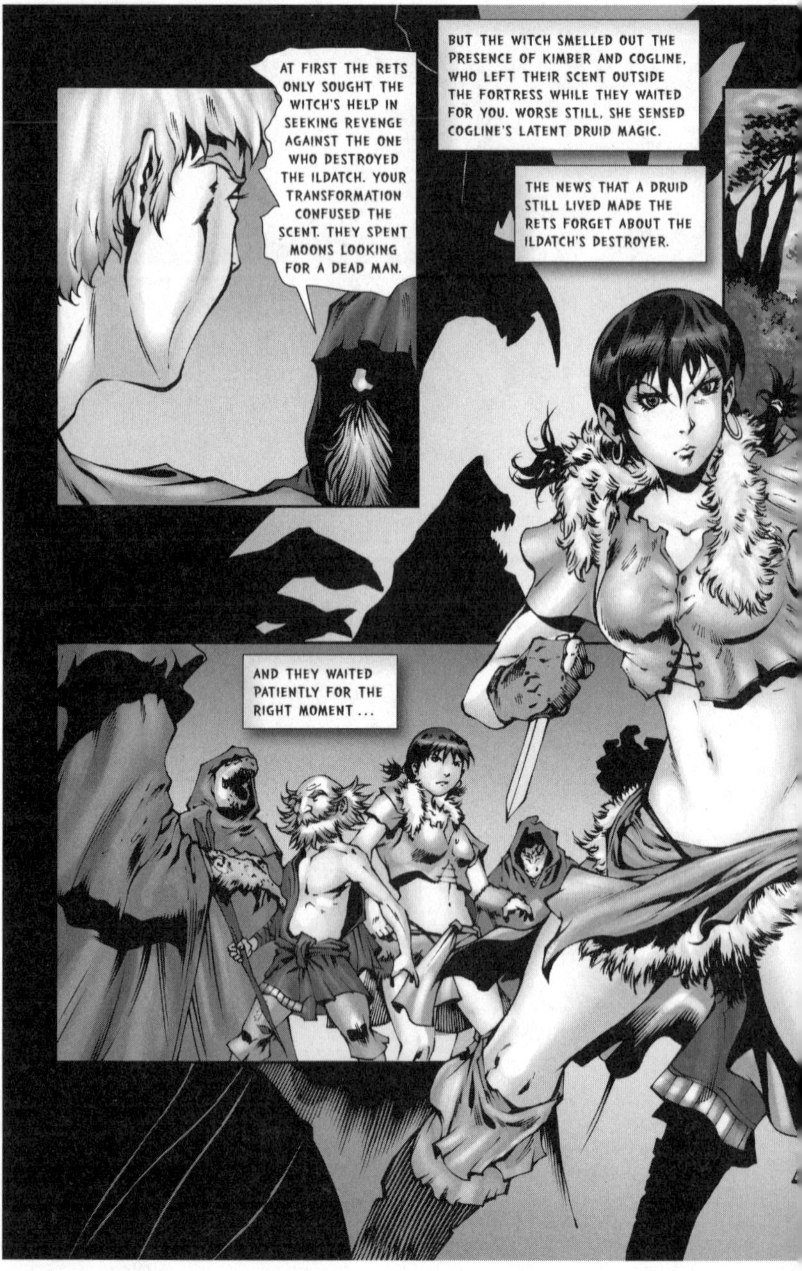
AT FIRST THE RETS ONLY SOUGHT THE WITCH'S HELP IN SEEKING REVENGE AGAINST THE ONE WHO DESTROYED THE ILDATCH. YOUR TRANSFORMATION CONFUSED THE SCENT. THEY SPENT MOONS LOOKING FOR A DEAD MAN.
BUT THE WITCH SMELLED OUT THE PRESENCE OF KIMBER AND COGLINE, WHO LEFT THEIR SCENT OUTSIDE THE FORTRESS WHILE THEY WAITED FOR YOU. WORSE STILL, SHE SENSED COGLINE'S LATENT DRUID MAGIC.
THE NEWS THAT A DRUID STILL LIVED MADE THE RETS FORGET ABOUT THE ILDATCH'S DESTROYER.
AND THEY WAITED PATIENTLY FOR THE RIGHT MOMENT . . .

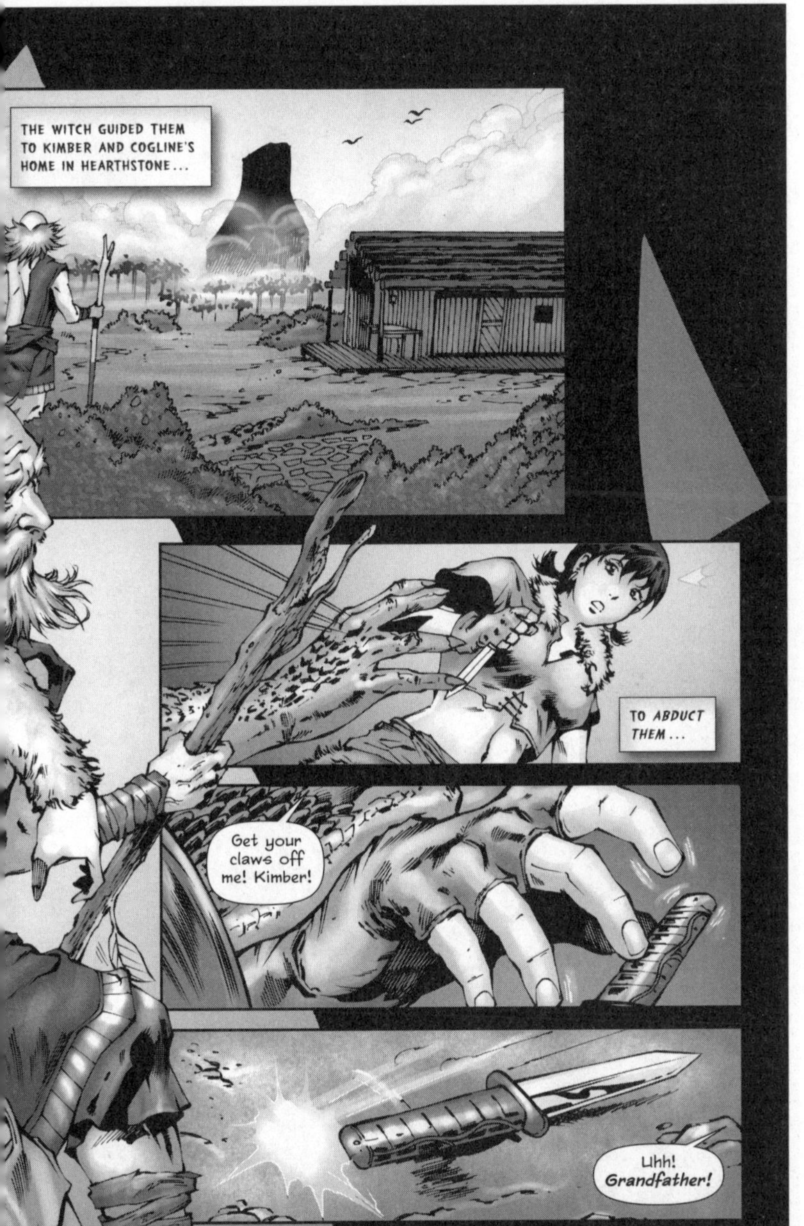
THE WITCH GUIDED THEM TO KIMBER AND COGLINE'S HOME IN HEARTHSTONE...
TO ABDUCT THEM...
Get your claws off me! Kimber!
Uhh! Grandfather!

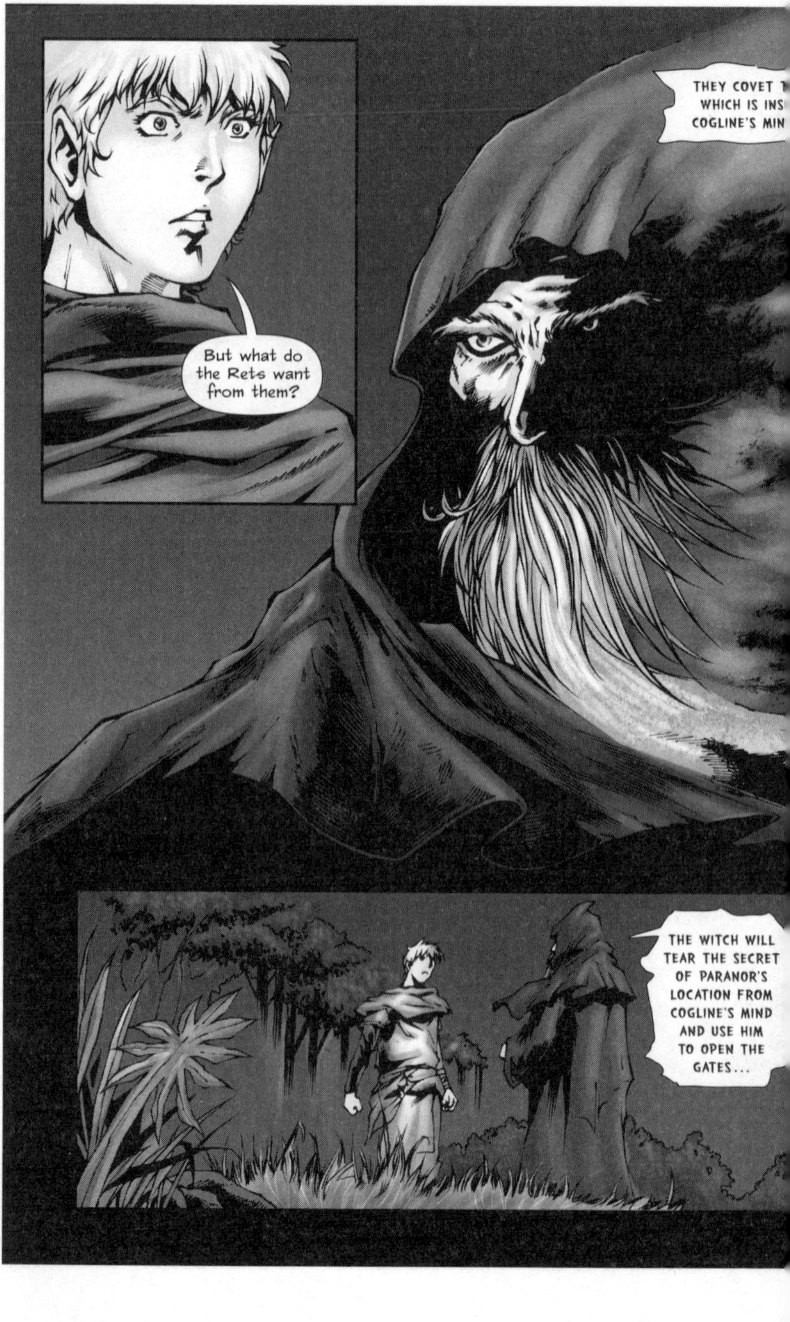
But what do the Rets want from them?
THEY COVET
WHICH IS
COGLINE'S
THE WITCH WILL TEAR THE SECRET OF PARANOR'S LOCATION FROM COGLINE'S MIND AND USE HIM TO OPEN THE GATES...

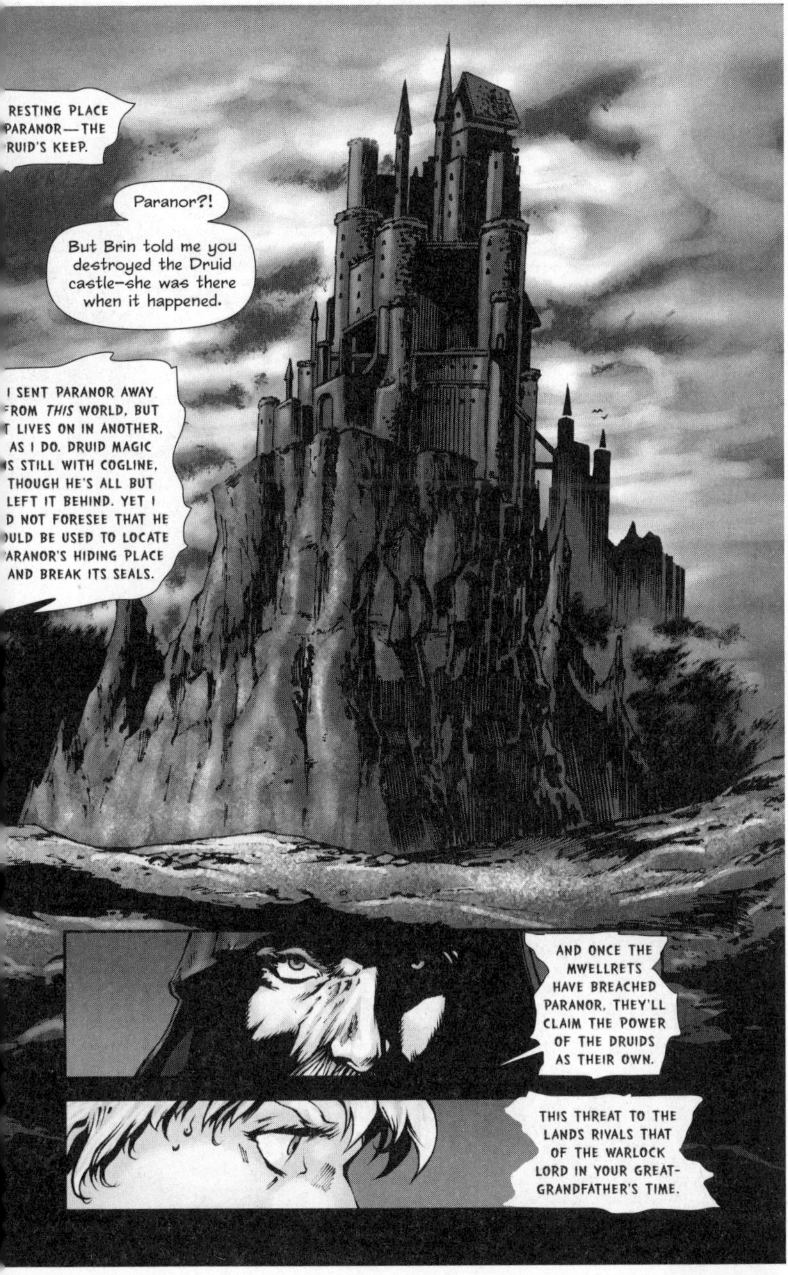
RESTING PLACE PARANOR—THE RUID'S KEEP.
Paranor?!
But Brin told me you destroyed the Druid castle—she was there when it happened.
I SENT PARANOR AWAY FROM THIS WORLD, BUT T LIVES ON IN ANOTHER, AS I DO. DRUID MAGIC IS STILL WITH COGLINE, THOUGH HE'S ALL BUT LEFT IT BEHIND. YET I D NOT FORESEE THAT HE OULD BE USED TO LOCATE ARANOR'S HIDING PLACE AND BREAK ITS SEALS.
AND ONCE THE MWELLRETS HAVE BREACHED PARANOR, THEY'LL CLAIM THE POWER OF THE DRUIDS AS THEIR OWN.
THIS THREAT TO THE LANDS RIVALS THAT OF THE WARLOCK LORD IN YOUR GREAT-GRANDFATHER'S TIME.

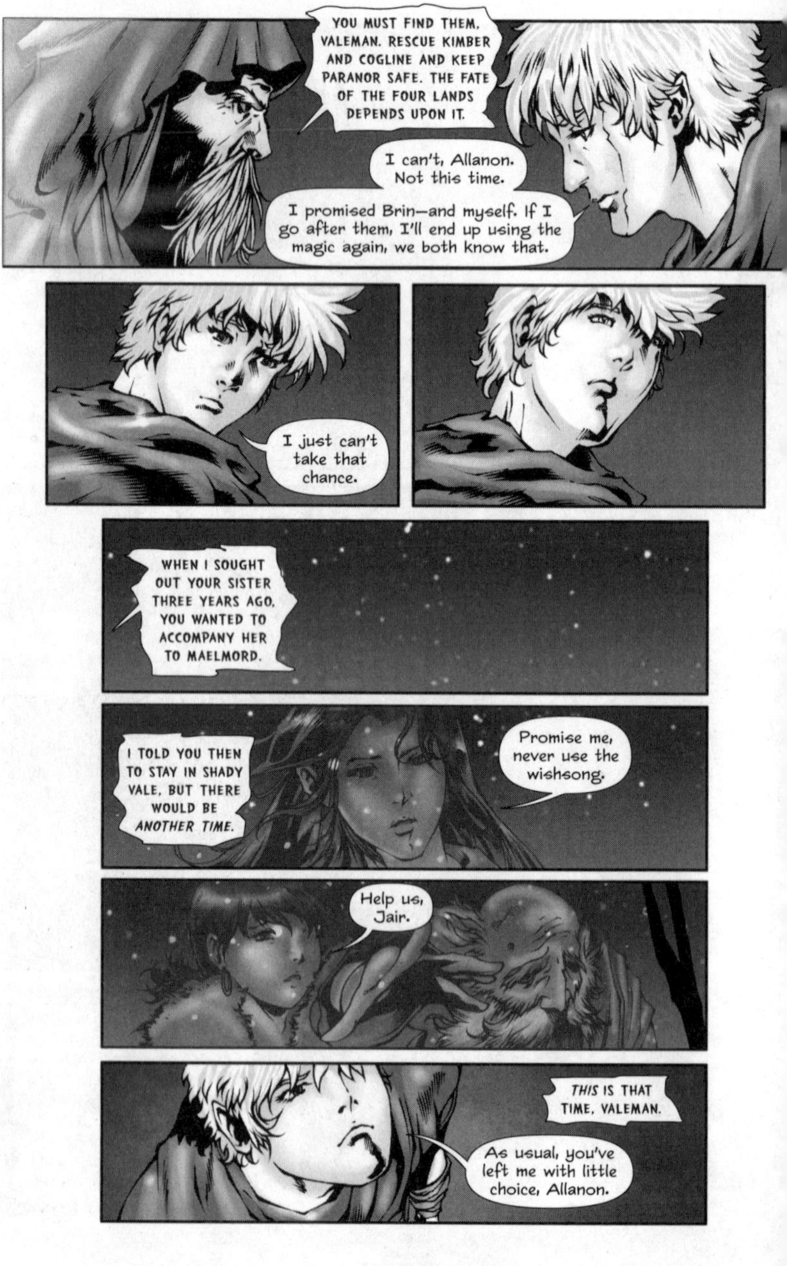
YOU MUST FIND THEM, VALEMAN. RESCUE KIMBER AND COGLINE AND KEEP PARANOR SAFE. THE FATE OF THE FOUR LANDS DEPENDS UPON IT.
I can't, Allanon. Not this time.
I promised Brin—and myself. If I go after them, I'll end up using the magic again, we both know that.
I just can't take that chance.
WHEN I SOUGHT OUT YOUR SISTER THREE YEARS AGO, YOU WANTED TO ACCOMPANY HER TO MAELMORD.
I TOLD YOU THEN TO STAY IN SHADY VALE, BUT THERE WOULD BE *ANOTHER TIME.*
Promise me, never use the wishsong.
Help us, Jair.
THIS IS THAT TIME, VALEMAN.
As usual, you've left me with little choice, Allanon.

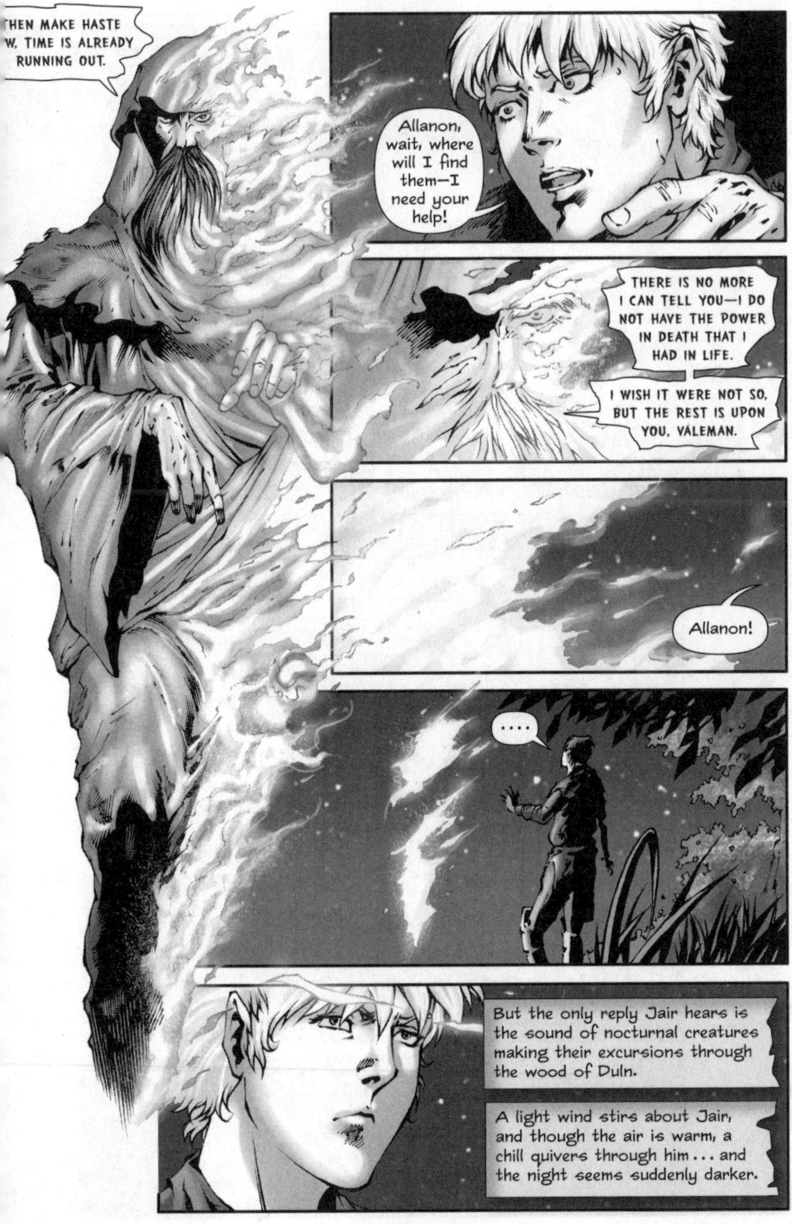
THEN MAKE HASTE W, TIME IS ALREADY RUNNING OUT.
Allanon, wait, where will I find them—I need your help!
THERE IS NO MORE I CAN TELL YOU—I DO NOT HAVE THE POWER IN DEATH THAT I HAD IN LIFE.
I WISH IT WERE NOT SO, BUT THE REST IS UPON YOU, VALEMAN.
Allanon!
....
But the only reply Jair hears is the sound of nocturnal creatures making their excursions through the wood of Duln.
A light wind stirs about Jair, and though the air is warm, a chill quivers through him . . . and the night seems suddenly darker.

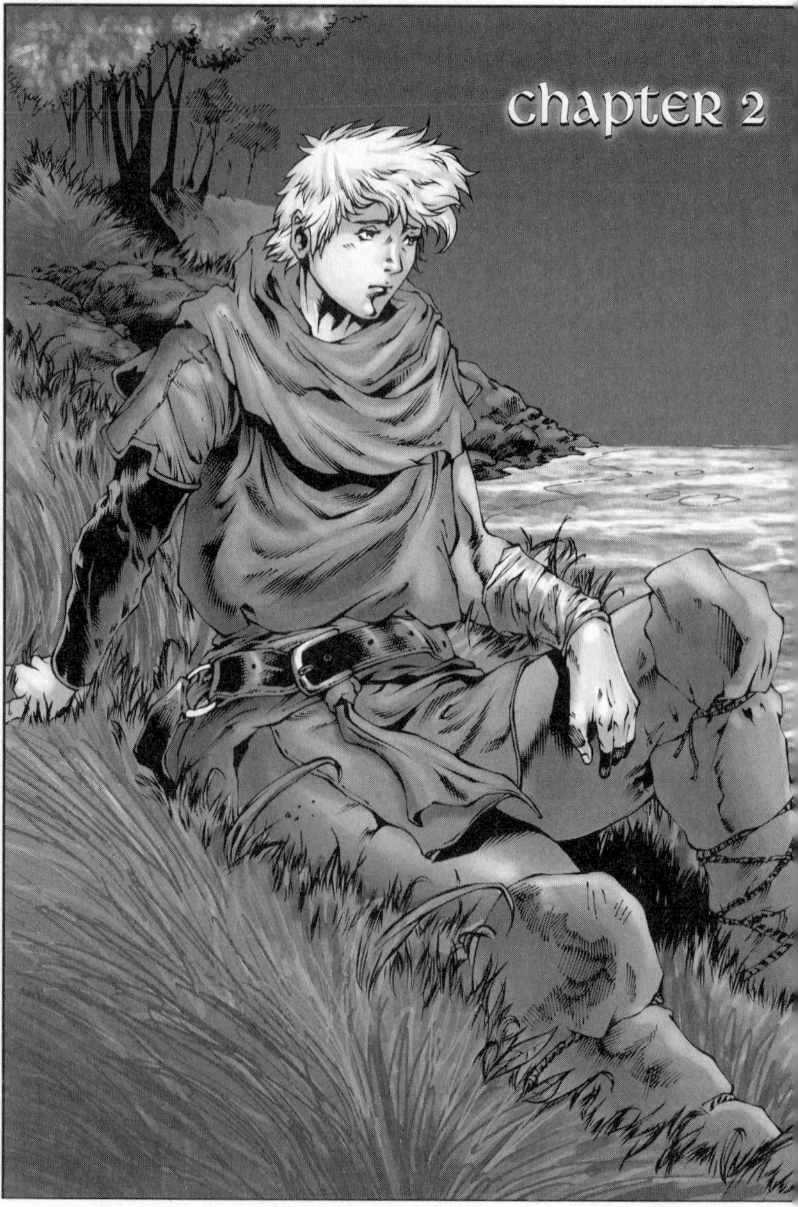
chapter 2

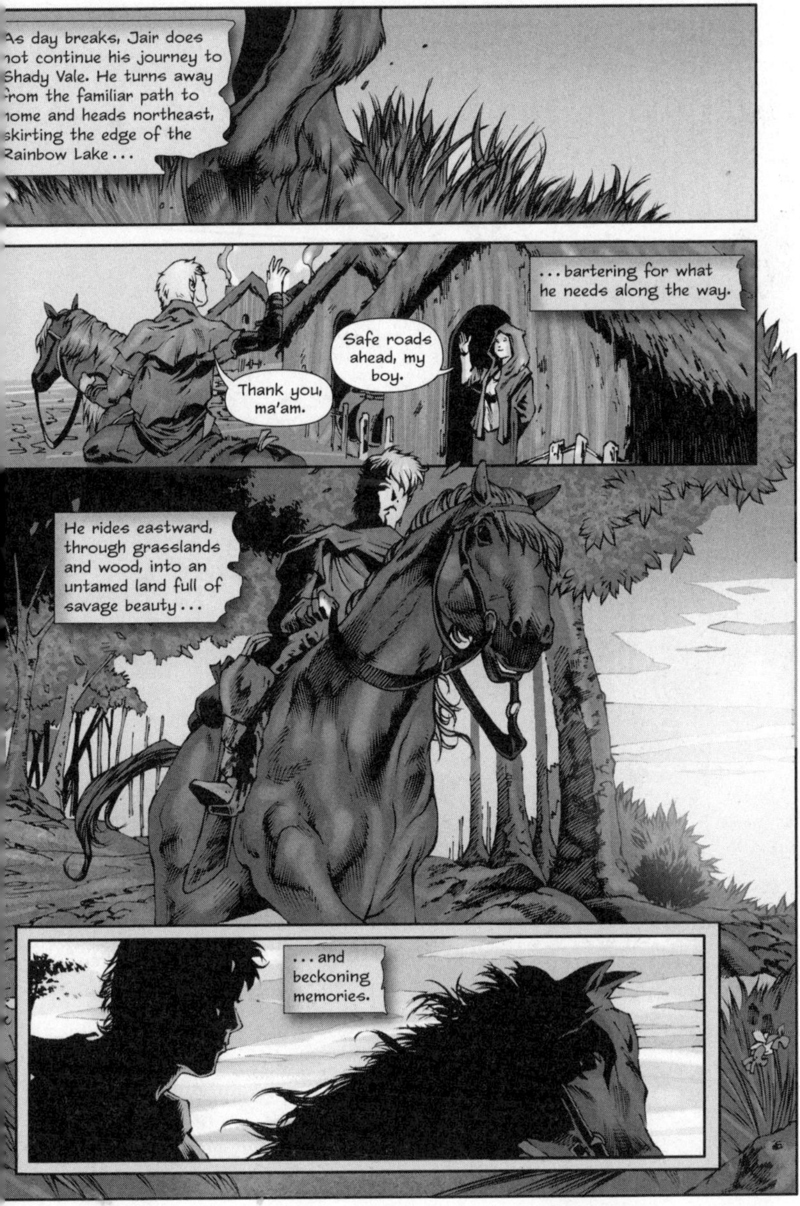
As day breaks, Jair does not continue his journey to Shady Vale. He turns away from the familiar path to home and heads northeast, skirting the edge of the Rainbow Lake . . .
. . . bartering for what he needs along the way.
Safe roads ahead, my boy.
Thank you, ma'am.
He rides eastward, through grasslands and wood, into an untamed land full of savage beauty . . .
. . . and beckoning memories.

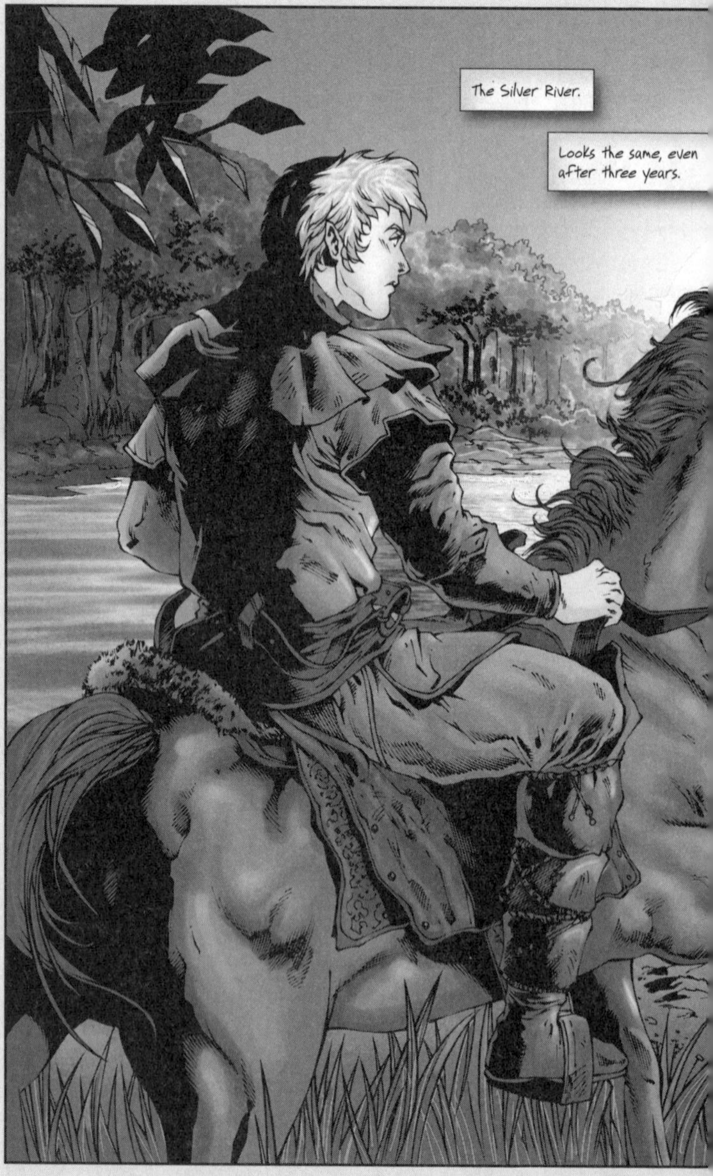
The Silver River.
Looks the same, even after three years.

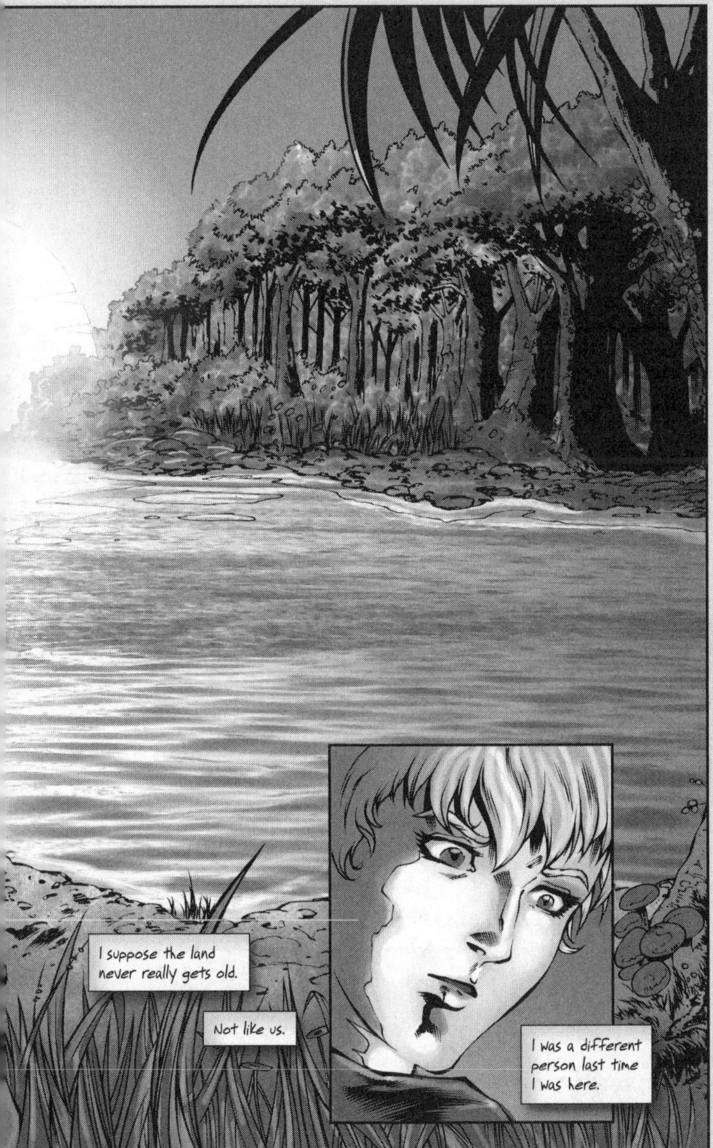
I suppose the land
never really gets old.
Not like us.
I was a different
person last time
I was here.

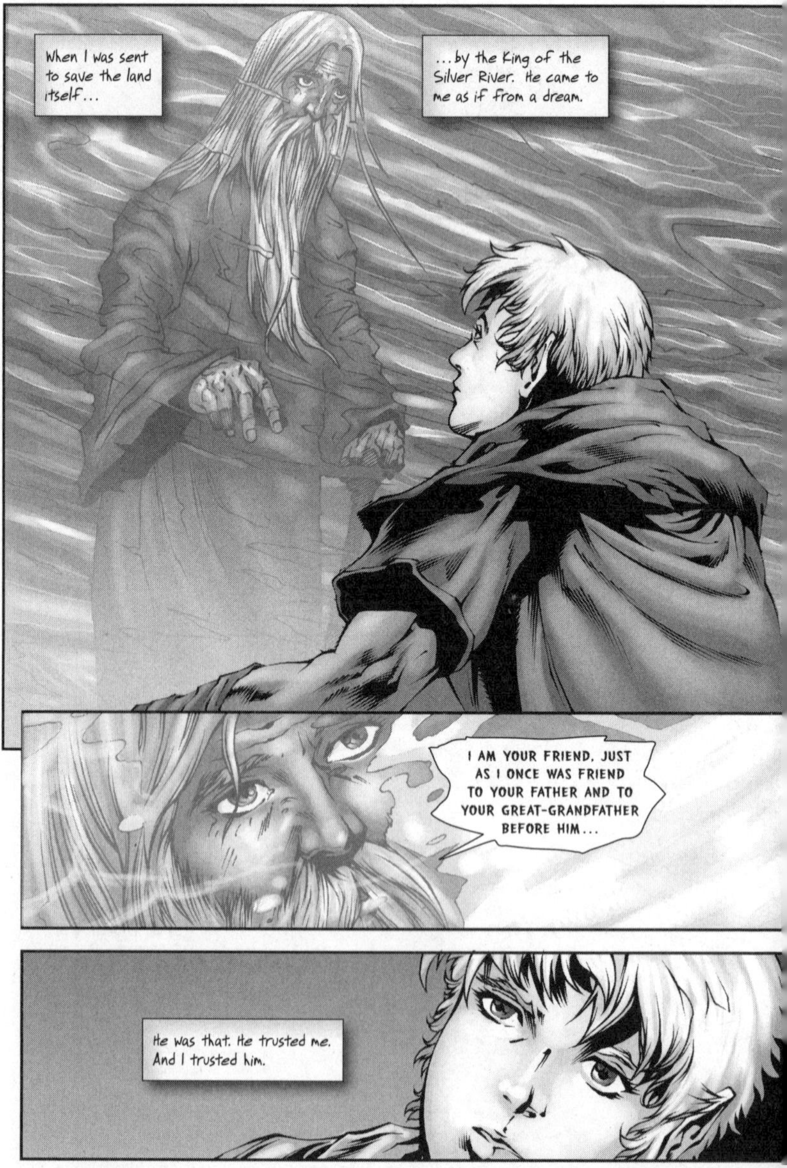
When I was sent to save the land itself...
...by the King of the Silver River. He came to me as if from a dream.
I AM YOUR FRIEND, JUST AS I ONCE WAS FRIEND TO YOUR FATHER AND TO YOUR GREAT-GRANDFATHER BEFORE HIM...
He was that. He trusted me. And I trusted him.

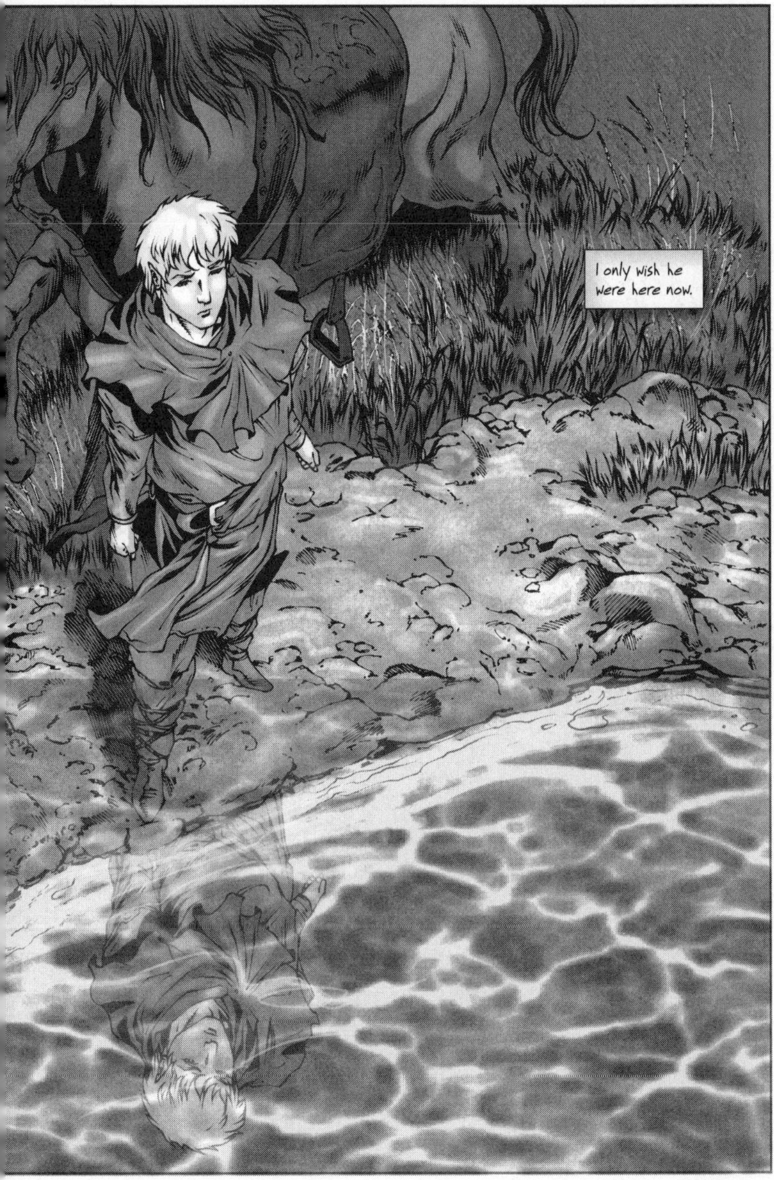
I only wish he were here now.

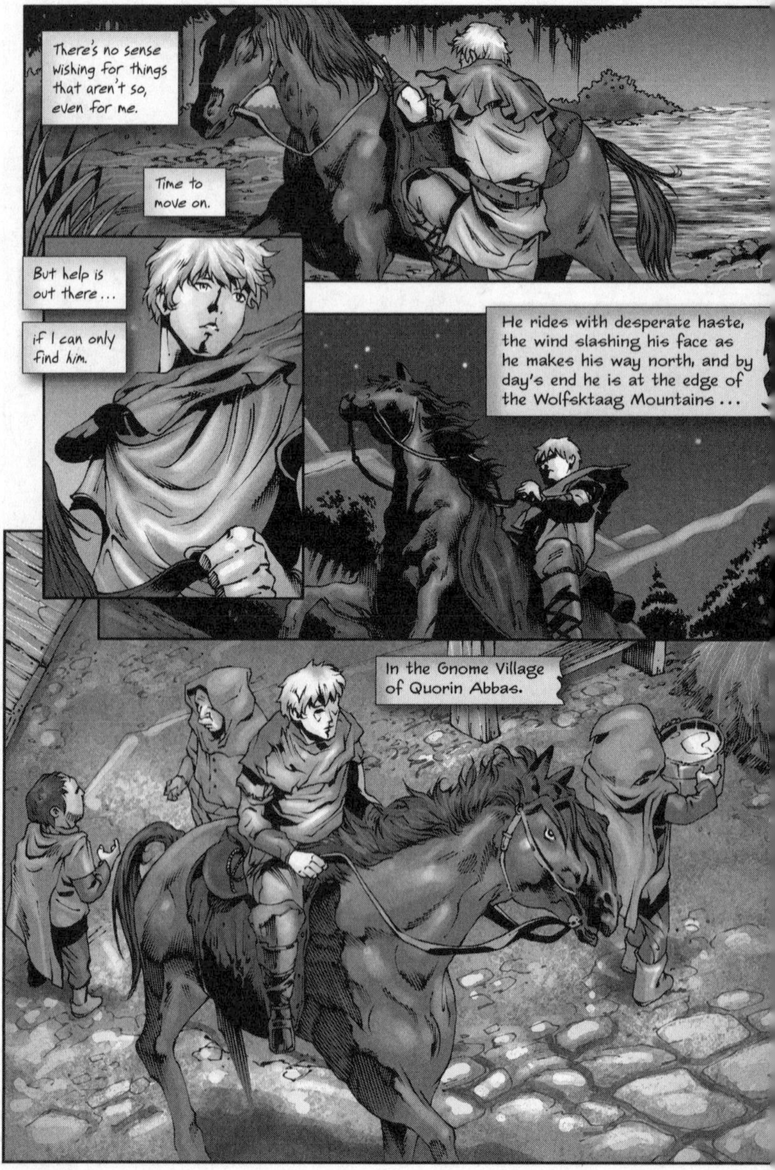
There's no sense wishing for things that aren't so, even for me.
Time to move on.
But help is out there . . .
if I can only find him.
He rides with desperate haste, the wind slashing his face as he makes his way north, and by day's end he is at the edge of the Wolfsktaag Mountains . . .
In the Gnome Village of Quorin Abbas.

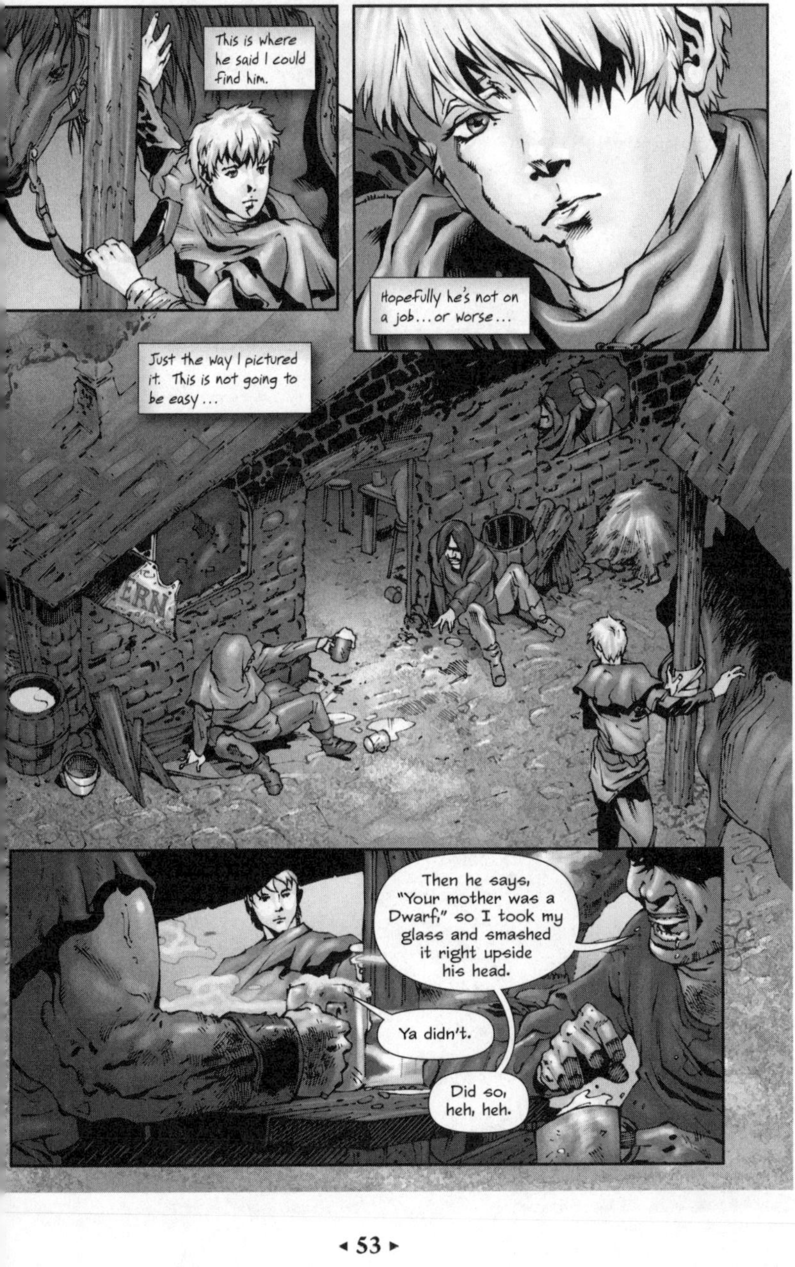
This is where he said I could find him.
Hopefully he's not on a job... or worse...
Just the way I pictured it. This is not going to be easy...
ERN
Then he says, "Your mother was a Dwarf," so I took my glass and smashed it right upside his head.
Ya didn't.
Did so, heh, heh.

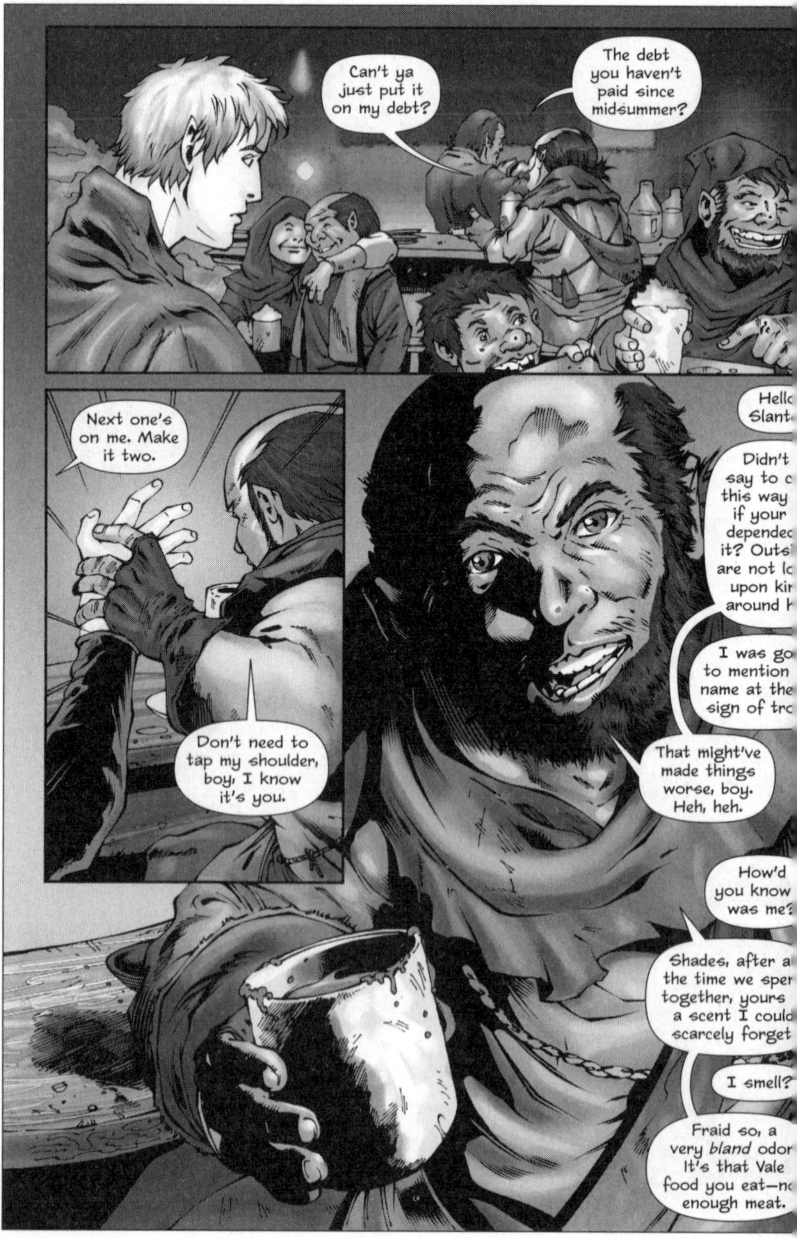

Can't ya just put it on my debt?
The debt you haven't paid since midsummer?
Next one's on me. Make it two.
Don't need to tap my shoulder, boy, I know it's you.
Hell Slant
Didn't say to c this way if your depende it? Outs are not l upon ki around h
I was go to mention name at the sign of tr
That might've made things worse, boy. Heh, heh.
How'd you know was me?
Shades, after a the time we spe together, yours a scent I coul scarcely forget
I smell?
Fraid so, a very *bland* odor It's that Vale food you eat—n enough meat.

...guess that big nose of yours comes in handy.

Sure enough. So what ya want, boy?

That nose, in fact.

So it is business that brings you.

Well, got plenty of work right now. Not interested.

Give me a chance, you don't even know what it is.

Trouble, that's what it is.

Always trouble when you're around, boy. Don't like saying it, but it's true.

GULP!

Not interested.

It's important, or I wouldn't be here.

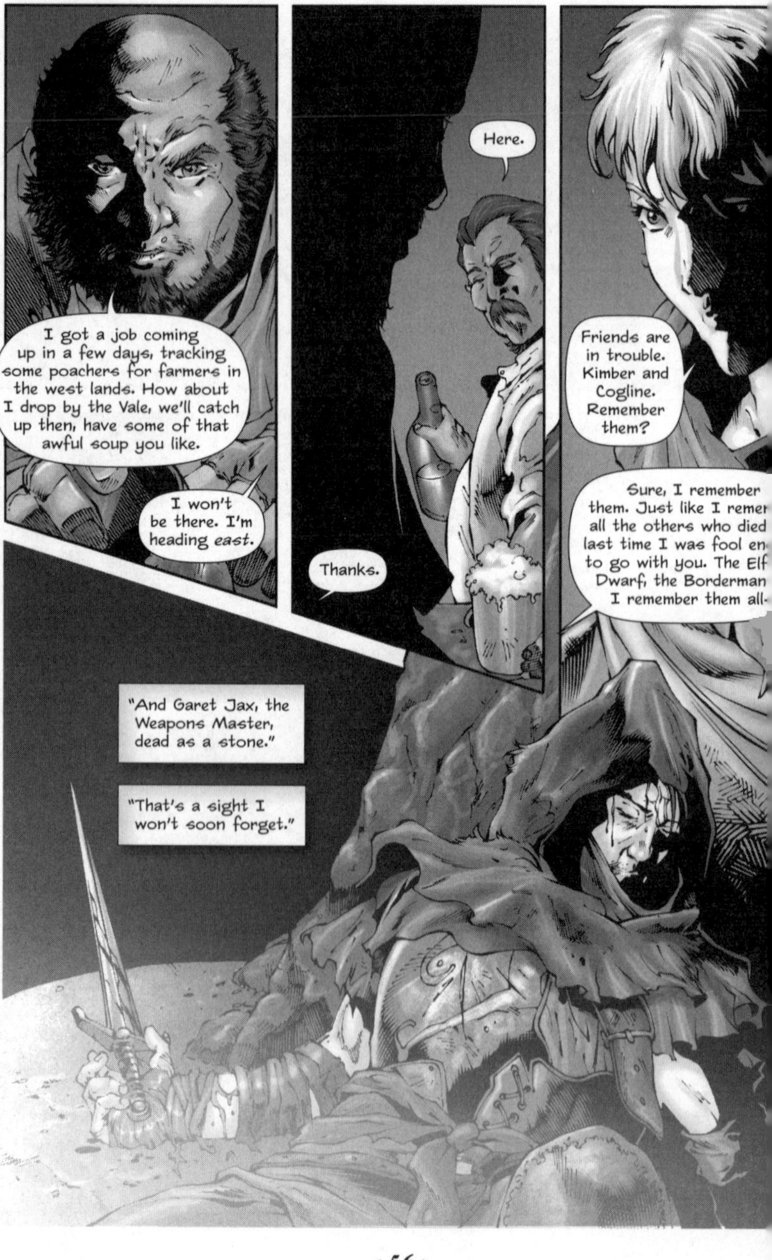
I got a job coming up in a few days, tracking some poachers for farmers in the west lands. How about I drop by the Vale, we'll catch up then, have some of that awful soup you like.
I won't be there. I'm heading *east*.
Here.
Thanks.
Friends are in trouble. Kimber and Cogline. Remember them?
Sure, I remember them. Just like I remer all the others who died last time I was fool en to go with you. The Elf Dwarf, the Borderman I remember them all-
"And Garet Jax, the Weapons Master, dead as a stone."
"That's a sight I won't soon forget."

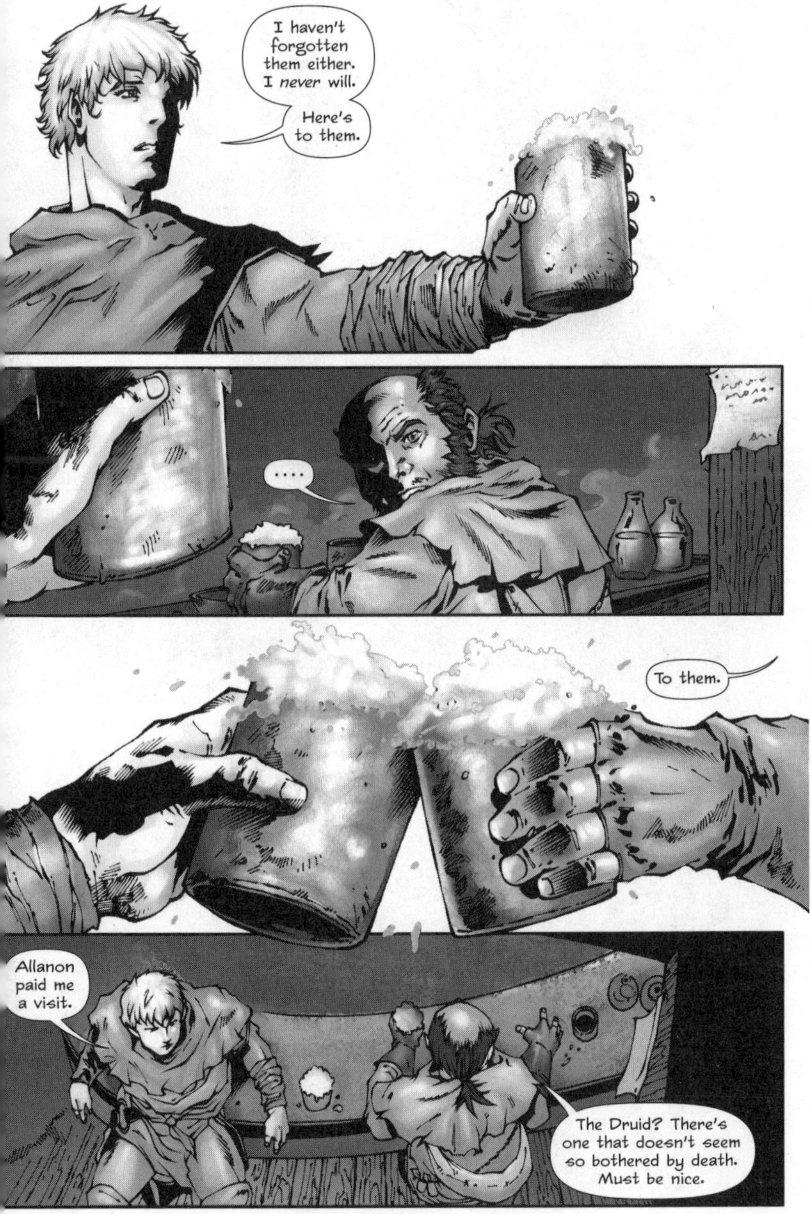
I haven't forgotten them either. I *never* will.
Here's to them.
....
To them.
Allanon paid me a visit.
The Druid? There's one that doesn't seem so bothered by death. Must be nice.

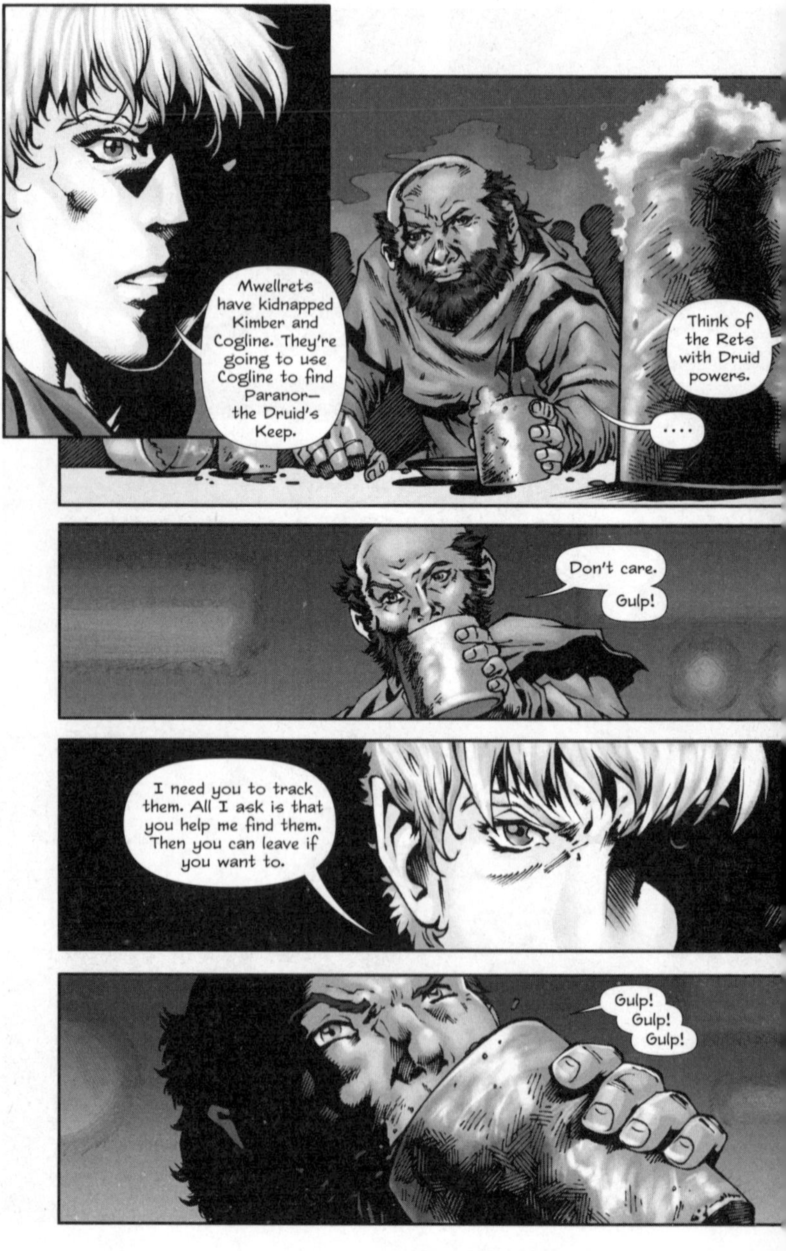
Mwellrets have kidnapped Kimber and Cogline. They're going to use Cogline to find Paranor—the Druid's Keep.
Think of the Rets with Druid powers.
....
Don't care.
Gulp!
I need you to track them. All I ask is that you help me find them. Then you can leave if you want to.
Gulp! Gulp! Gulp!

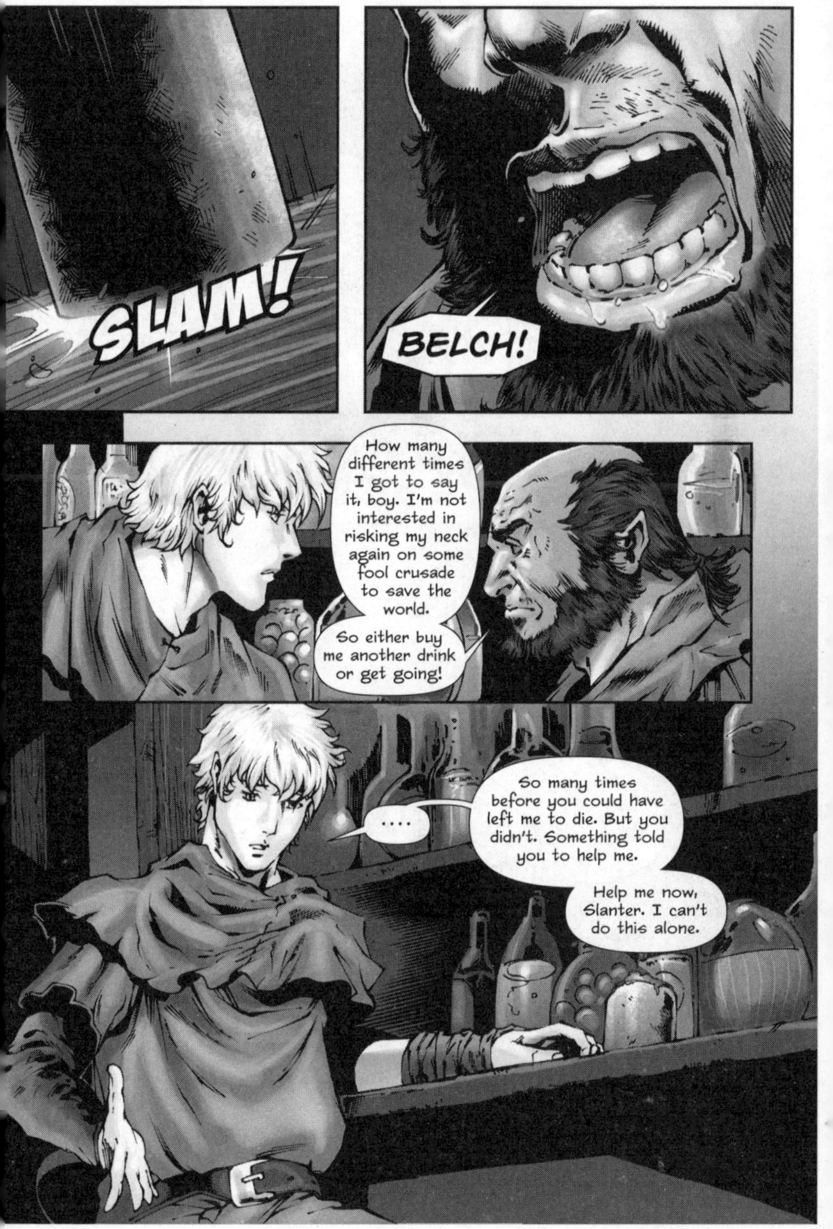
SLAM!
BELCH!
How many different times I got to say it, boy. I'm not interested in risking my neck again on some fool crusade to save the world.
So either buy me another drink or get going!
....
So many times before you could have left me to die. But you didn't. Something told you to help me.
Help me now, Slanter. I can't do this alone.

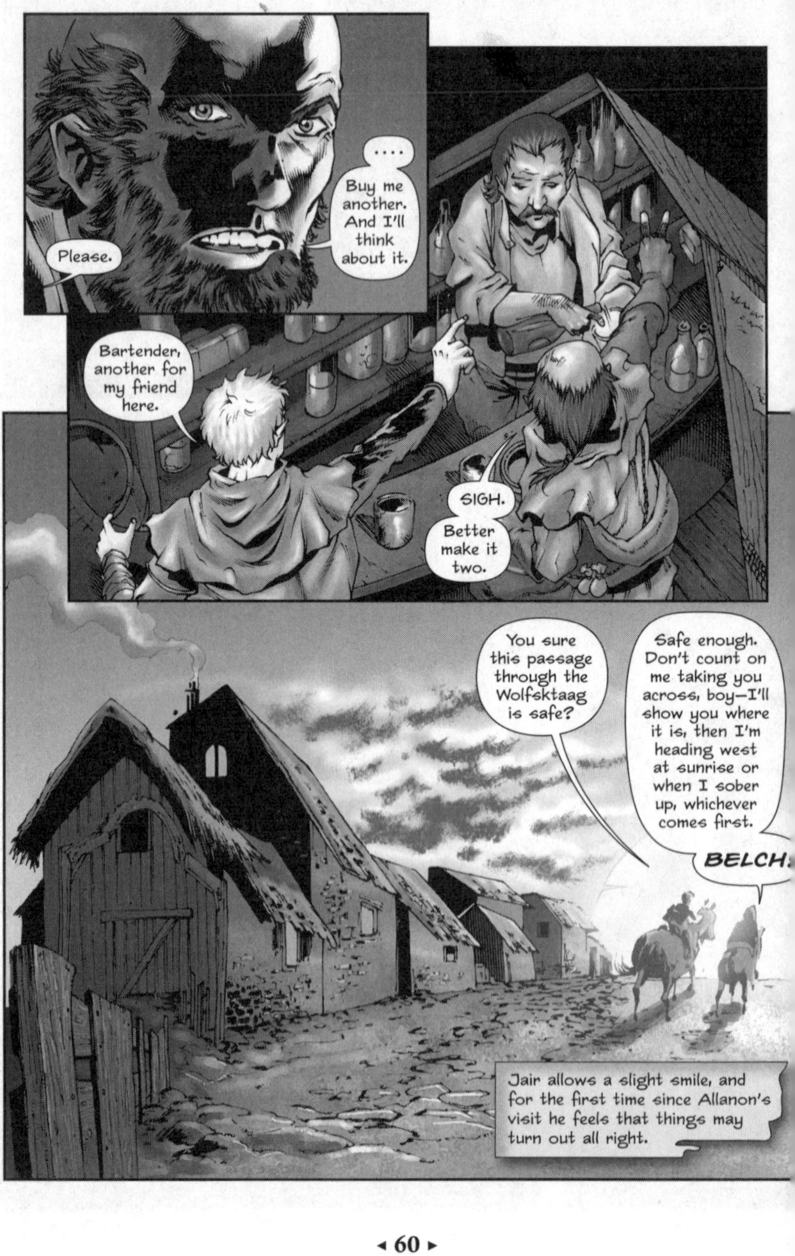
....
Buy me another. And I'll think about it.
Please.
Bartender, another for my friend here.
SIGH.
Better make it two.
You sure this passage through the Wolfsktaag is safe?
Safe enough. Don't count on me taking you across, boy—I'll show you where it is, then I'm heading west at sunrise or when I sober up, whichever comes first.
BELCH!
Jair allows a slight smile, and for the first time since Allanon's visit he feels that things may turn out all right.

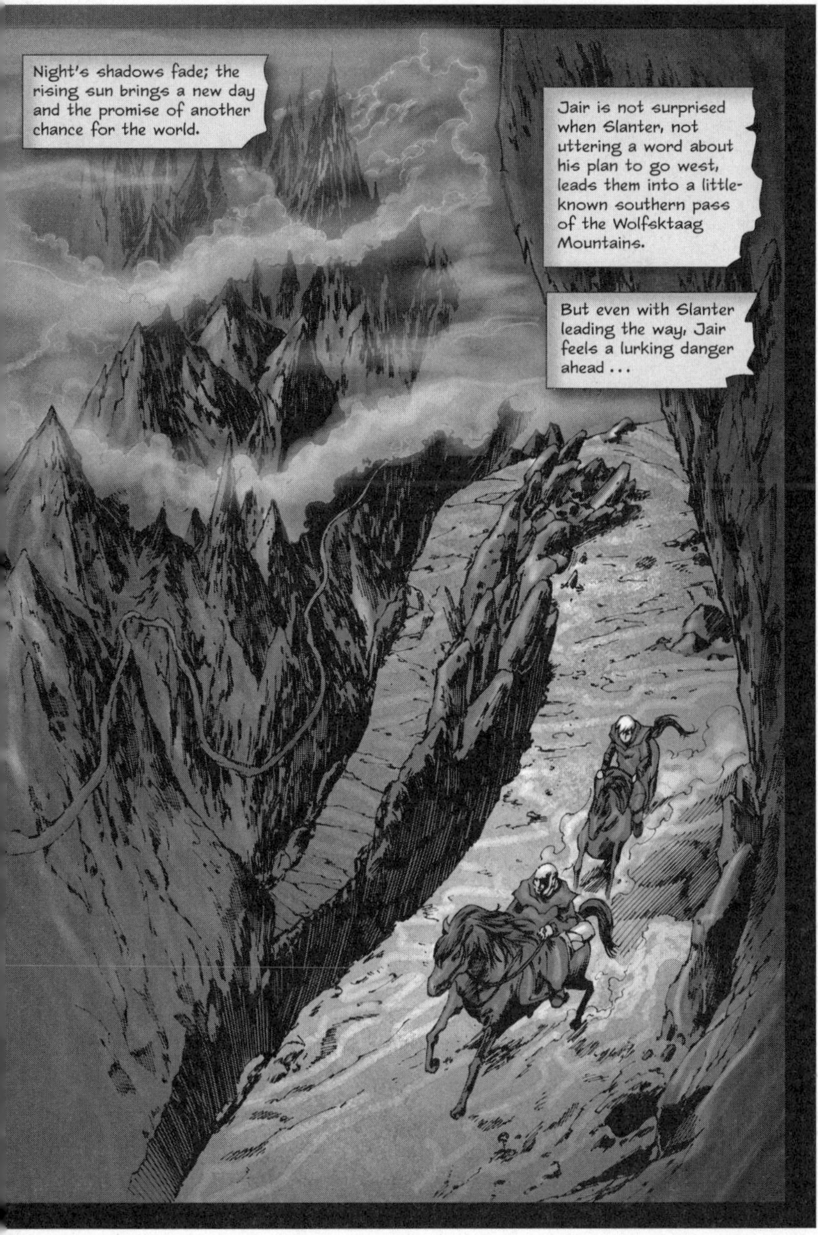
Night's shadows fade; the rising sun brings a new day and the promise of another chance for the world.
Jair is not surprised when Slanter, not uttering a word about his plan to go west, leads them into a little-known southern pass of the Wolfsktaag Mountains.
But even with Slanter leading the way, Jair feels a lurking danger ahead . . .

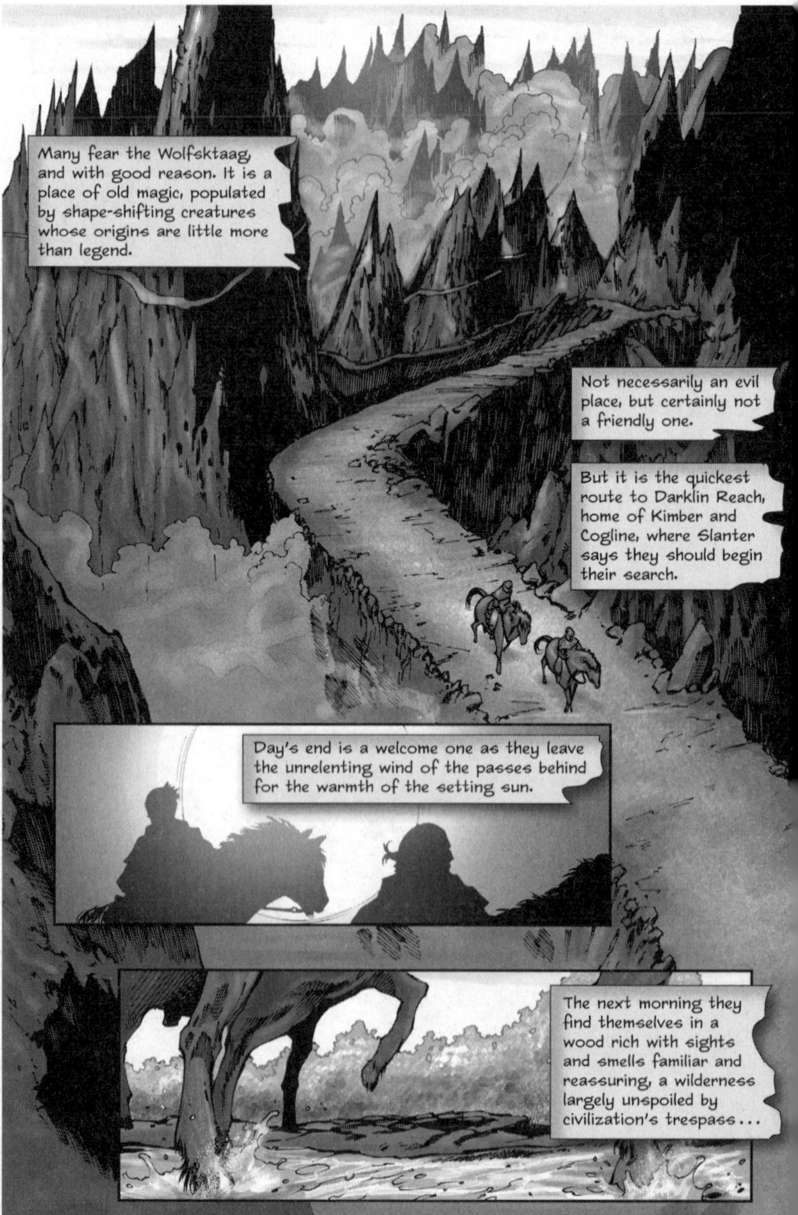
Many fear the Wolfsktaag, and with good reason. It is a place of old magic, populated by shape-shifting creatures whose origins are little more than legend.
Not necessarily an evil place, but certainly not a friendly one.
But it is the quickest route to Darklin Reach, home of Kimber and Cogline, where Slanter says they should begin their search.
Day's end is a welcome one as they leave the unrelenting wind of the passes behind for the warmth of the setting sun.
The next morning they find themselves in a wood rich with sights and smells familiar and reassuring, a wilderness largely unspoiled by civilization's trespass...

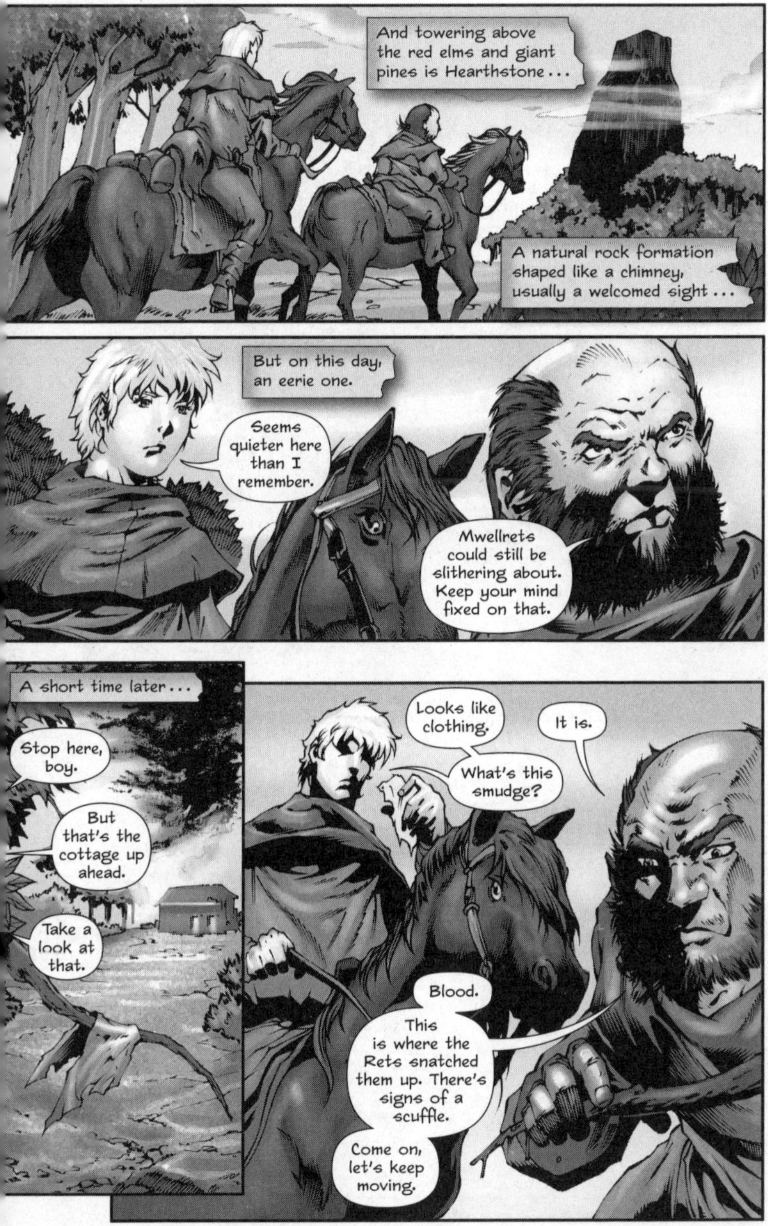
And towering above the red elms and giant pines is Hearthstone . . .
A natural rock formation shaped like a chimney, usually a welcomed sight . . .
But on this day, an eerie one.
Seems quieter here than I remember.
Mwellrets could still be slithering about. Keep your mind fixed on that.
A short time later . . .
Stop here, boy.
But that's the cottage up ahead.
Take a look at that.
Looks like clothing.
What's this smudge?
It is.
Blood.
This is where the Rets snatched them up. There's signs of a scuffle.
Come on, let's keep moving.

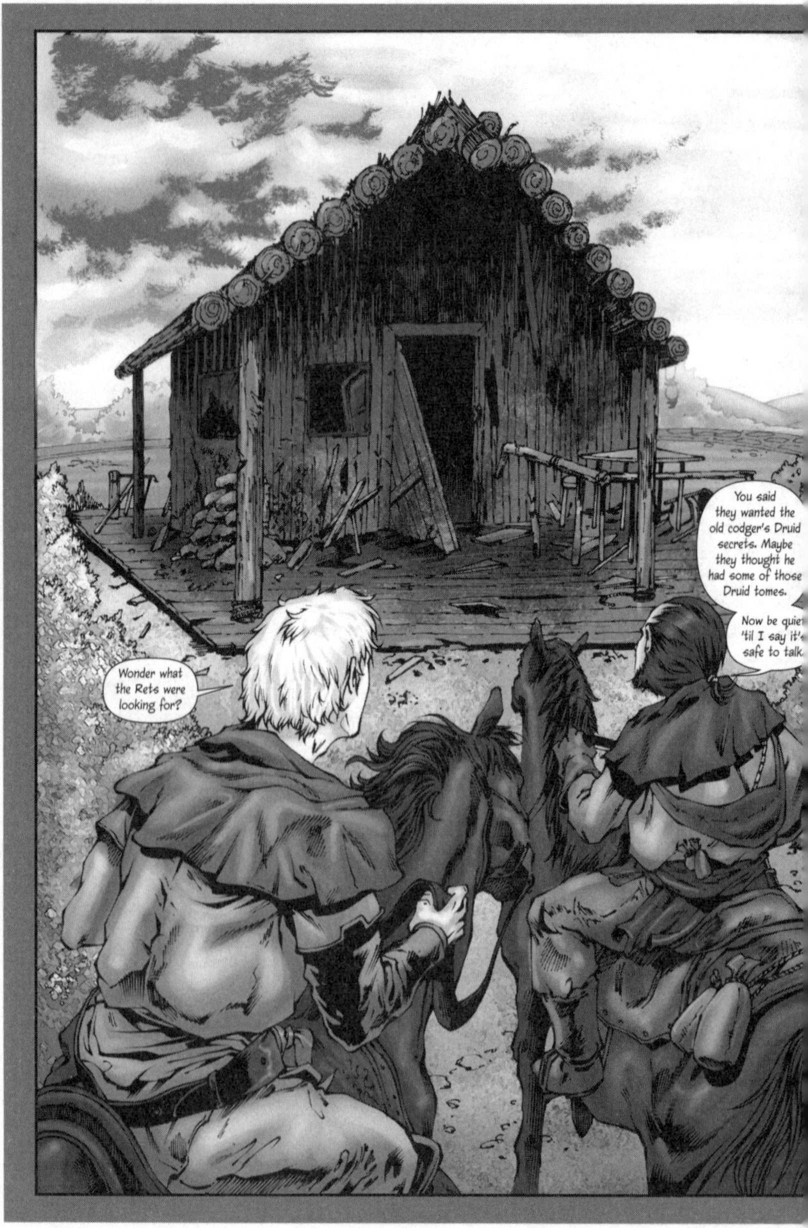
Wonder what the Rets were looking for?
You said they wanted the old codger's Druid secrets. Maybe they thought he had some of those Druid tomes.
Now be quie 'til I say it safe to talk.

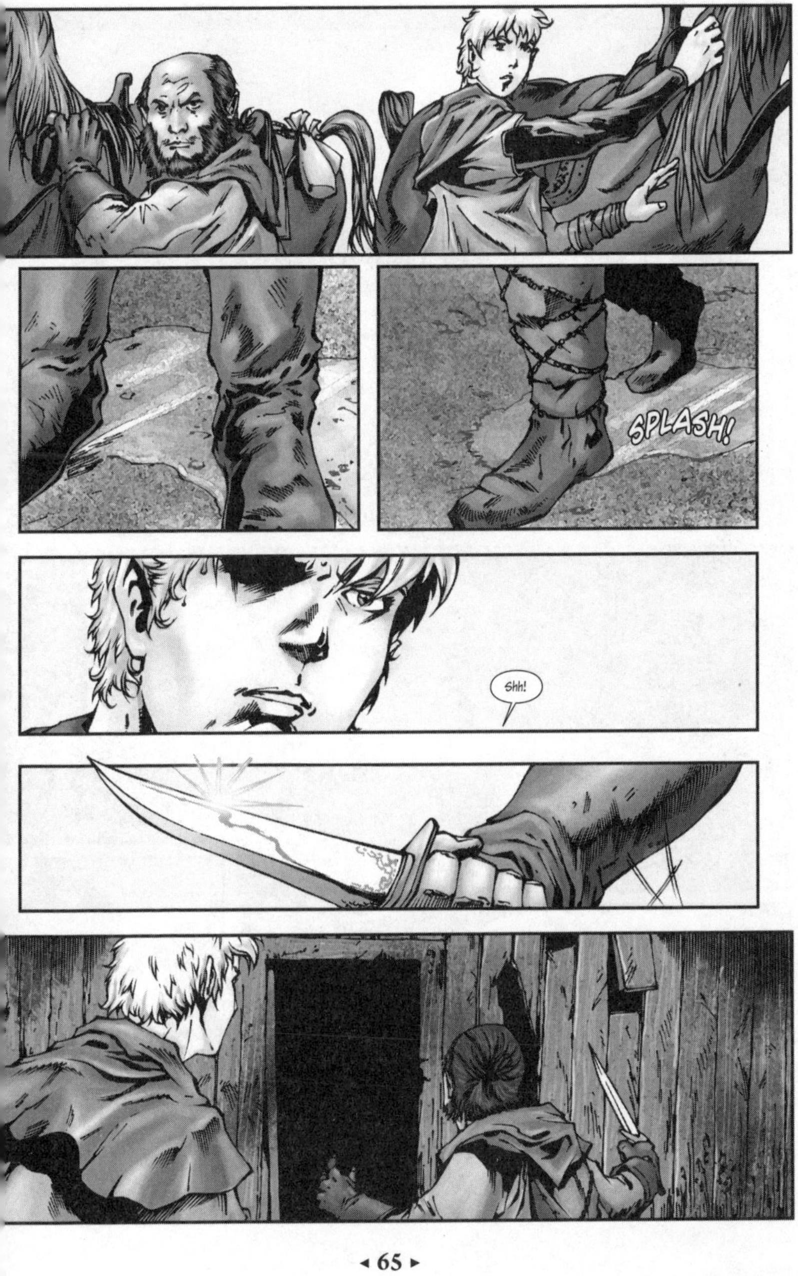
SPLASH!
Shh!

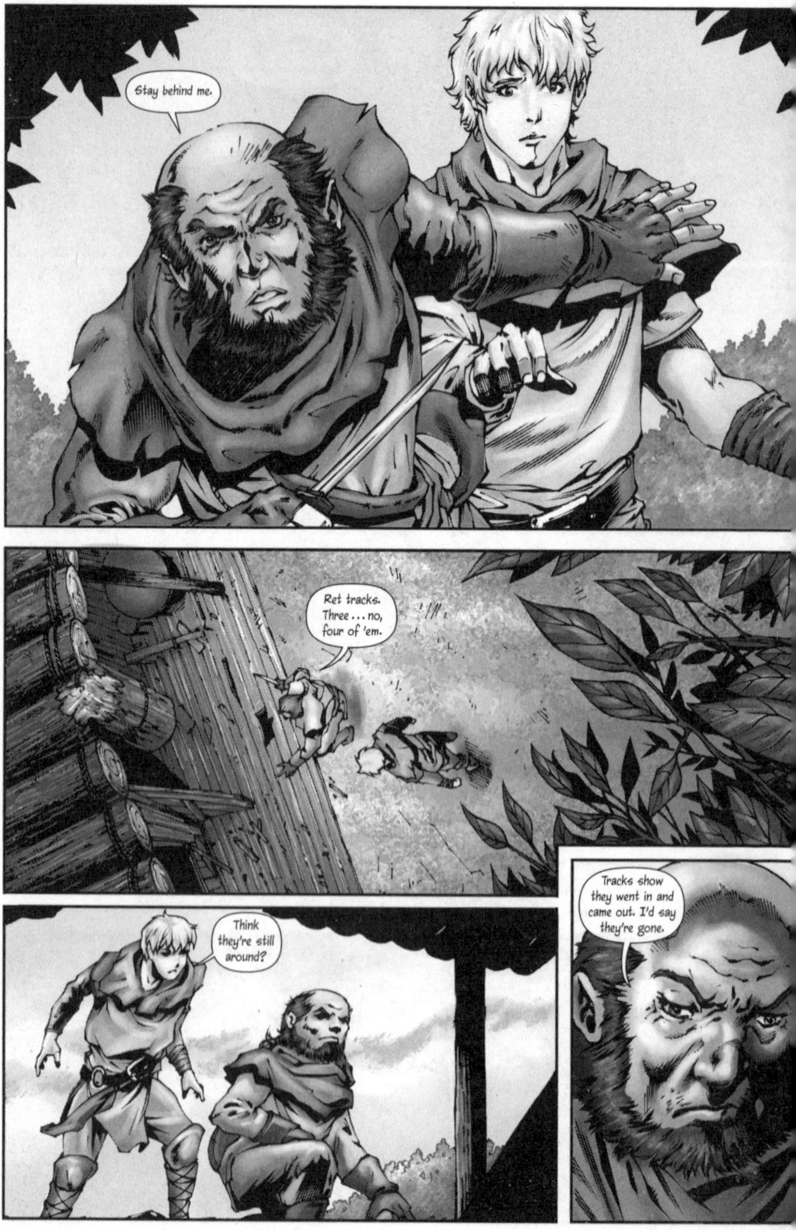
Stay behind me.
Ret tracks. Three ... no, four of 'em.
Think they're still around?
Tracks show they went in and came out. I'd say they're gone.

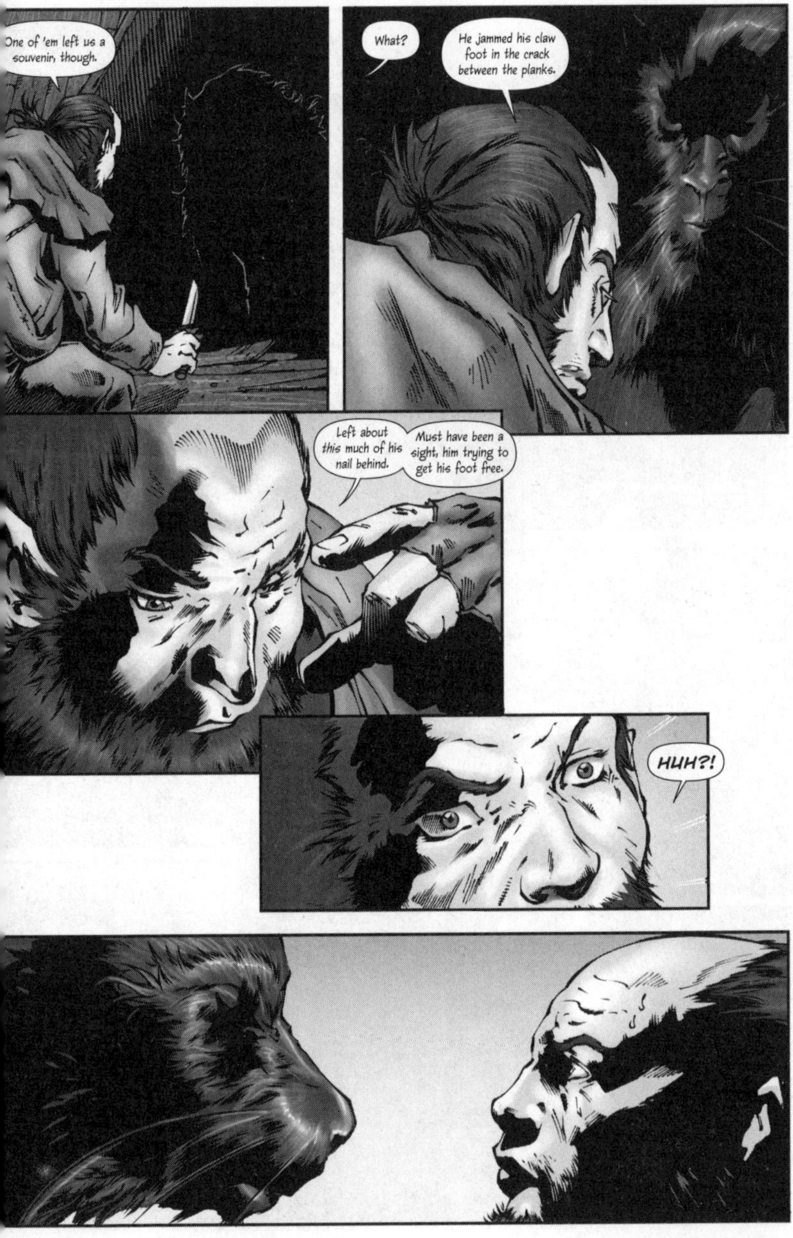
One of 'em left us a souvenir, though.
What?
He jammed his claw foot in the crack between the planks.
Left about this much of his nail behind.
Must have been a sight, him trying to get his foot free.
HUH?!

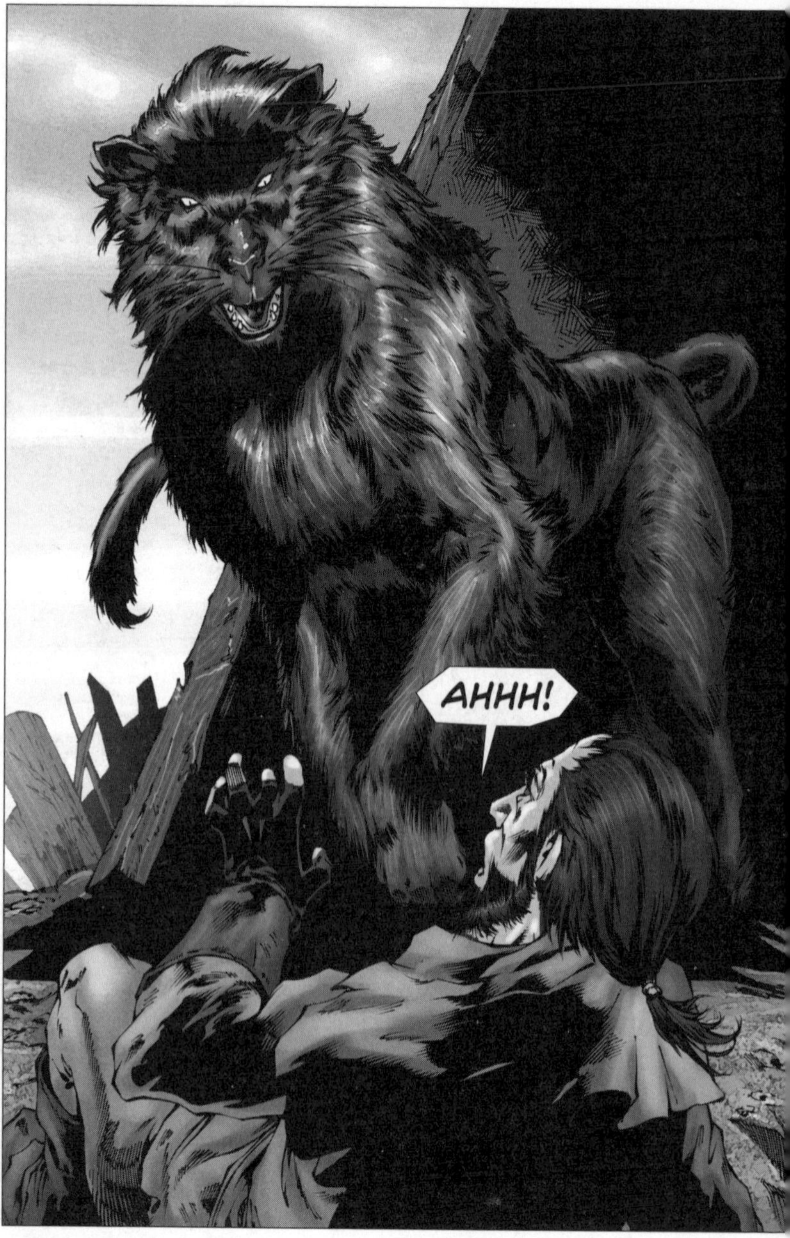
AHHH!

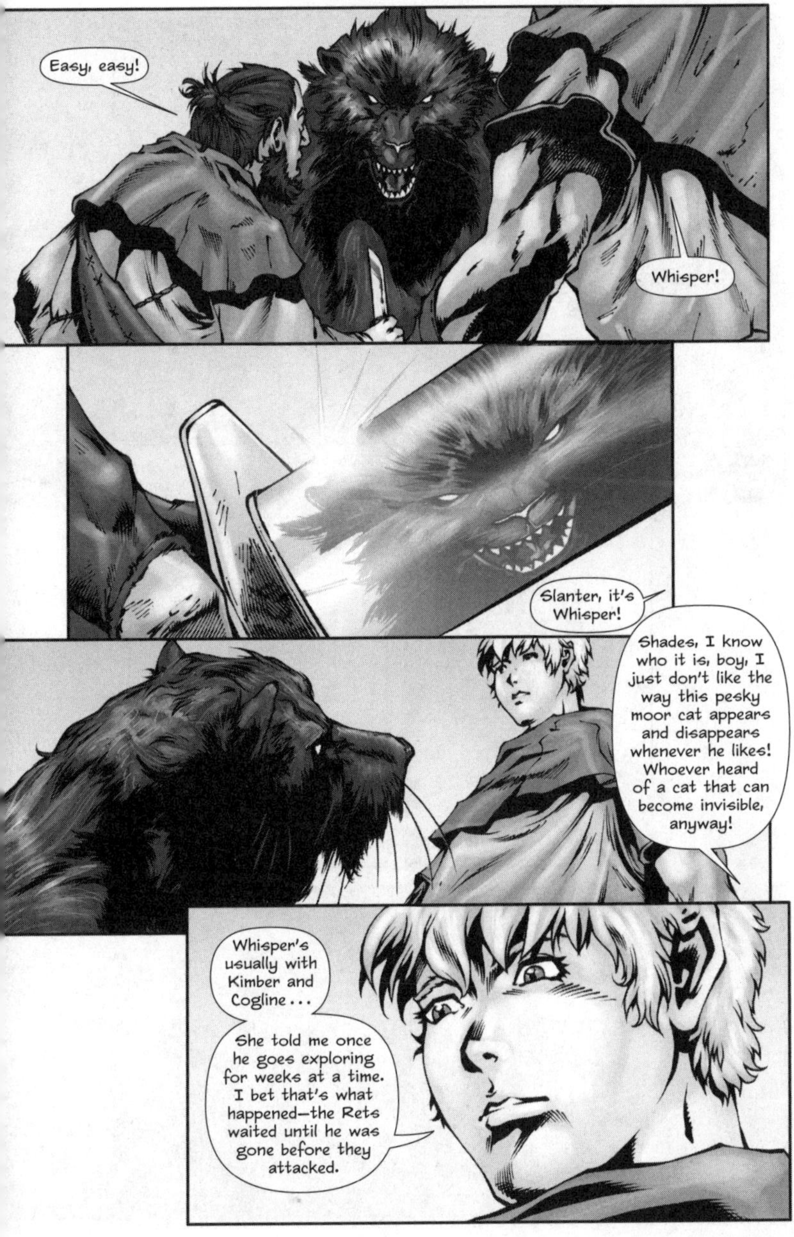
Easy, easy!
Whisper!
Slanter, it's Whisper!
Shades, I know who it is, boy, I just don't like the way this pesky moor cat appears and disappears whenever he likes! Whoever heard of a cat that can become invisible, anyway!
Whisper's usually with Kimber and Cogline . . .
She told me once he goes exploring for weeks at a time. I bet that's what happened—the Rets waited until he was gone before they attacked.

Well, he picked a bad time to go roamin' the countryside.

Hey, you remember me—I'm Brin's brother.

It's good to see you, too.

No time fo reunions, be If we're luck Rets left tracks that lead us rig to the old and Kimbe

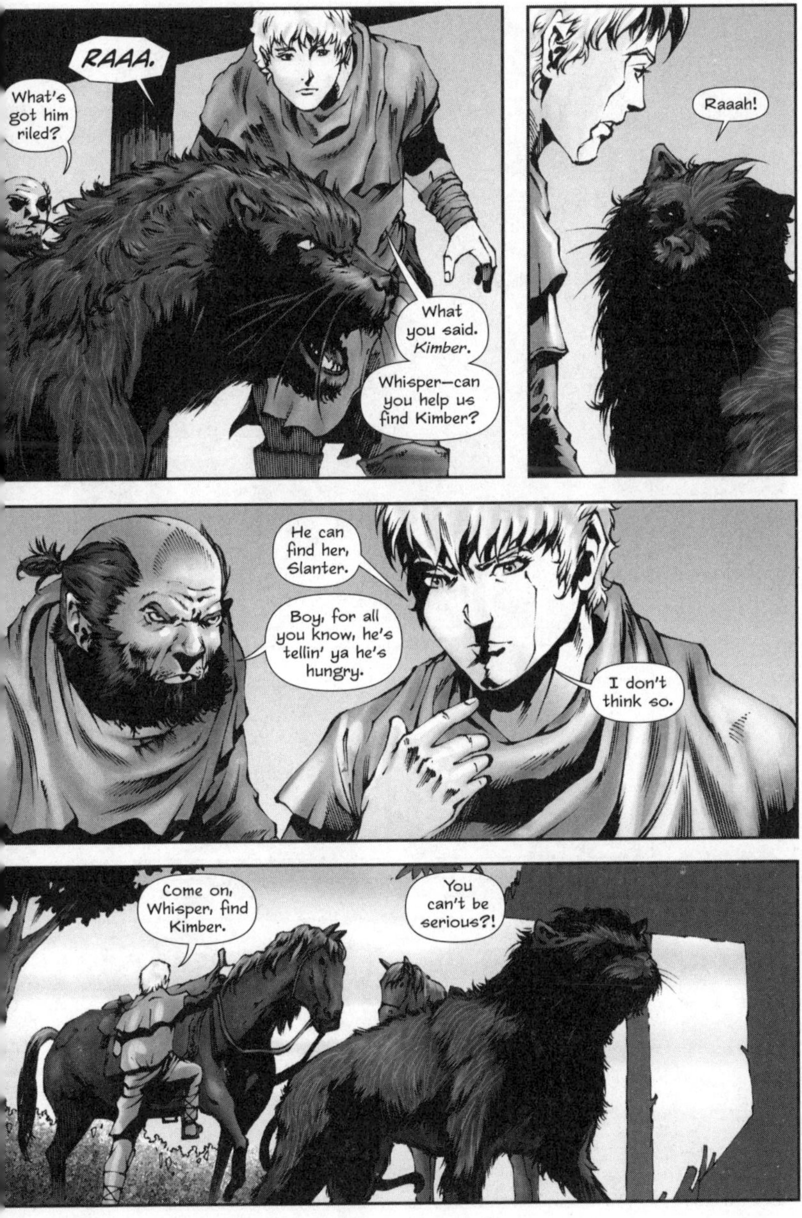
RAAA.
What's got him riled?
What you said. *Kimber*.
Whisper—can you help us find Kimber?
Raaah!
He can find her, Slanter.
Boy, for all you know, he's tellin' ya he's hungry.
I don't think so.
Come on, Whisper, find Kimber.
You can't be serious?!

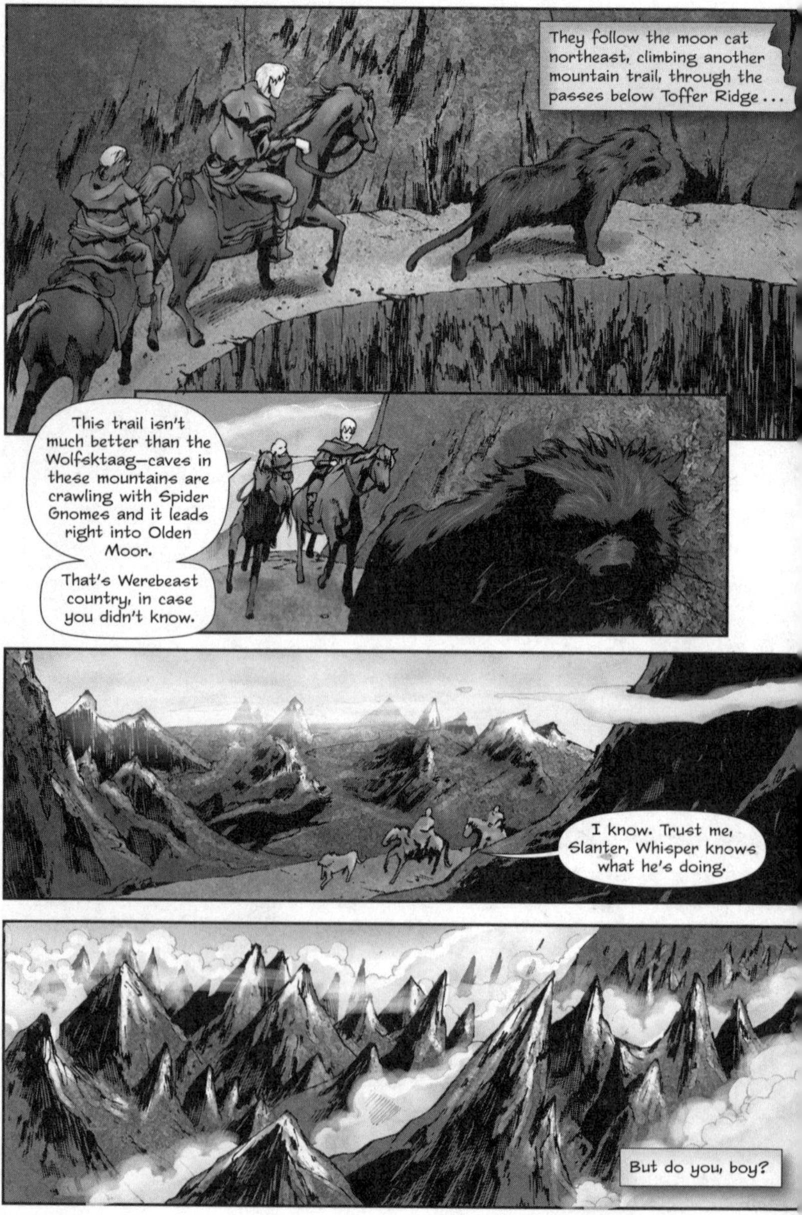
They follow the moor cat northeast, climbing another mountain trail, through the passes below Toffer Ridge . . .
This trail isn't much better than the Wolfsktaag—caves in these mountains are crawling with Spider Gnomes and it leads right into Olden Moor.
That's Werebeast country, in case you didn't know.
I know. Trust me, Slanter, Whisper knows what he's doing.
But do you, boy?

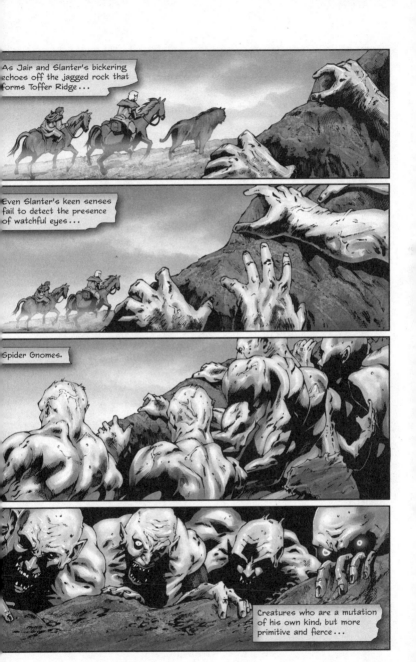

As Jair and Slanter's bickering echoes off the jagged rock that forms Toffer Ridge...

Even Slanter's keen senses fail to detect the presence of watchful eyes...

Spider Gnomes.

Creatures who are a mutation of his own kind, but more primitive and fierce...

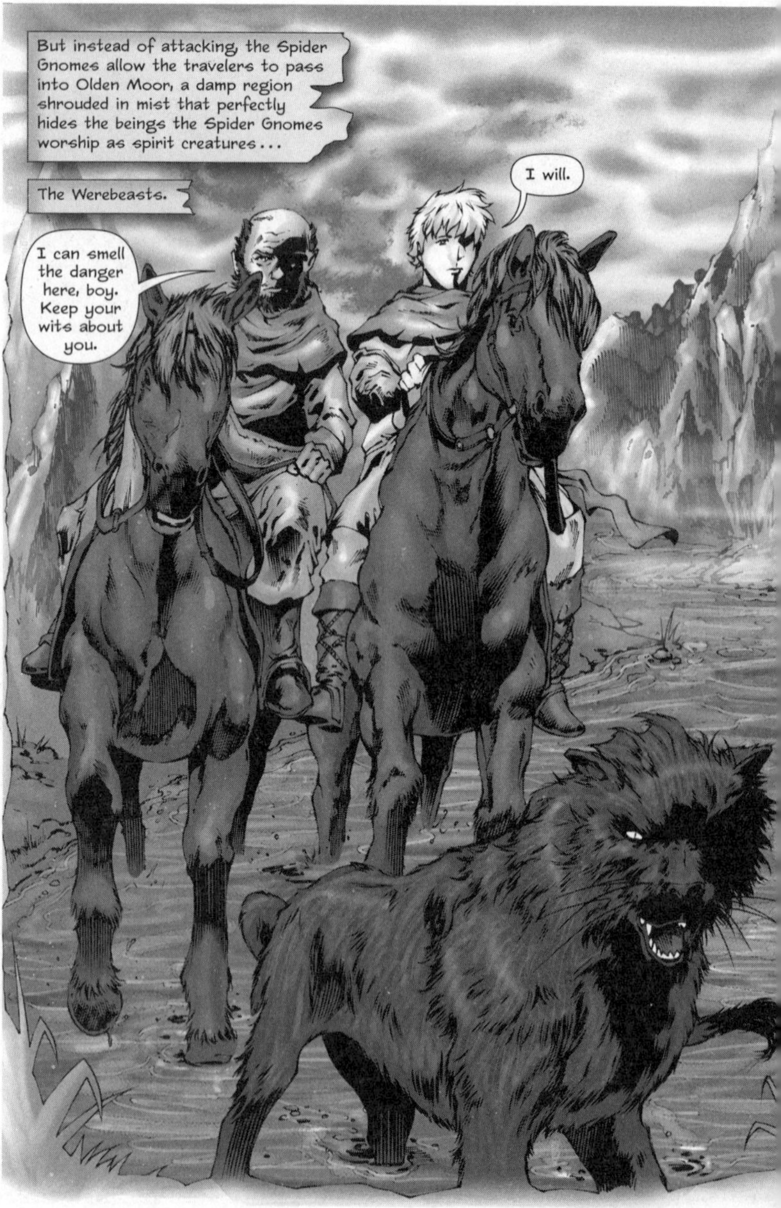

But instead of attacking, the Spider Gnomes allow the travelers to pass into Olden Moor, a damp region shrouded in mist that perfectly hides the beings the Spider Gnomes worship as spirit creatures...
The Werebeasts.
I can smell the danger here, boy. Keep your wits about you.
I will.

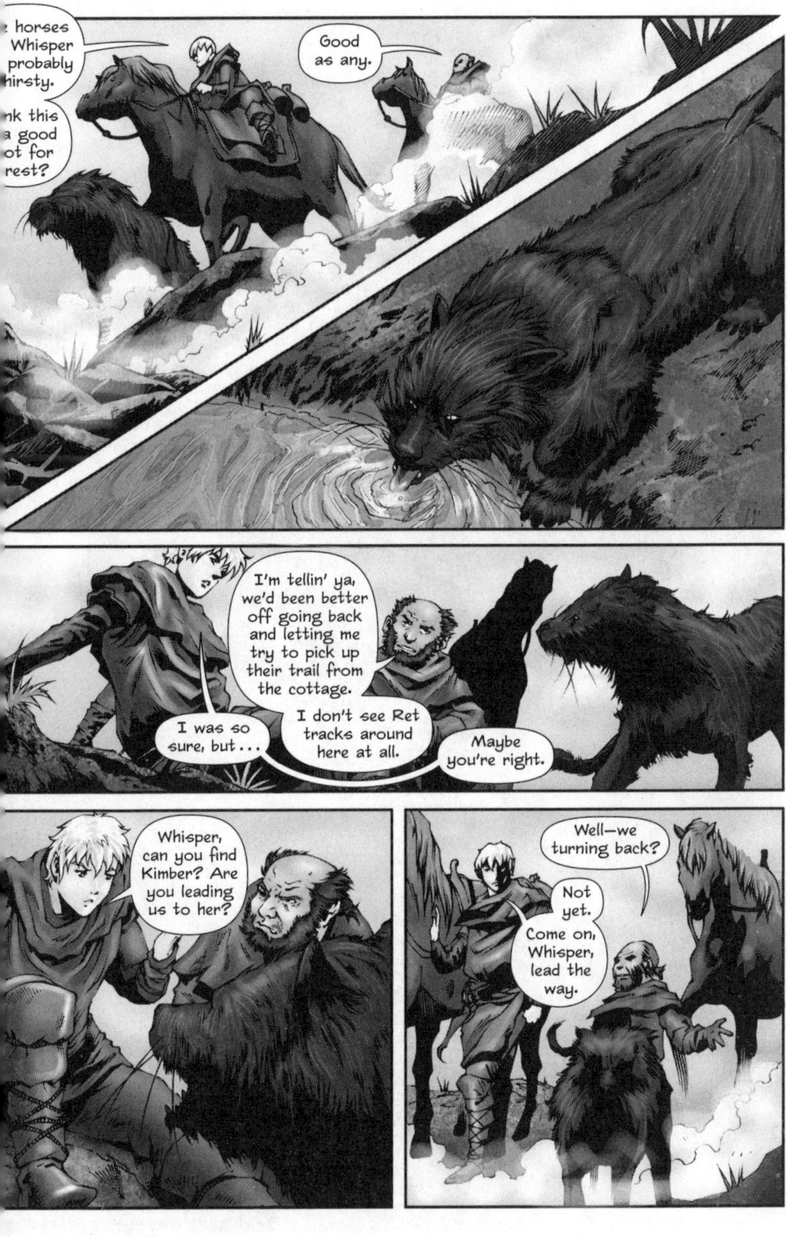

horses Whisper probably hirsty.
nk this a good ot for rest?
Good as any.
I'm tellin' ya, we'd been better off going back and letting me try to pick up their trail from the cottage.
I don't see Ret tracks around here at all.
I was so sure, but...
Maybe you're right.
Whisper, can you find Kimber? Are you leading us to her?
Well—we turning back?
Not yet.
Come on, Whisper, lead the way.

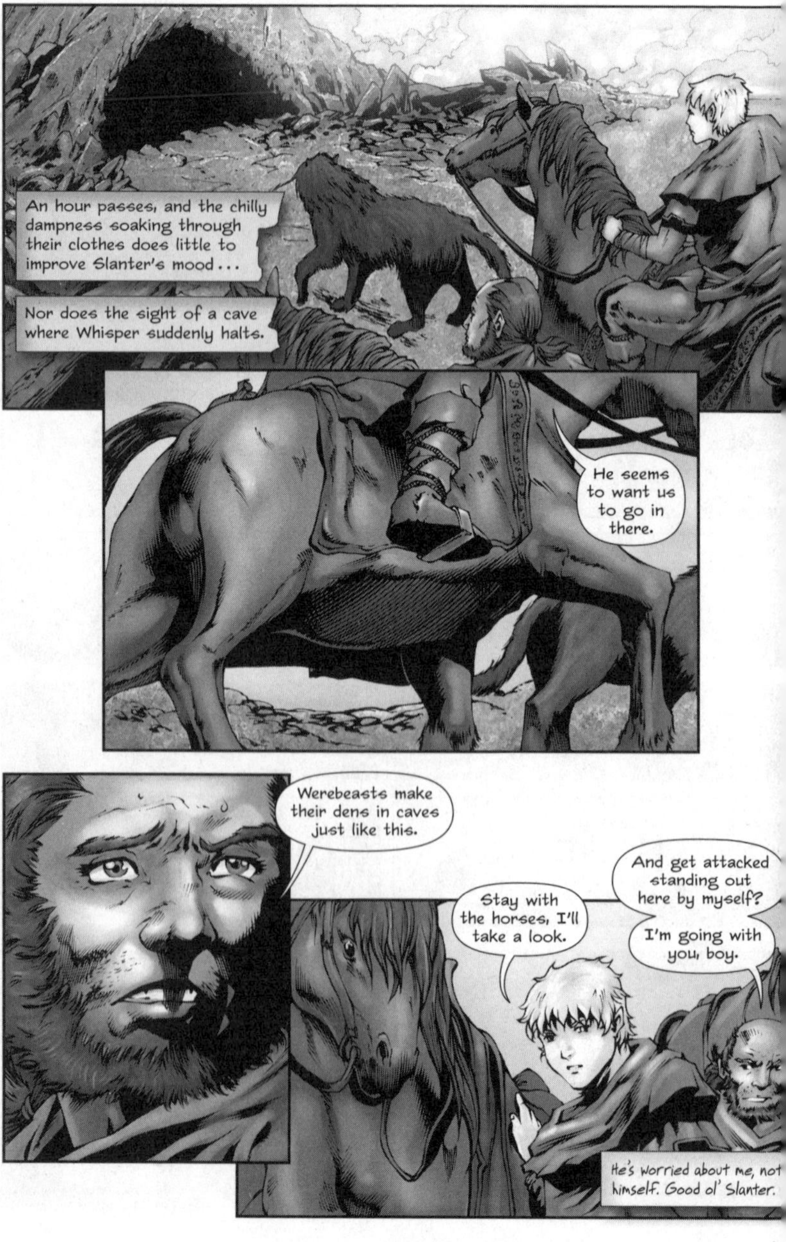

An hour passes, and the chilly dampness soaking through their clothes does little to improve Slanter's mood...
Nor does the sight of a cave where Whisper suddenly halts.
He seems to want us to go in there.
Werebeasts make their dens in caves just like this.
Stay with the horses, I'll take a look.
And get attacked standing out here by myself?
I'm going with you, boy.
He's worried about me, not himself. Good ol' Slanter.

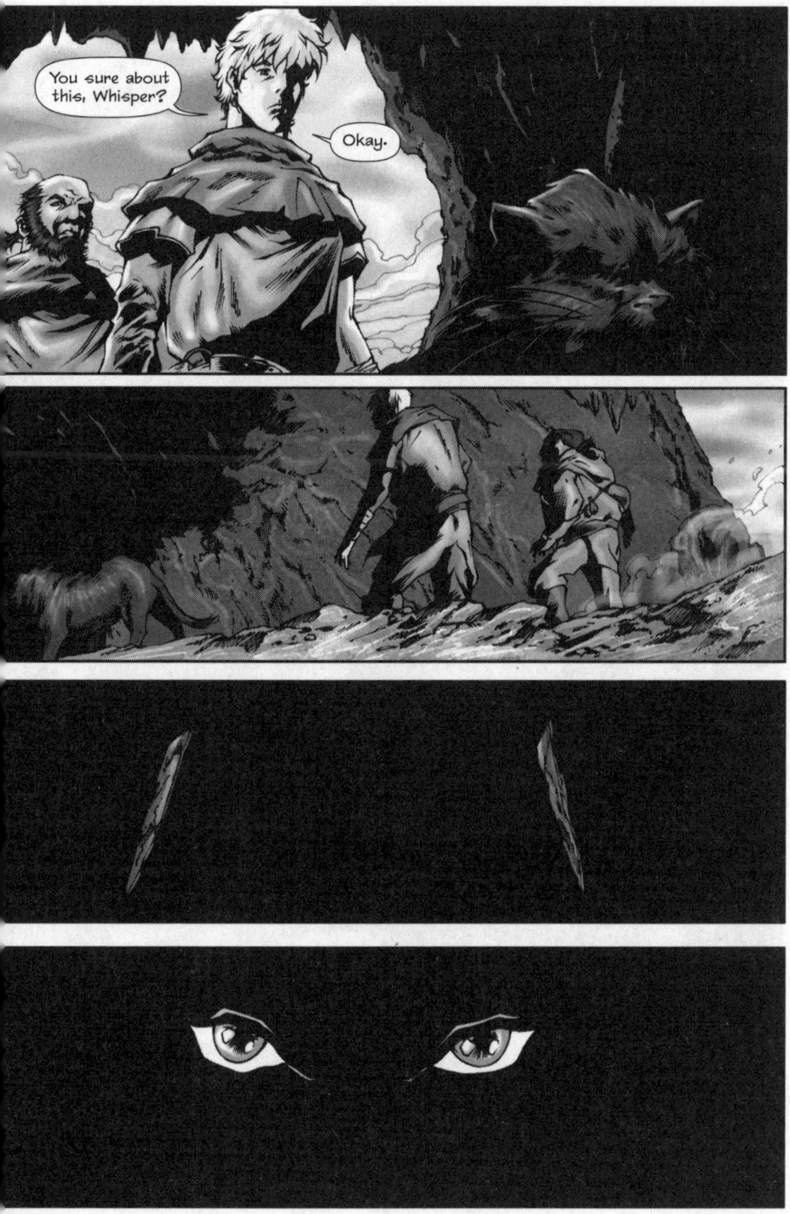
You sure about this, Whisper?
Okay.

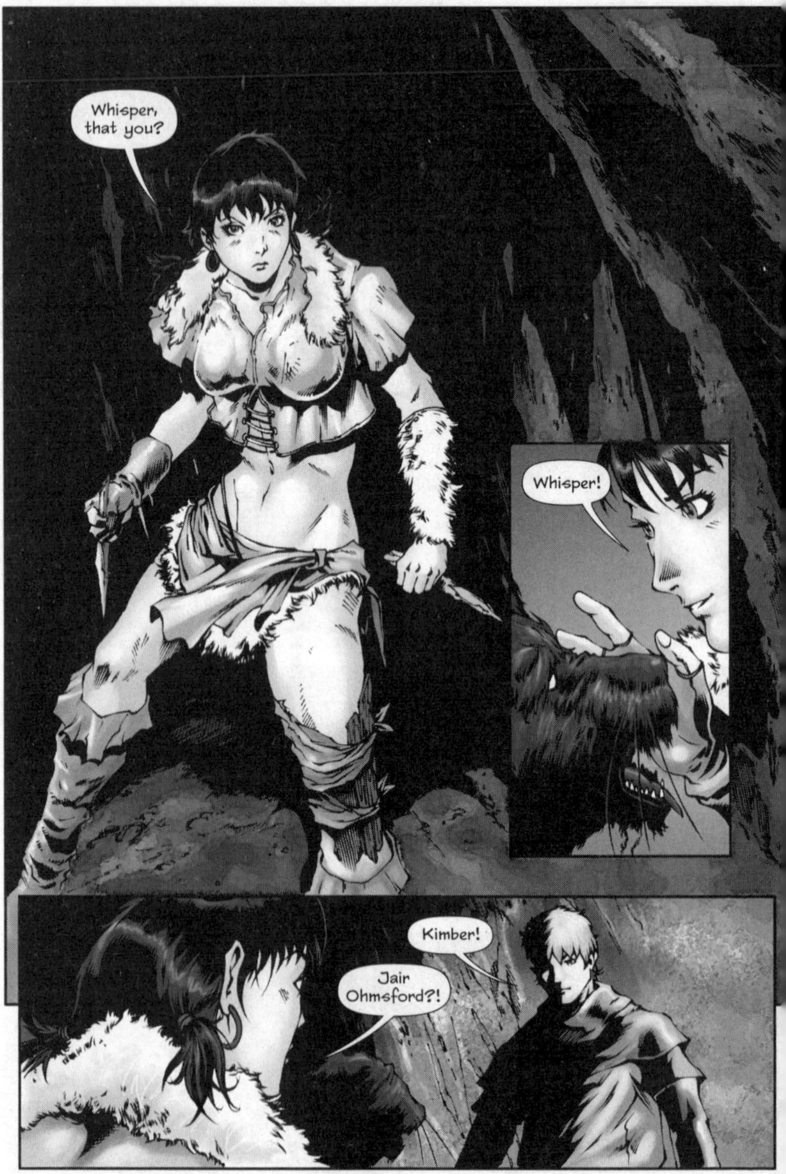
Whisper, that you?
Whisper!
Kimber!
Jair Ohmsford?!

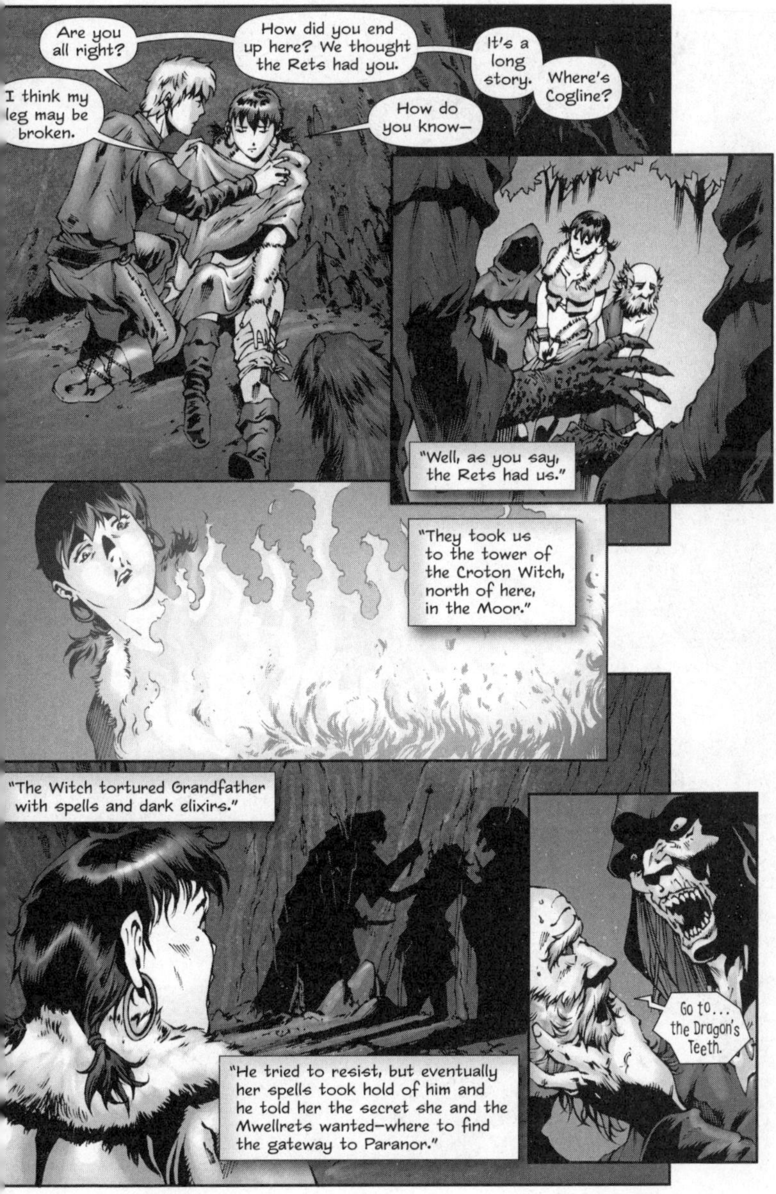
Are you all right?
I think my leg may be broken.
How did you end up here? We thought the Rets had you.
How do you know—
It's a long story.
Where's Cogline?
"Well, as you say, the Rets had us."
"They took us to the tower of the Croton Witch, north of here, in the Moor."
"The Witch tortured Grandfather with spells and dark elixirs."
"He tried to resist, but eventually her spells took hold of him and he told her the secret she and the Mwellrets wanted—where to find the gateway to Paranor."
Go to... the Dragon's Teeth.

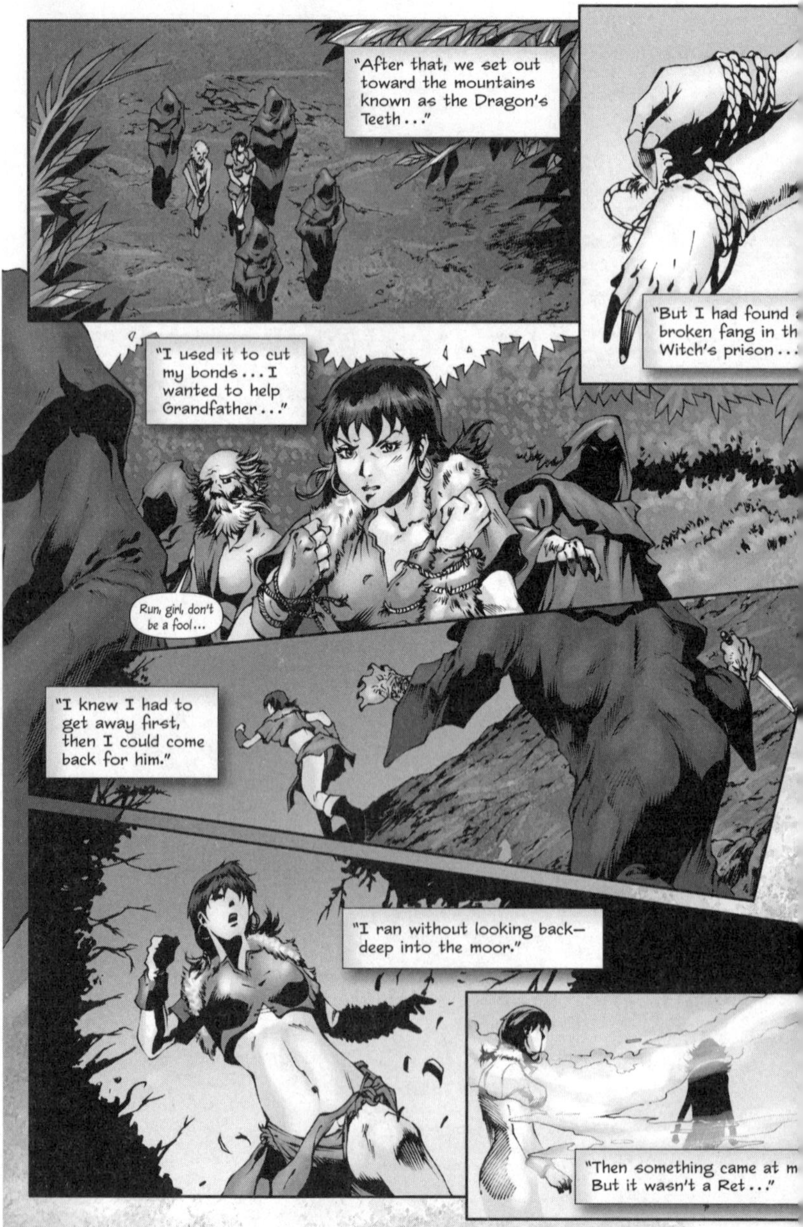
"After that, we set out toward the mountains known as the Dragon's Teeth..."
"But I had found a broken fang in th Witch's prison...
"I used it to cut my bonds...I wanted to help Grandfather..."
Run, girl, don't be a fool...
"I knew I had to get away first, then I could come back for him."
"I ran without looking back—deep into the moor."
"Then something came at m But it wasn't a Ret..."

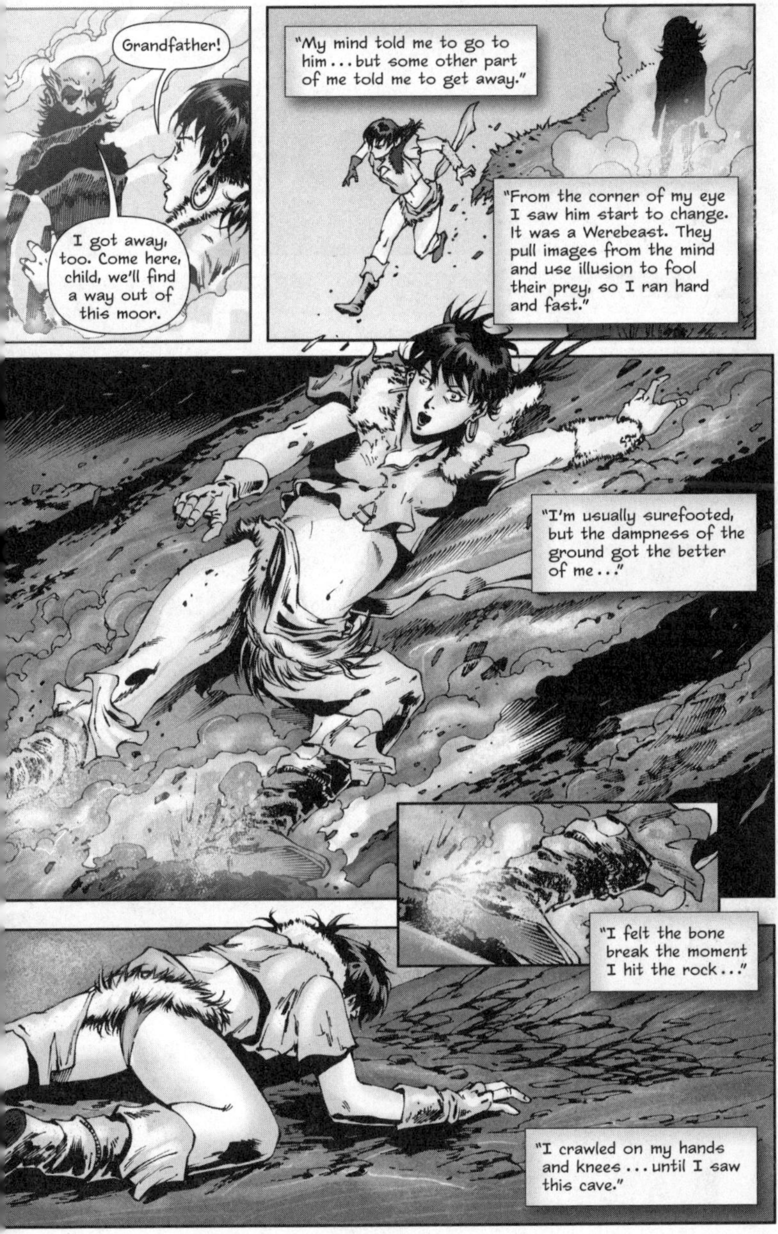
Grandfather!
I got away, too. Come here, child, we'll find a way out of this moor.
"My mind told me to go to him . . . but some other part of me told me to get away."
"From the corner of my eye I saw him start to change. It was a Werebeast. They pull images from the mind and use illusion to fool their prey, so I ran hard and fast."
"I'm usually surefooted, but the dampness of the ground got the better of me . ."
"I felt the bone break the moment I hit the rock . . ."
"I crawled on my hands and knees . . . until I saw this cave."

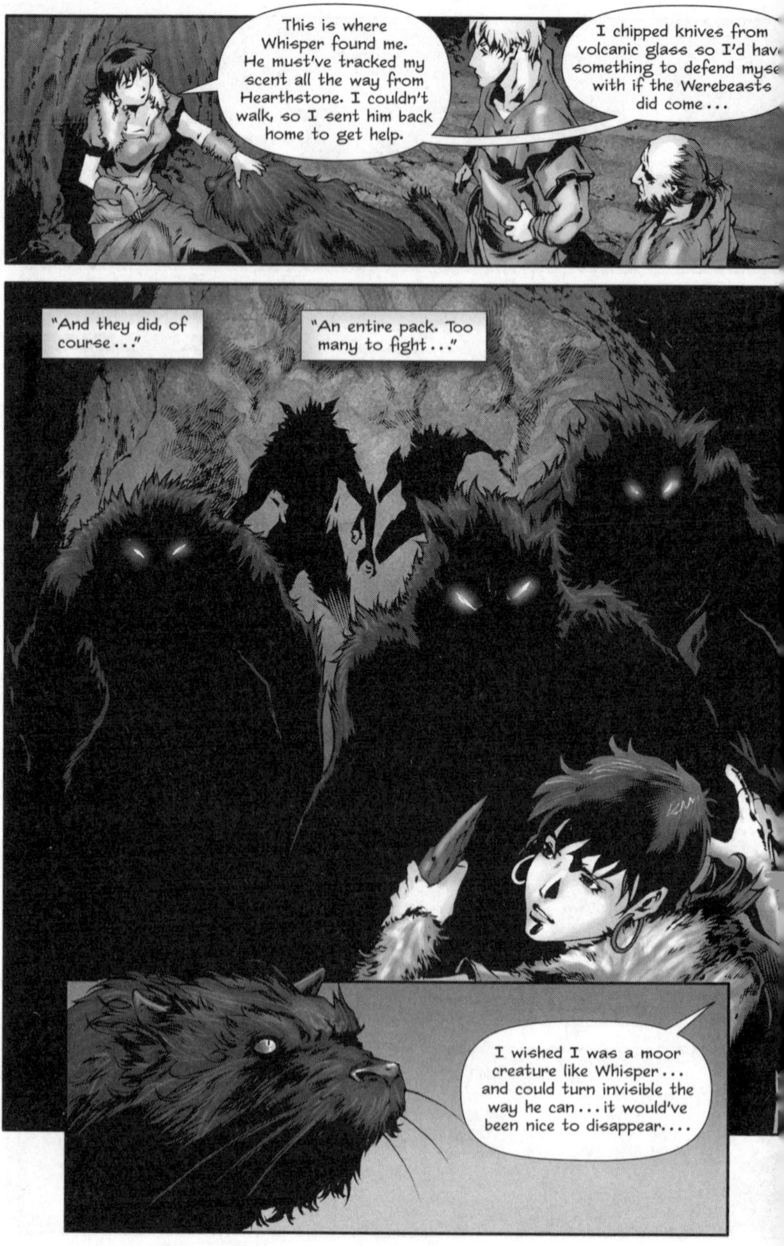
This is where Whisper found me. He must've tracked my scent all the way from Hearthstone. I couldn't walk, so I sent him back home to get help.
I chipped knives from volcanic glass so I'd hav something to defend myse with if the Werebeasts did come...
"And they did, of course..."
"An entire pack. Too many to fight..."
I wished I was a moor creature like Whisper... and could turn invisible the way he can... it would've been nice to disappear....

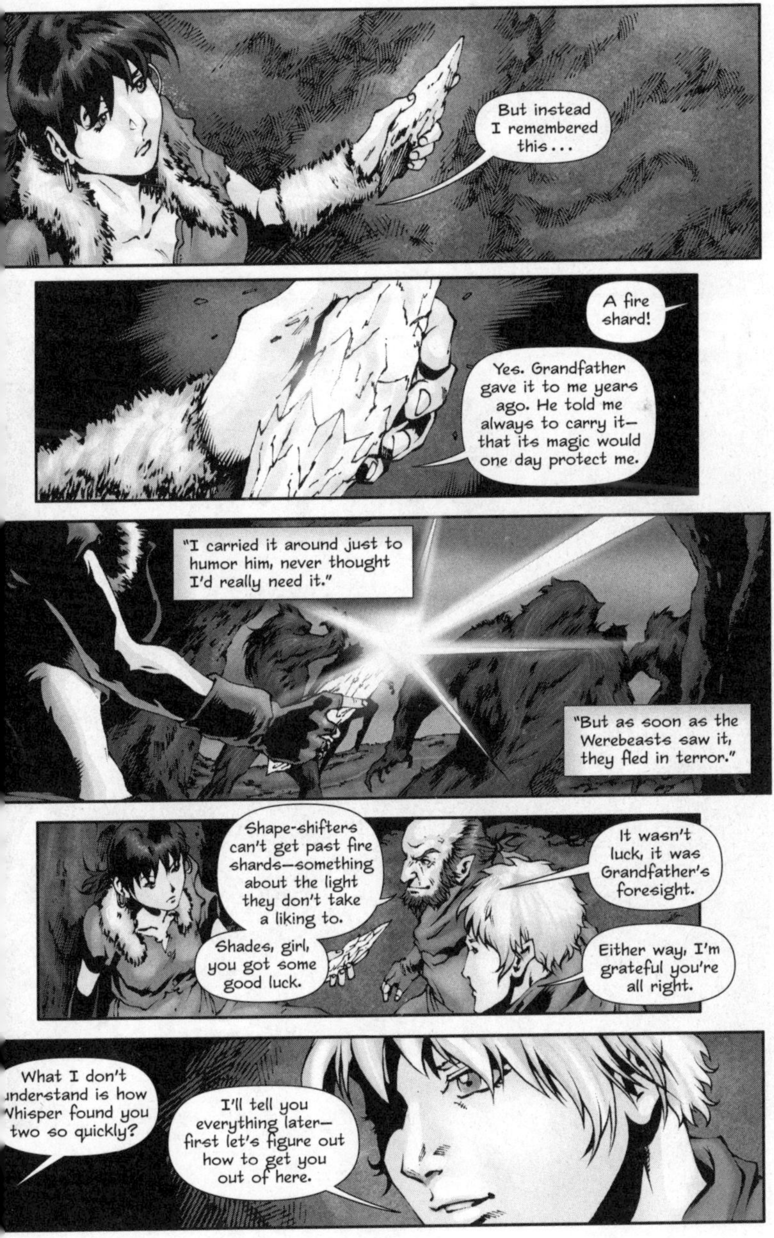
But instead I remembered this . . .
A fire shard!
Yes. Grandfather gave it to me years ago. He told me always to carry it— that its magic would one day protect me.
"I carried it around just to humor him, never thought I'd really need it."
"But as soon as the Werebeasts saw it, they fled in terror."
Shape-shifters can't get past fire shards—something about the light they don't take a liking to.
Shades, girl, you got some good luck.
It wasn't luck, it was Grandfather's foresight.
Either way, I'm grateful you're all right.
What I don't nderstand is how Vhisper found you two so quickly?
I'll tell you everything later— first let's figure out how to get you out of here.

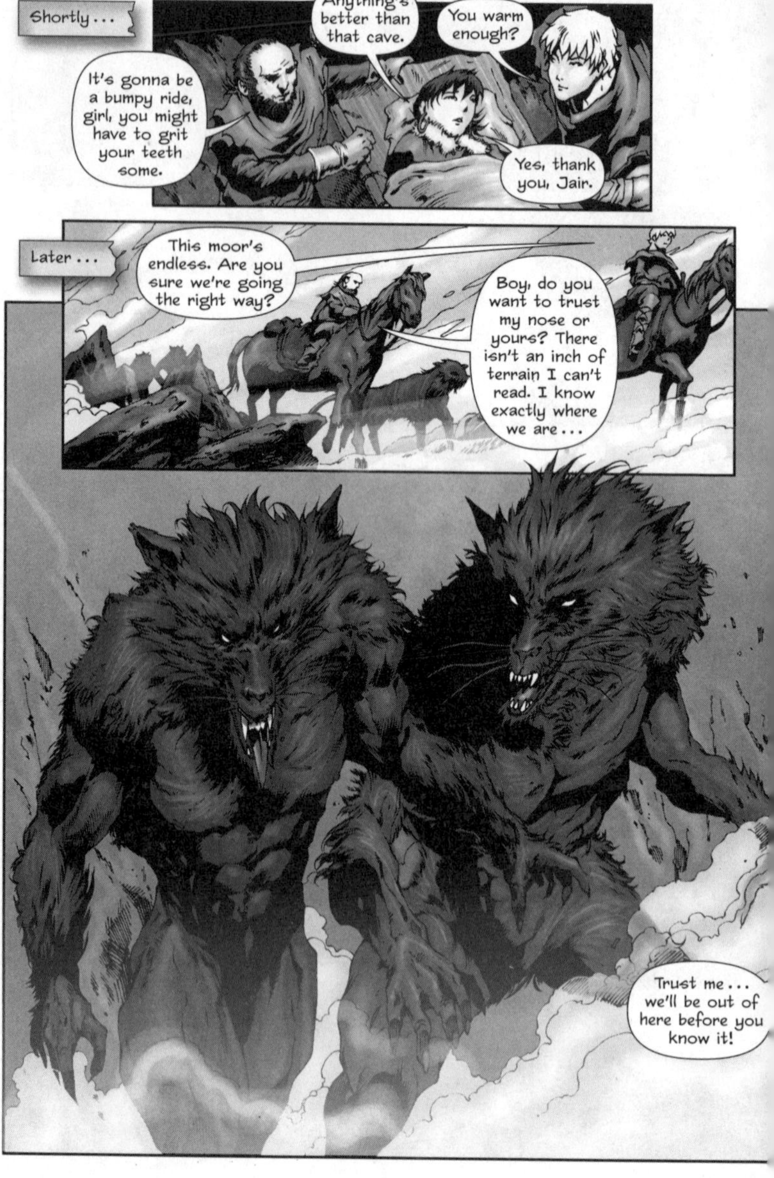
Shortly . . .
Anything's better than that cave.
You warm enough?
It's gonna be a bumpy ride, girl, you might have to grit your teeth some.
Yes, thank you, Jair.
Later . . .
This moor's endless. Are you sure we're going the right way?
Boy, do you want to trust my nose or yours? There isn't an inch of terrain I can't read. I know exactly where we are . . .
Trust me . . . we'll be out of here before you know it!

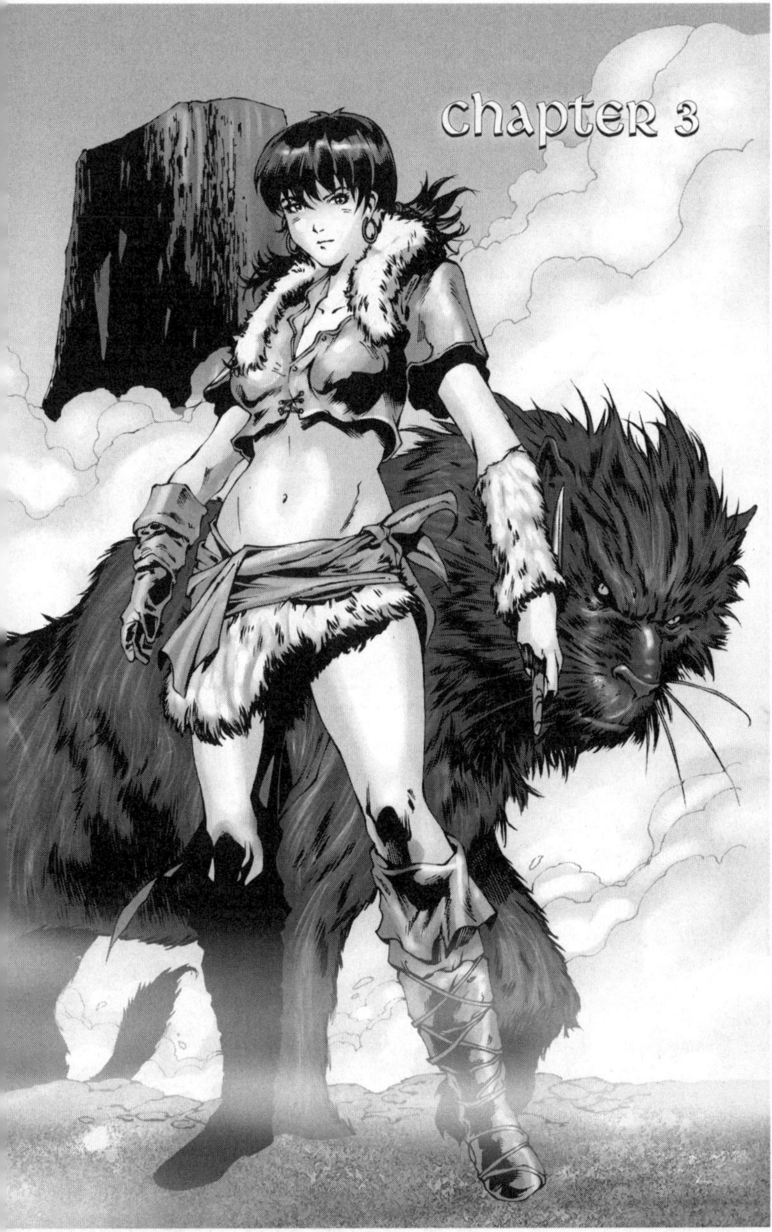
chapter 3

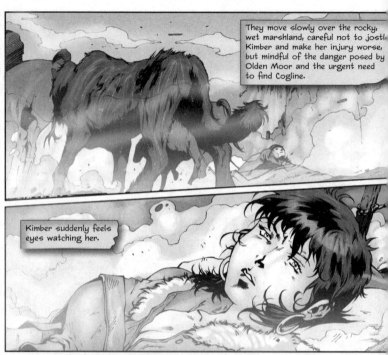

They move slowly over the rocky, wet marshland, careful not to jostl[e] Kimber and make her injury worse, but mindful of the danger posed by Olden Moor and the urgent need to find Cogline.

Kimber suddenly feels eyes watching her.

She peers into the mist ...

Her imagination and the thick miasma fuel her anxiety.

Even a gnarled branch becomes a threat ...

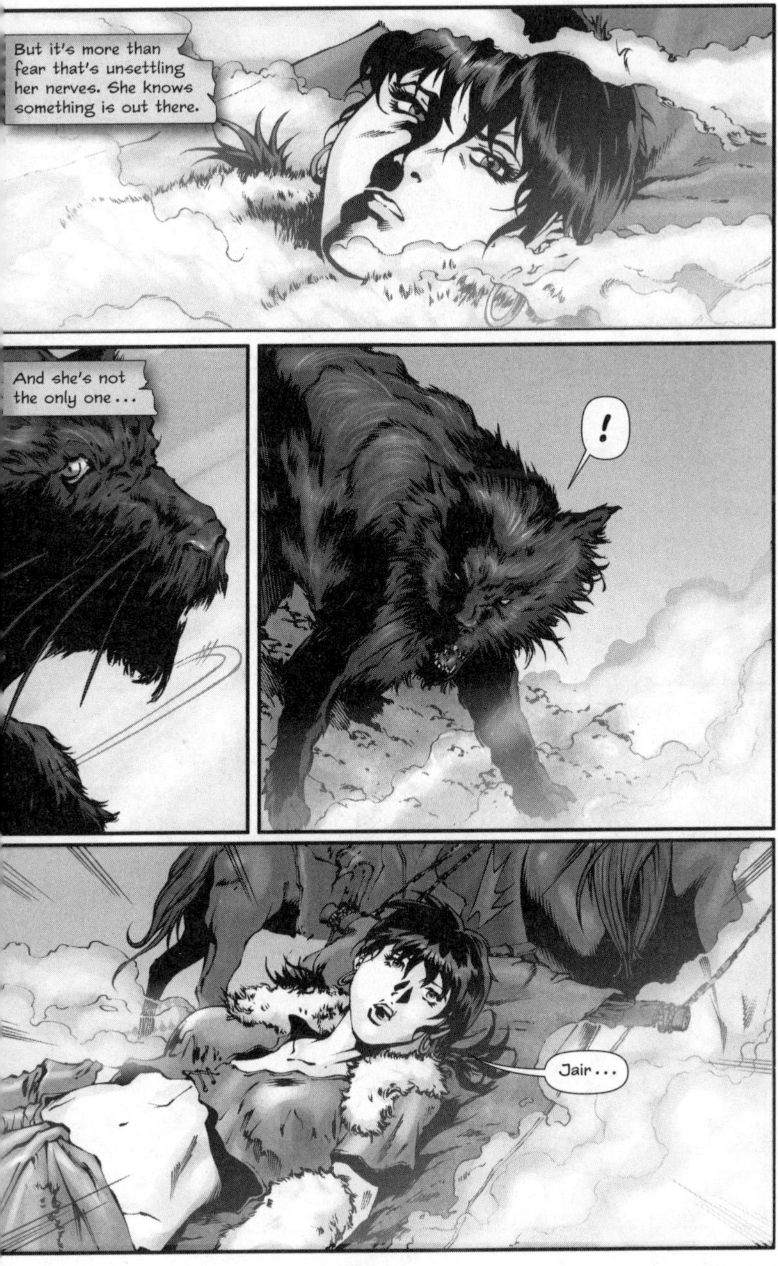
But it's more than fear that's unsettling her nerves. She knows something is out there.
And she's not the only one...
!
Jair...

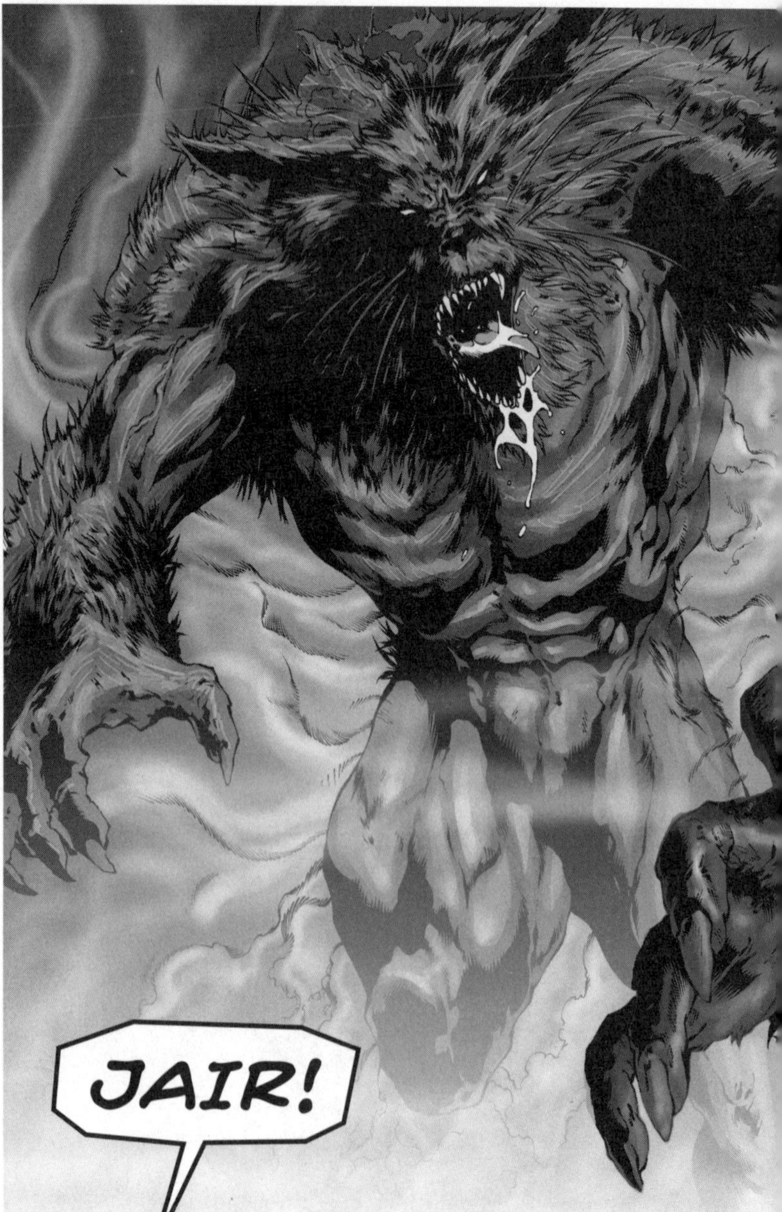
JAIR!

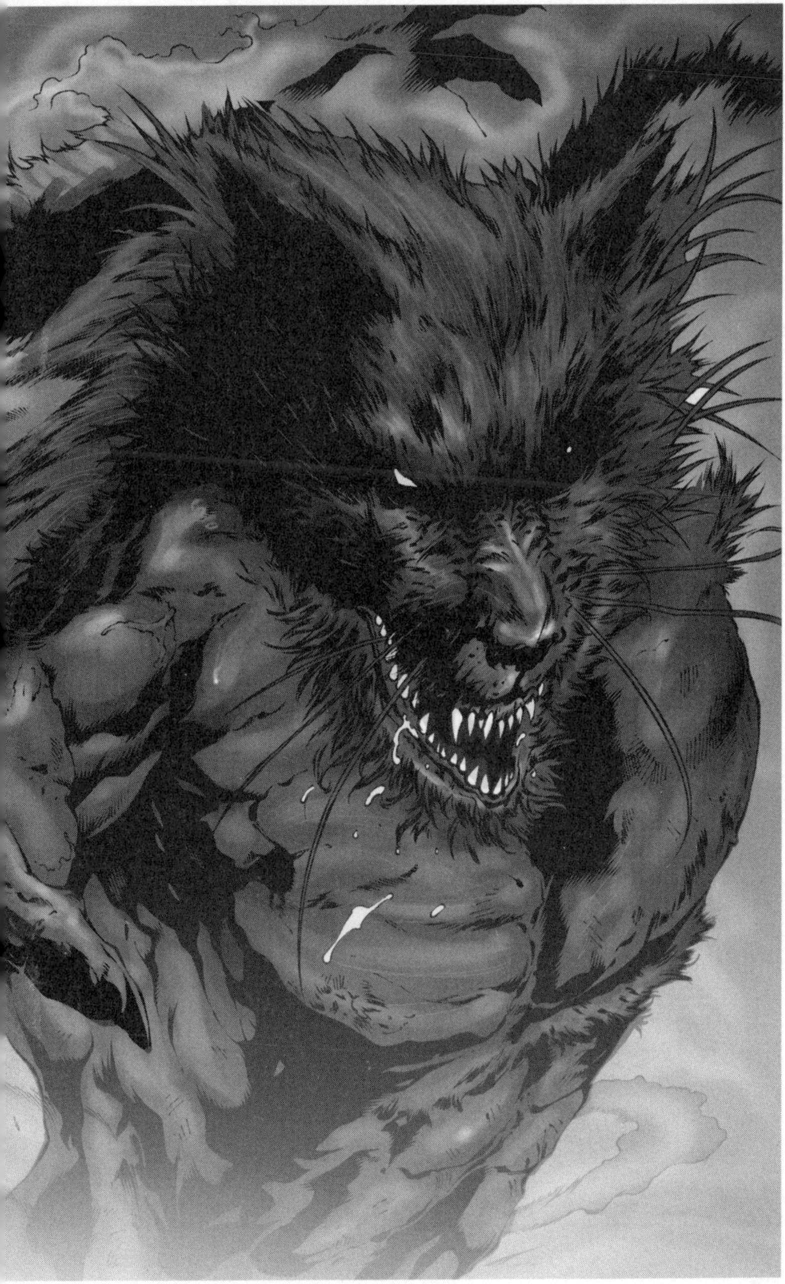

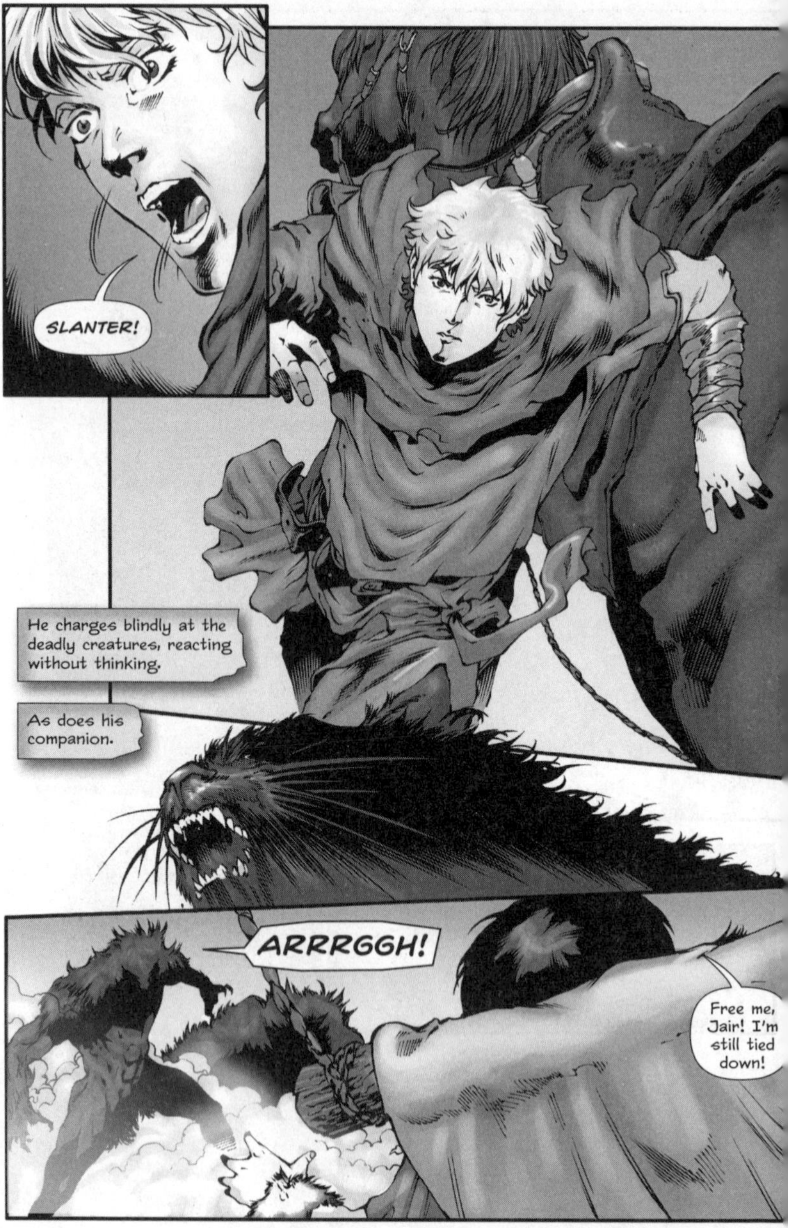
SLANTER!
He charges blindly at the deadly creatures, reacting without thinking.
As does his companion.
ARRRGGH!
Free me, Jair! I'm still tied down!

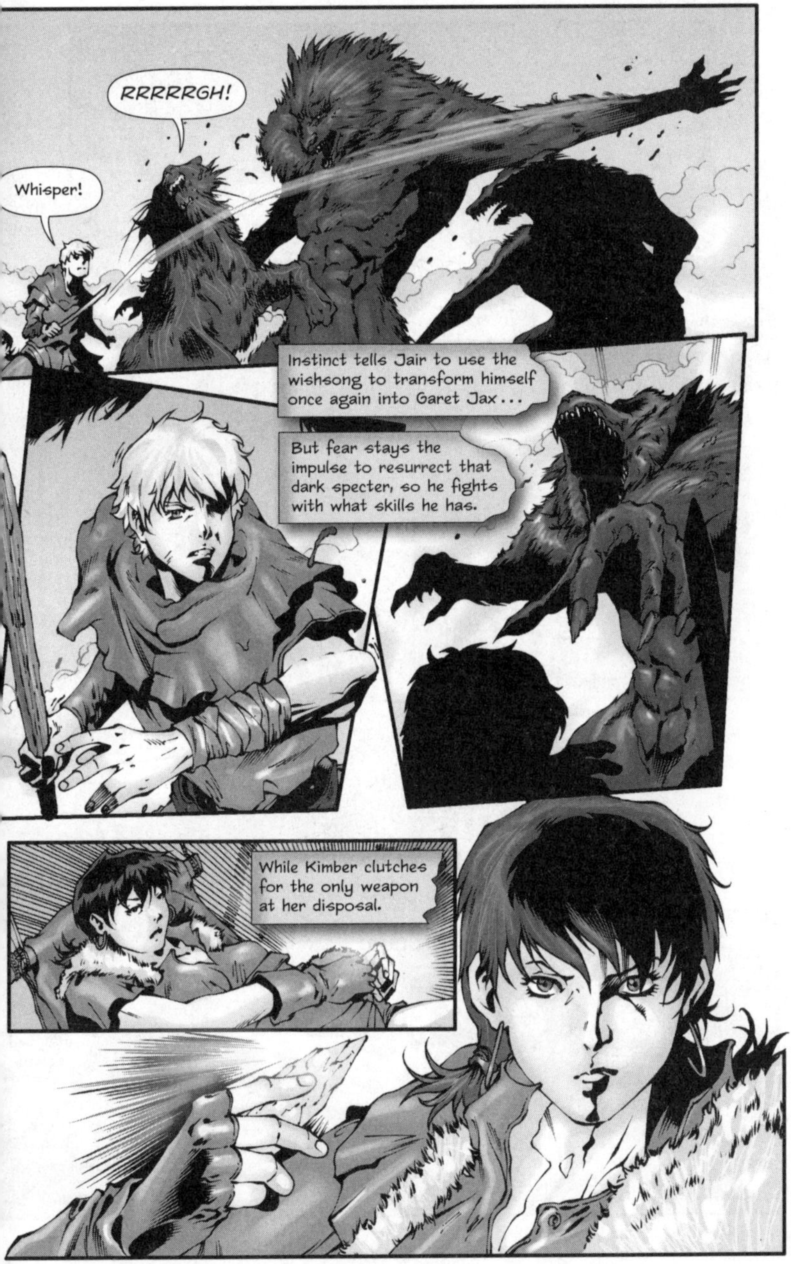
Whisper!
RRRRRGH!
Instinct tells Jair to use the wishsong to transform himself once again into Garet Jax . . .
But fear stays the impulse to resurrect that dark specter, so he fights with what skills he has.
While Kimber clutches for the only weapon at her disposal.

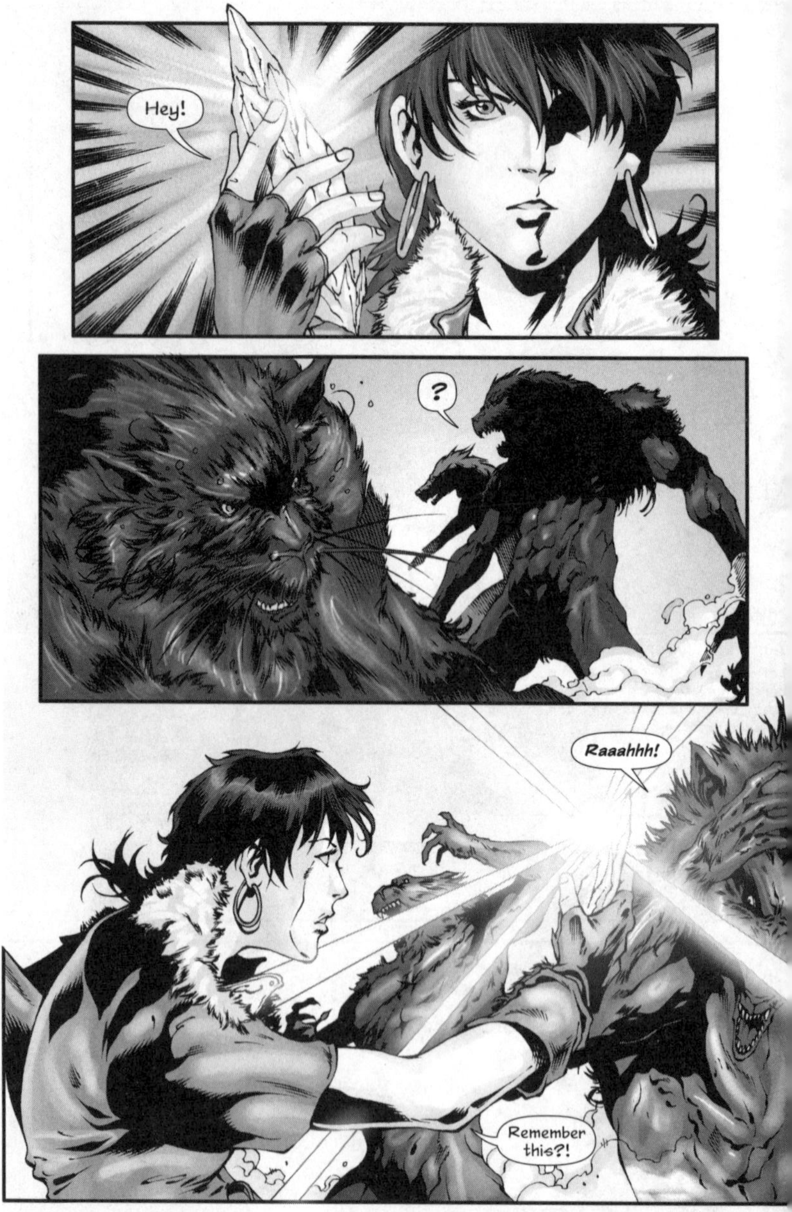
Hey!
?
Raaahhh!
Remember this?!

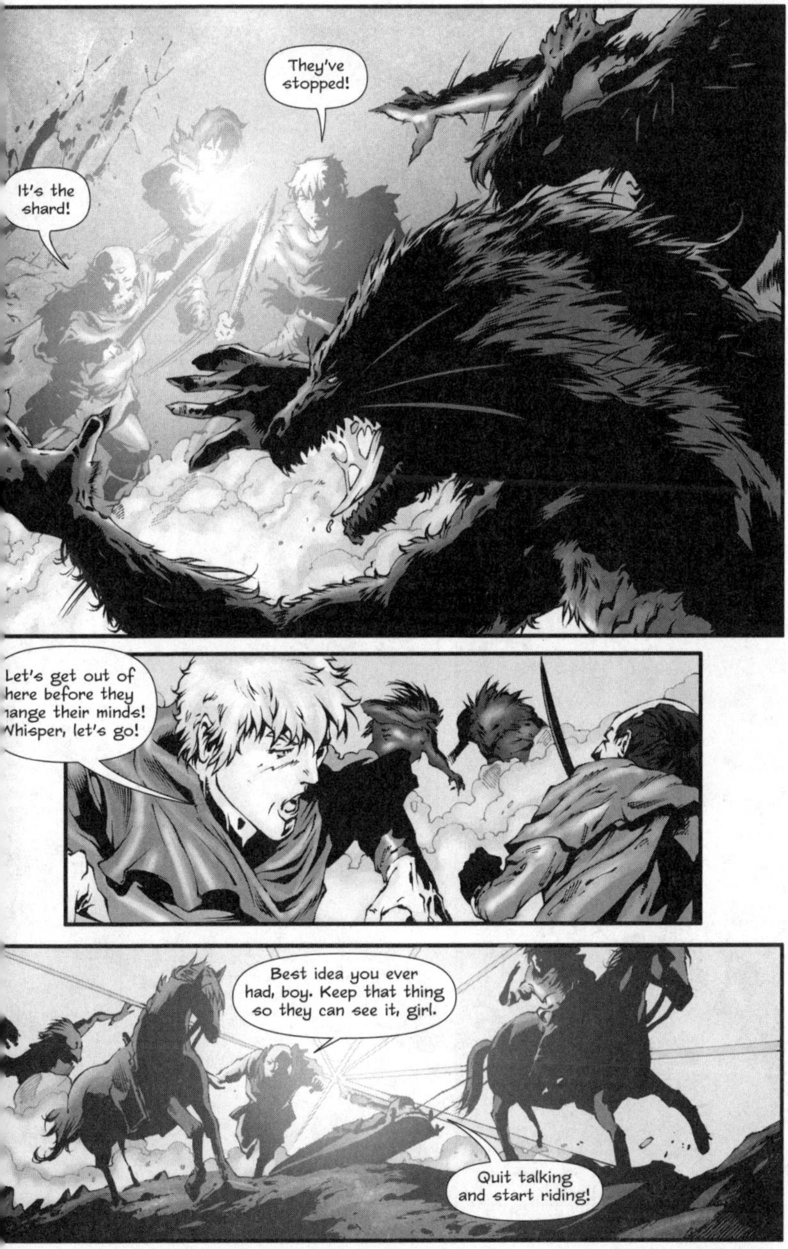
It's the shard!
They've stopped!
Let's get out of here before they hange their minds! Whisper, let's go!
Best idea you ever had, boy. Keep that thing so they can see it, girl.
Quit talking and start riding!

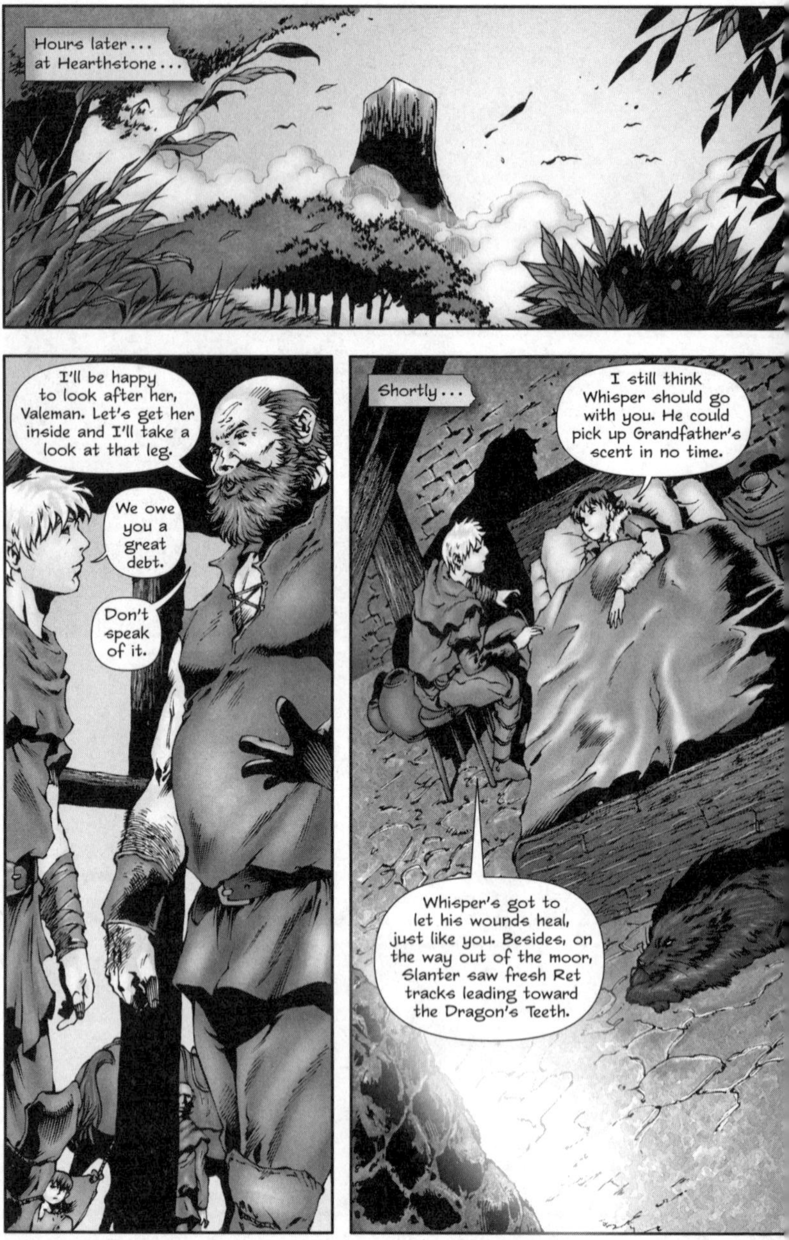

Hours later... at Hearthstone...
I'll be happy to look after her, Valeman. Let's get her inside and I'll take a look at that leg.
We owe you a great debt.
Don't speak of it.
Shortly...
I still think Whisper should go with you. He could pick up Grandfather's scent in no time.
Whisper's got to let his wounds heal, just like you. Besides, on the way out of the moor, Slanter saw fresh Ret tracks leading toward the Dragon's Teeth.

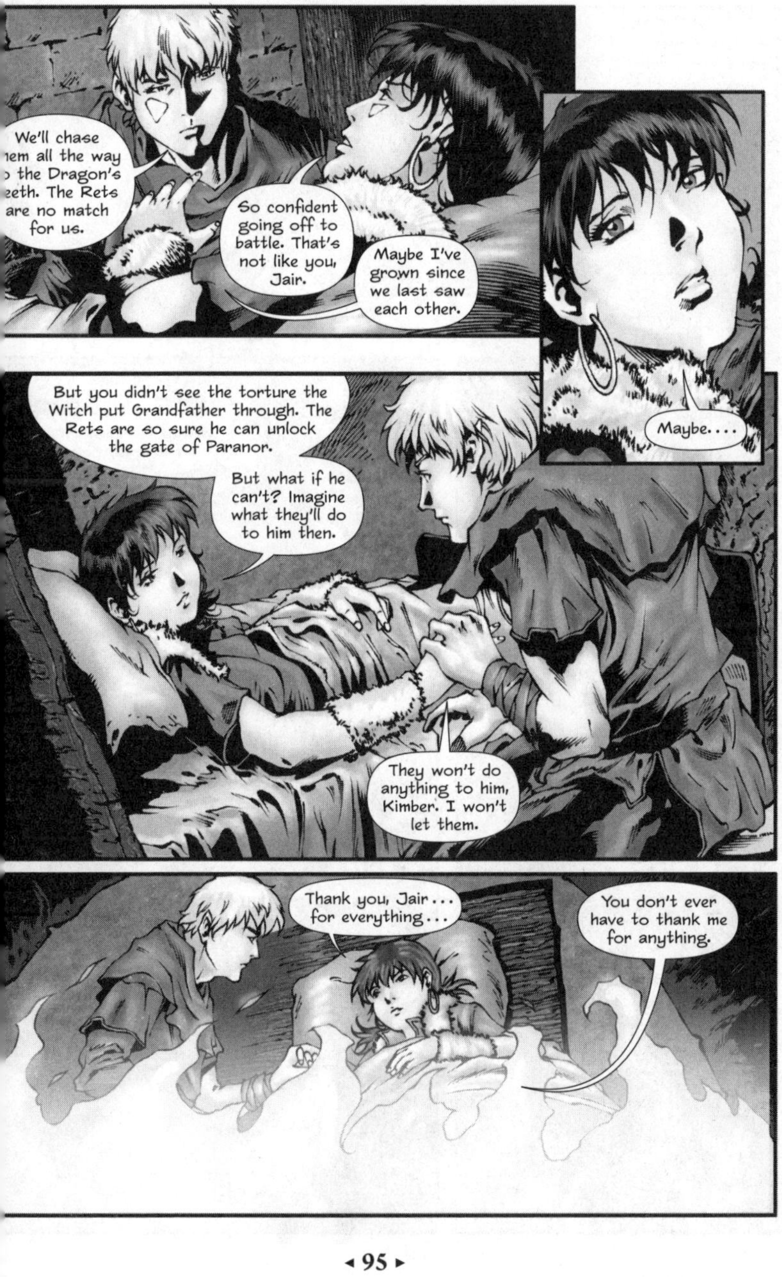
We'll chase
hem all the way
the Dragon's
eeth. The Rets
are no match
for us.
So confident going off to battle. That's not like you, Jair.
Maybe I've grown since we last saw each other.
Maybe....
But you didn't see the torture the Witch put Grandfather through. The Rets are so sure he can unlock the gate of Paranor.
But what if he can't? Imagine what they'll do to him then.
They won't do anything to him, Kimber. I won't let them.
Thank you, Jair... for everything...
You don't ever have to thank me for anything.

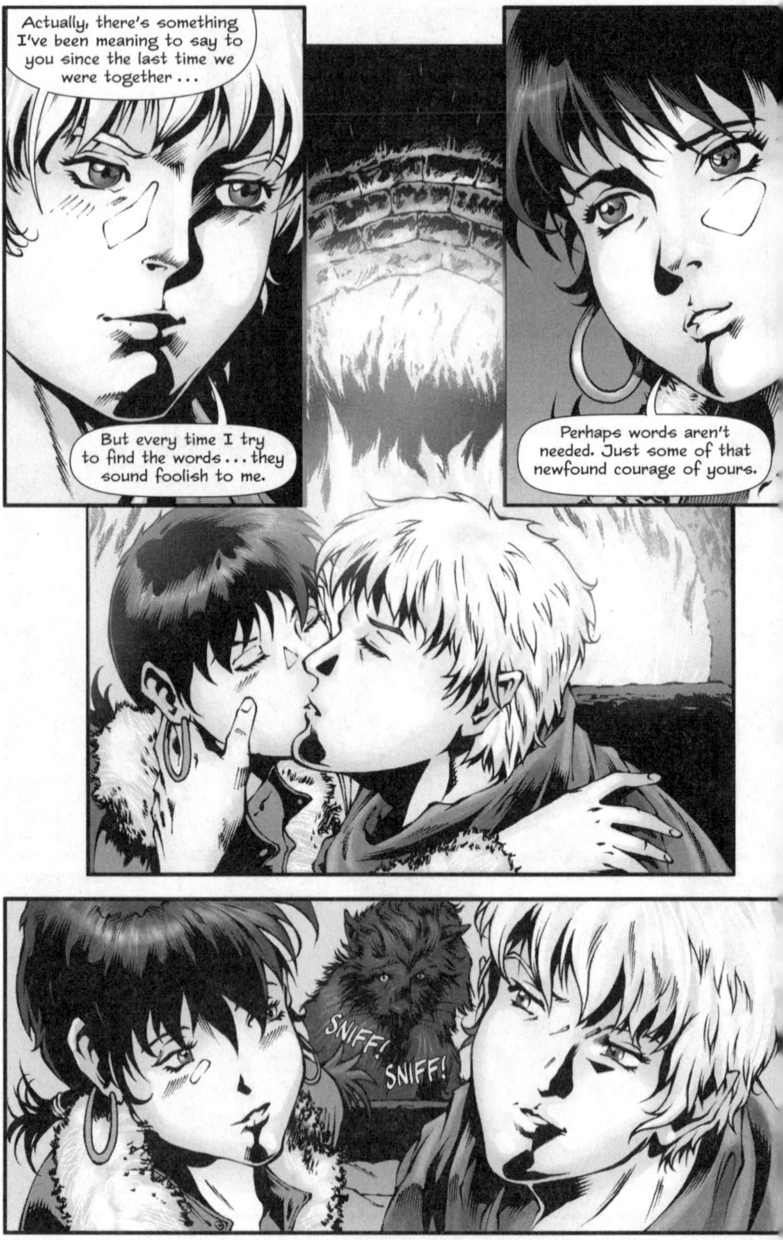

Actually, there's something I've been meaning to say to you since the last time we were together ...
But every time I try to find the words ... they sound foolish to me.
Perhaps words aren't needed. Just some of that newfound courage of yours.
SNIFF!
SNIFF!

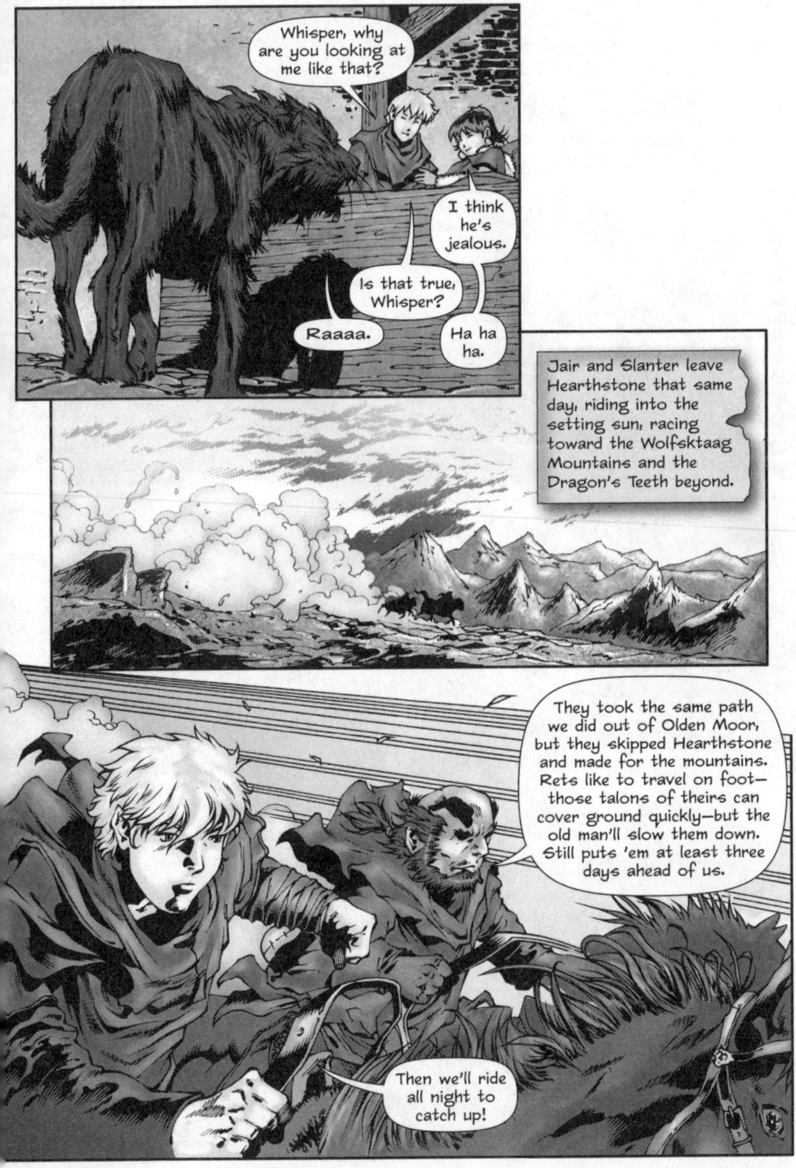

Whisper, why are you looking at me like that?
I think he's jealous.
Is that true, Whisper?
Raaaa.
Ha ha ha.
Jair and Slanter leave Hearthstone that same day, riding into the setting sun, racing toward the Wolfsktaag Mountains and the Dragon's Teeth beyond.
They took the same path we did out of Olden Moor, but they skipped Hearthstone and made for the mountains. Rets like to travel on foot—those talons of theirs can cover ground quickly—but the old man'll slow them down. Still puts 'em at least three days ahead of us.
Then we'll ride all night to catch up!

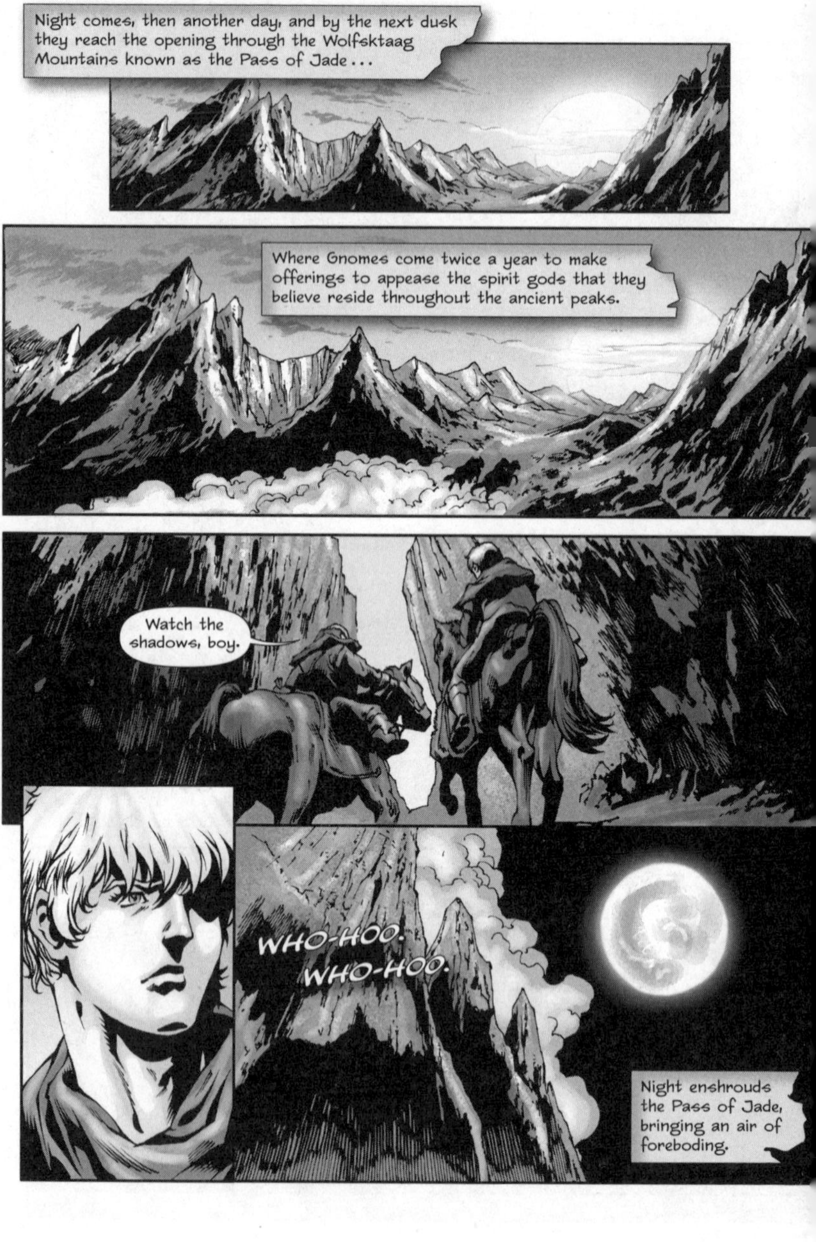
Night comes, then another day, and by the next dusk they reach the opening through the Wolfsktaag Mountains known as the Pass of Jade...
Where Gnomes come twice a year to make offerings to appease the spirit gods that they believe reside throughout the ancient peaks.
Watch the shadows, boy.
WHO-HOO.
WHO-HOO.
Night enshrouds the Pass of Jade, bringing an air of foreboding.

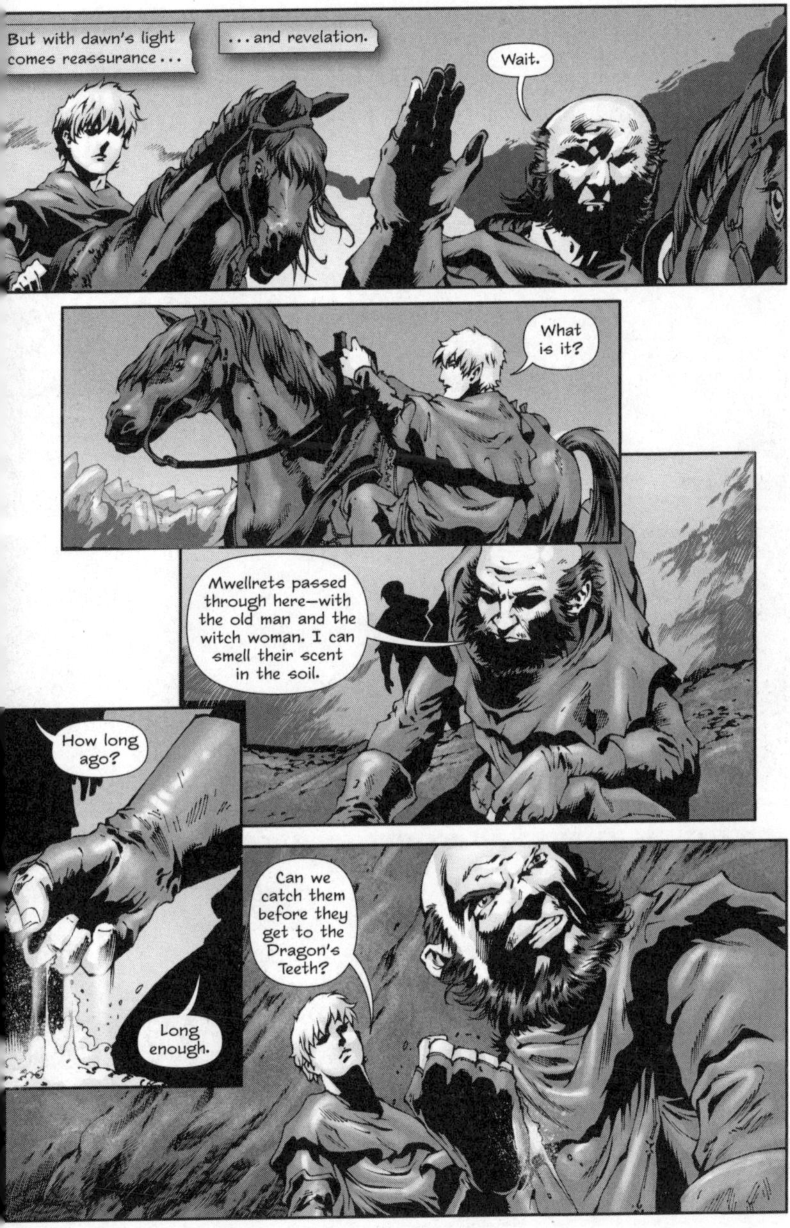

But with dawn's light comes reassurance...
...and revelation.
Wait.
What is it?
Mwellrets passed through here—with the old man and the witch woman. I can smell their scent in the soil.
How long ago?
Long enough.
Can we catch them before they get to the Dragon's Teeth?

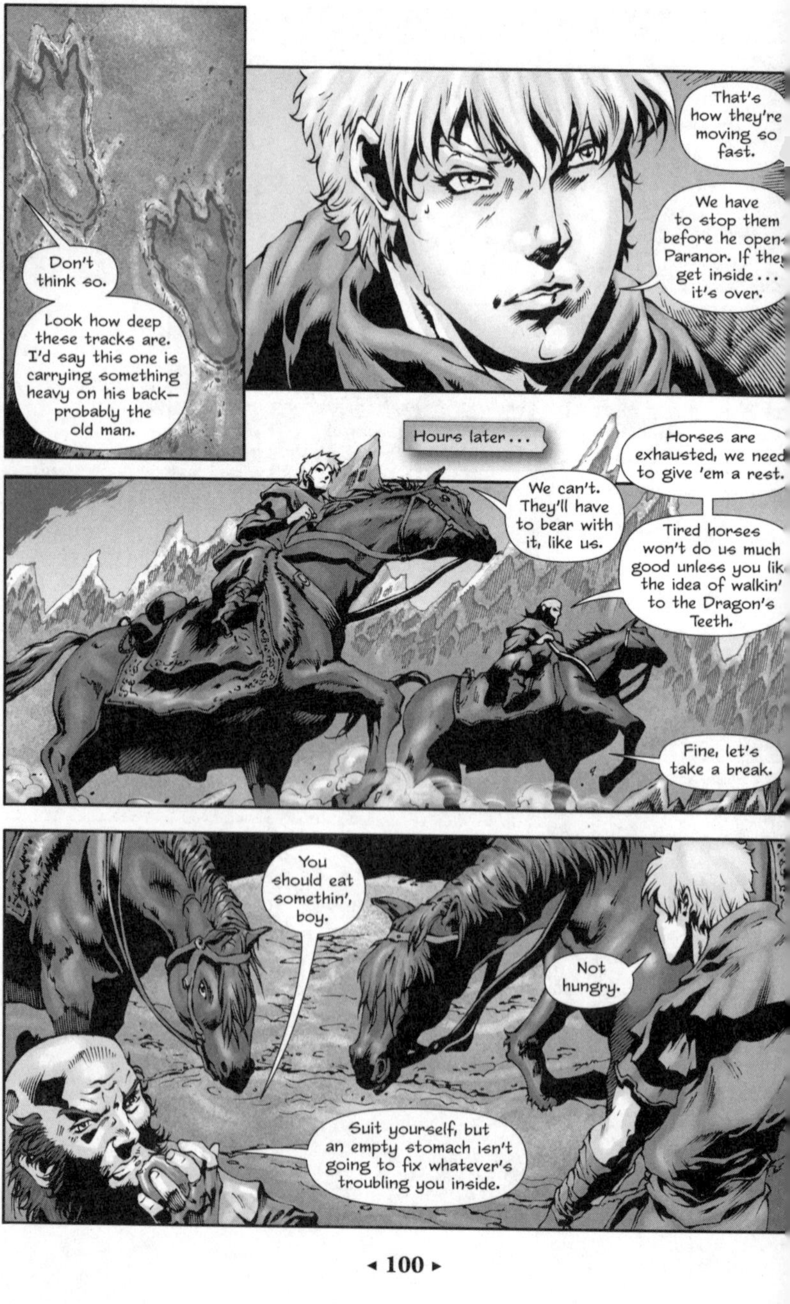
Don't think so.
Look how deep these tracks are. I'd say this one is carrying something heavy on his back—probably the old man.
That's how they're moving so fast.
We have to stop them before he open Paranor. If the get inside... it's over.
Hours later...
Horses are exhausted, we need to give 'em a rest.
We can't. They'll have to bear with it, like us.
Tired horses won't do us much good unless you lik the idea of walkin' to the Dragon's Teeth.
Fine, let's take a break.
You should eat somethin', boy.
Not hungry.
Suit yourself, but an empty stomach isn't going to fix whatever's troubling you inside.

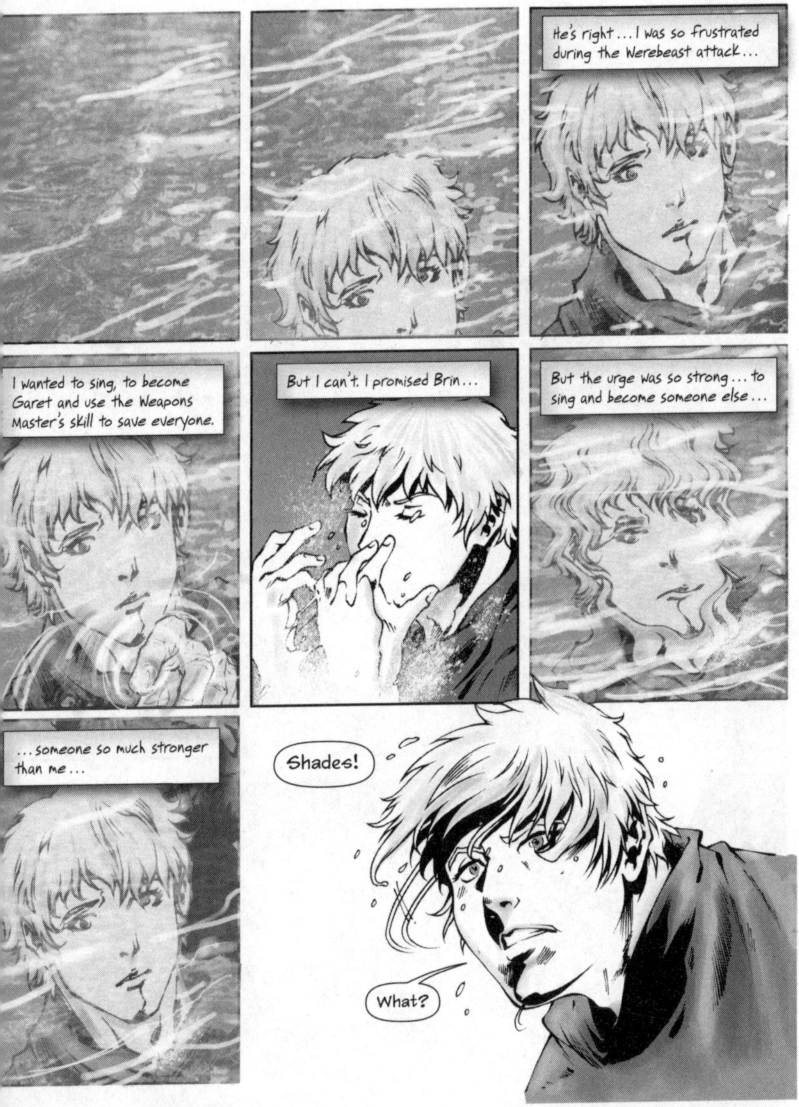
He's right . . . I was so frustrated during the Werebeast attack . . .
I wanted to sing, to become Garet and use the Weapons Master's skill to save everyone.
But I can't. I promised Brin . . .
But the urge was so strong . . . to sing and become someone else . . .
. . . someone so much stronger than me . . .
Shades!
What?

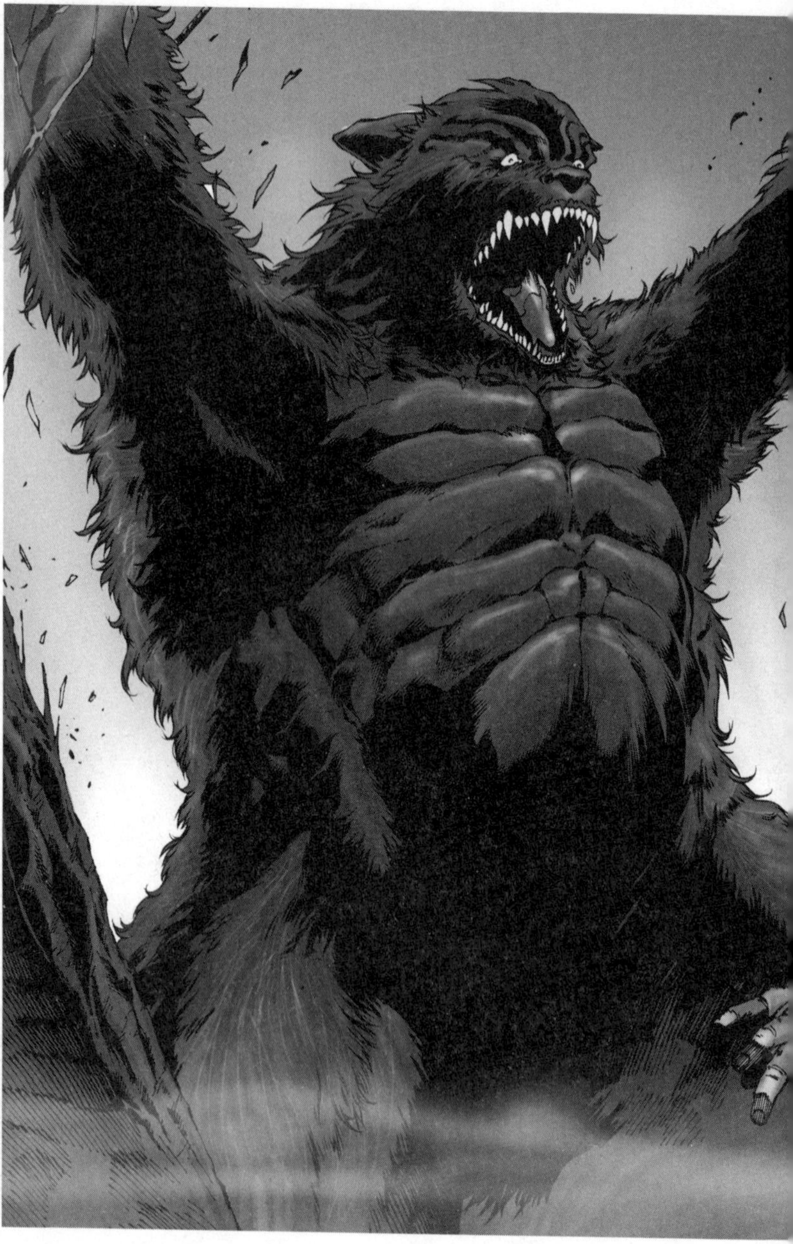

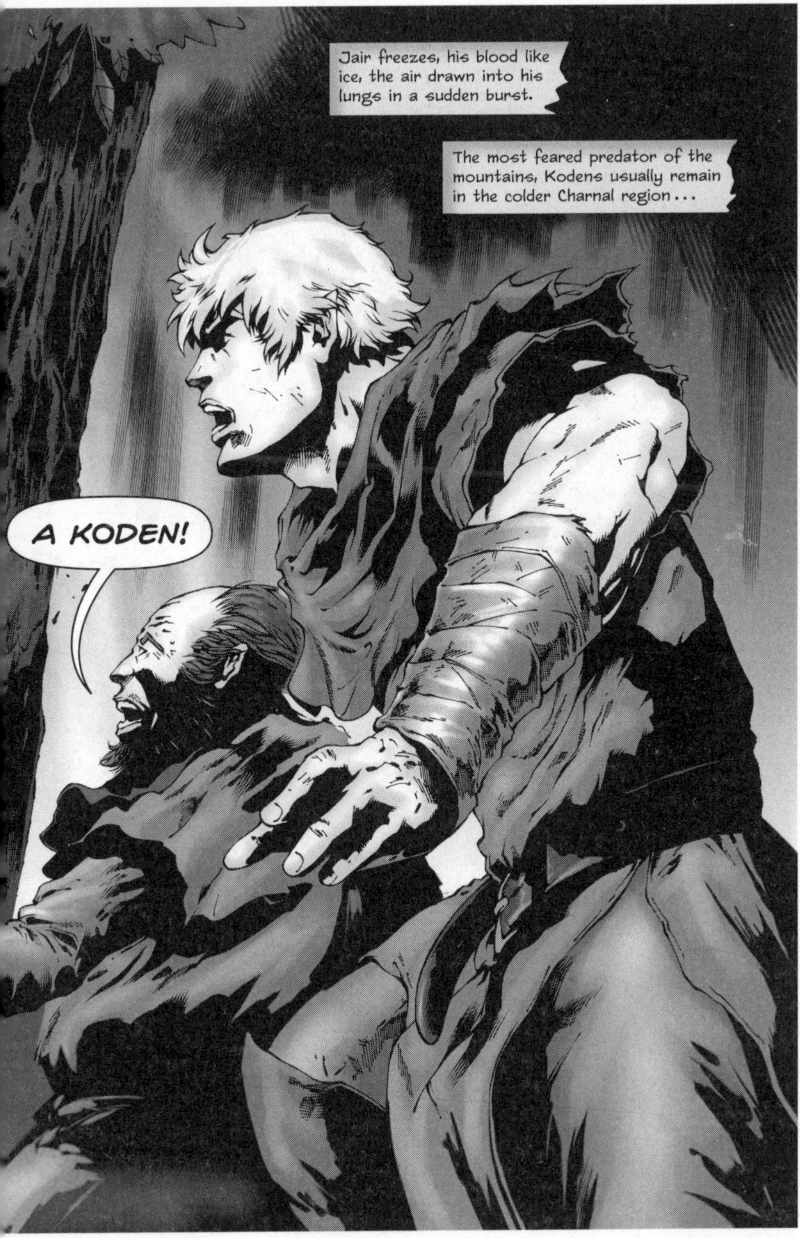
Jair freezes, his blood like ice, the air drawn into his lungs in a sudden burst.
The most feared predator of the mountains, Kodens usually remain in the colder Charnal region...
A KODEN!

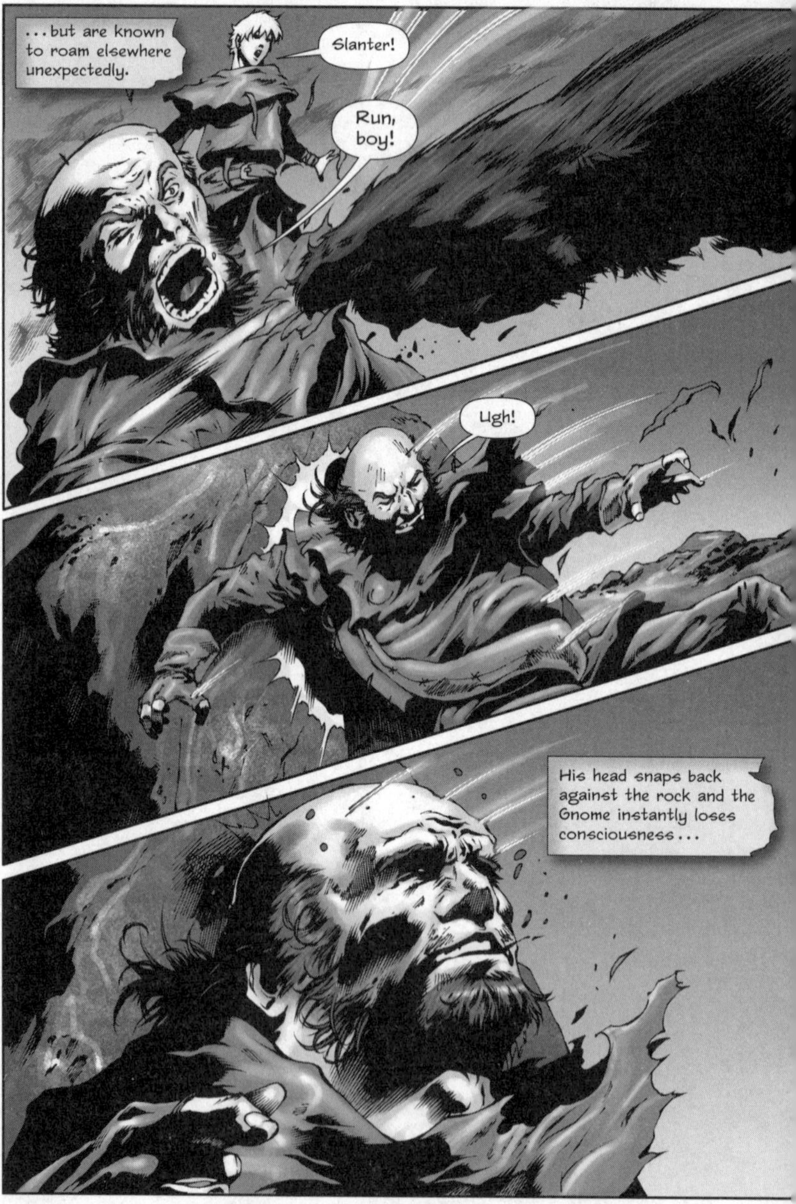
...but are known to roam elsewhere unexpectedly.
Slanter!
Run, boy!
Ugh!
His head snaps back against the rock and the Gnome instantly loses consciousness...

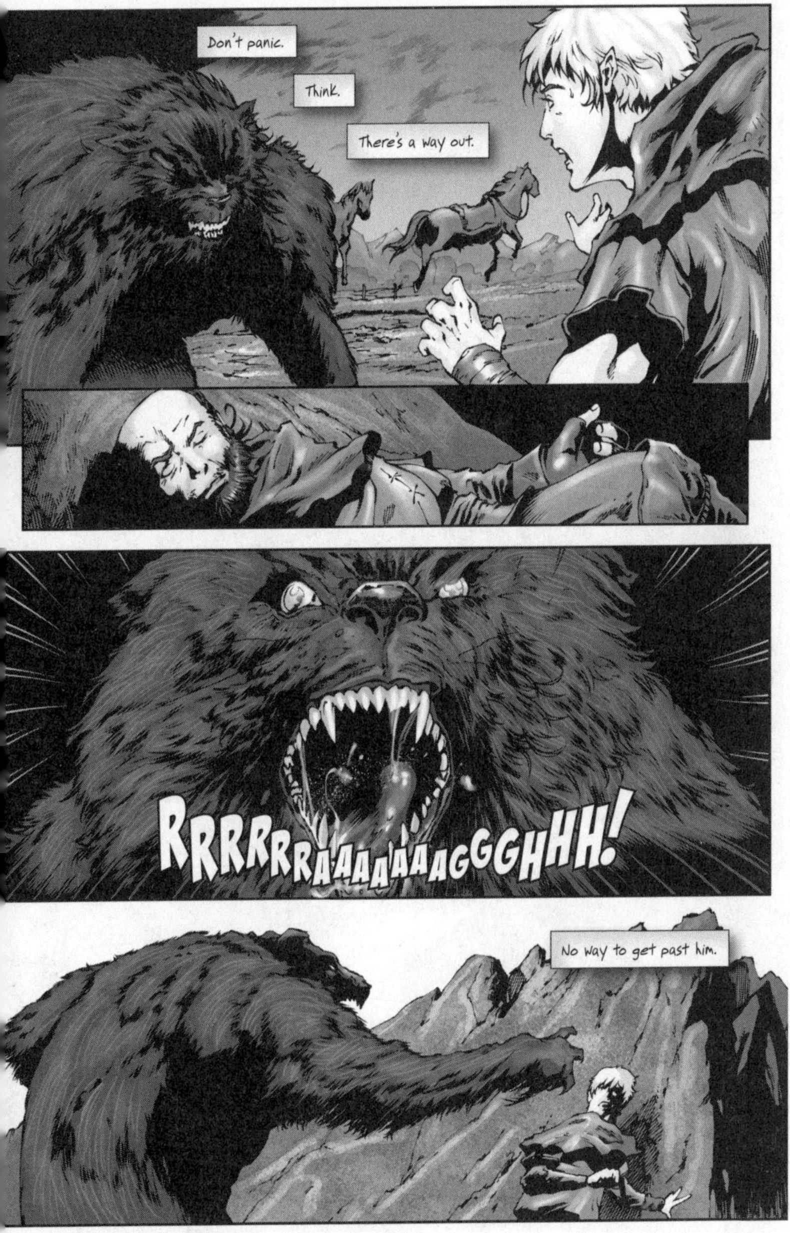
Don't panic.
Think.
There's a way out.
RRRRRRAAAAAAAGGGHHH!
No way to get past him.

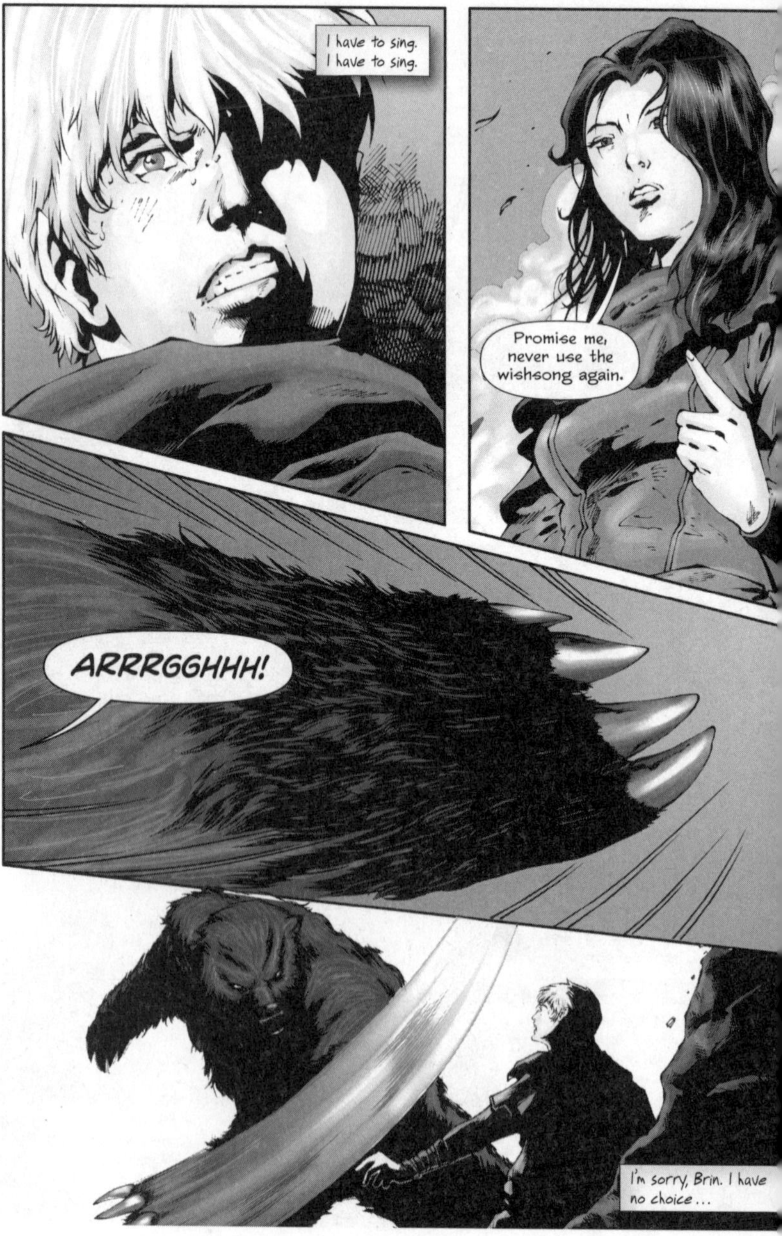
I have to sing.
I have to sing.
Promise me, never use the wishsong again.
ARRRGGHHH!
I'm sorry, Brin. I have no choice...

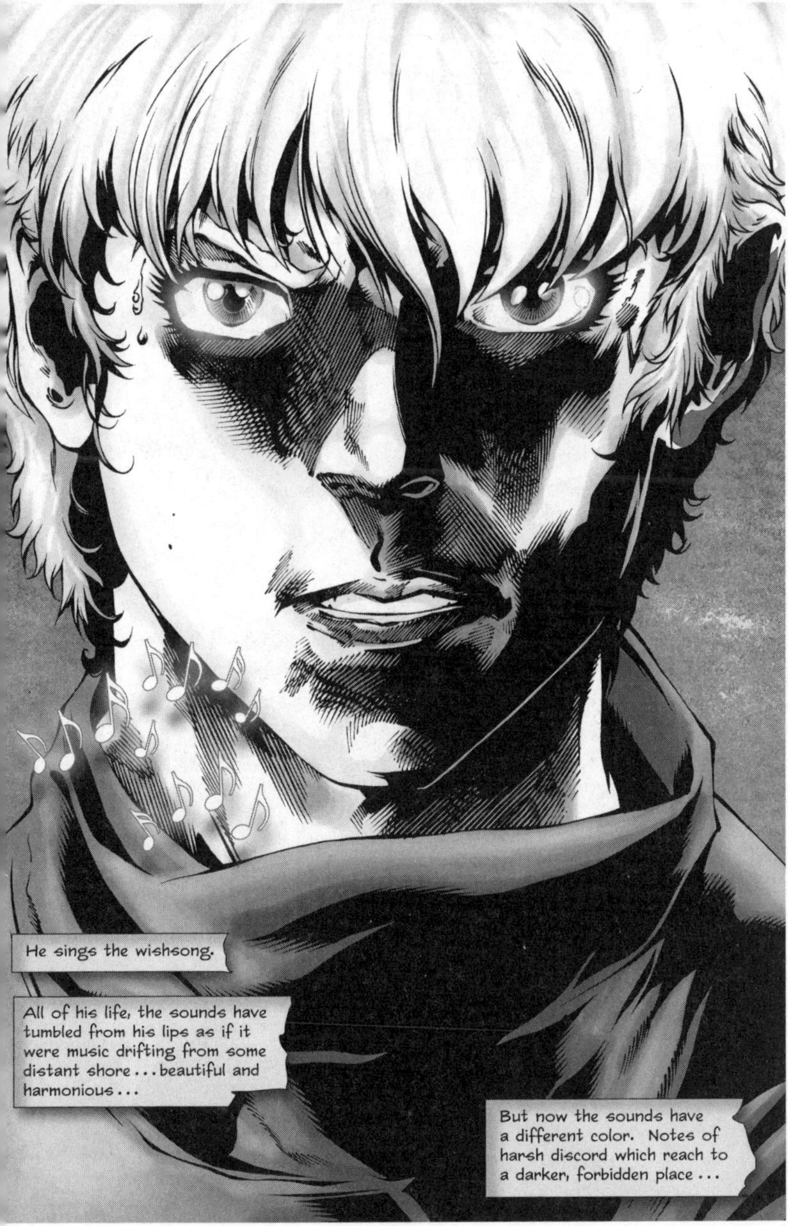
He sings the wishsong.
All of his life, the sounds have tumbled from his lips as if it were music drifting from some distant shore . . . beautiful and harmonious . . .
But now the sounds have a different color. Notes of harsh discord which reach to a darker, forbidden place . . .

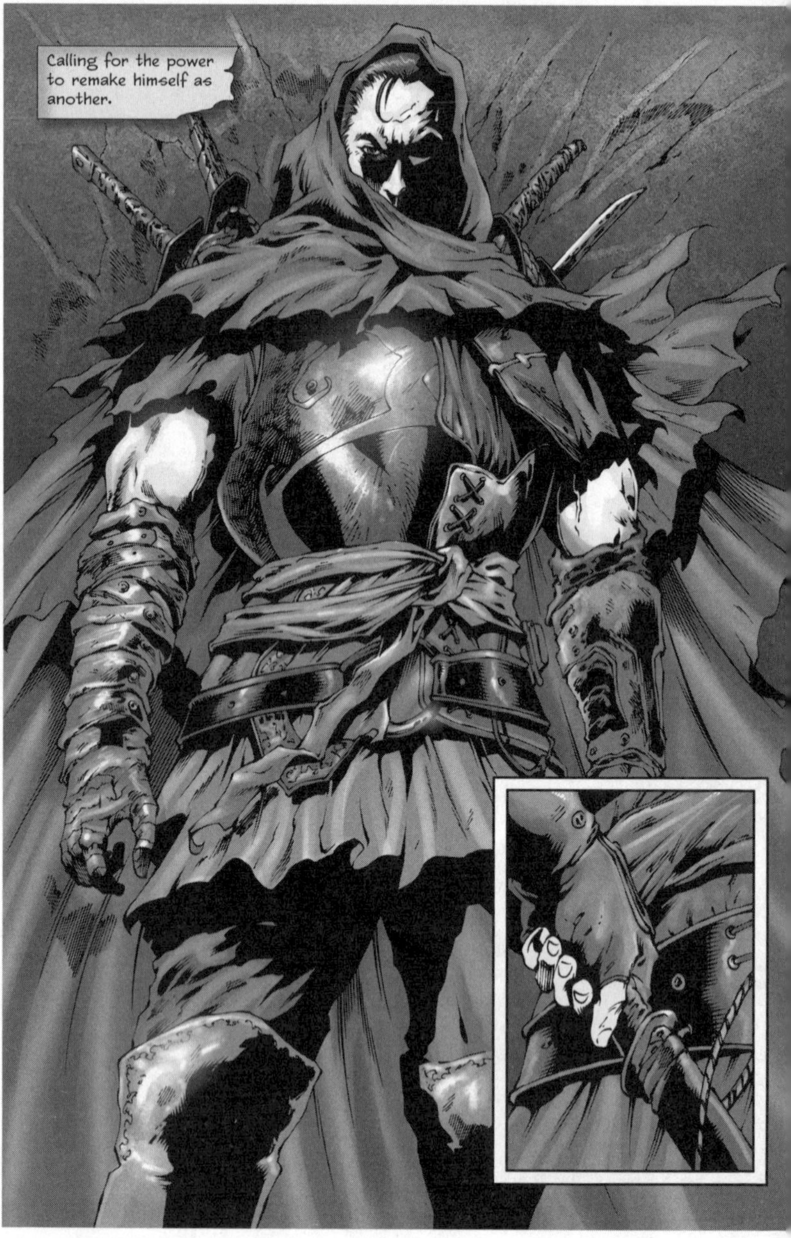
Calling for the power to remake himself as another.

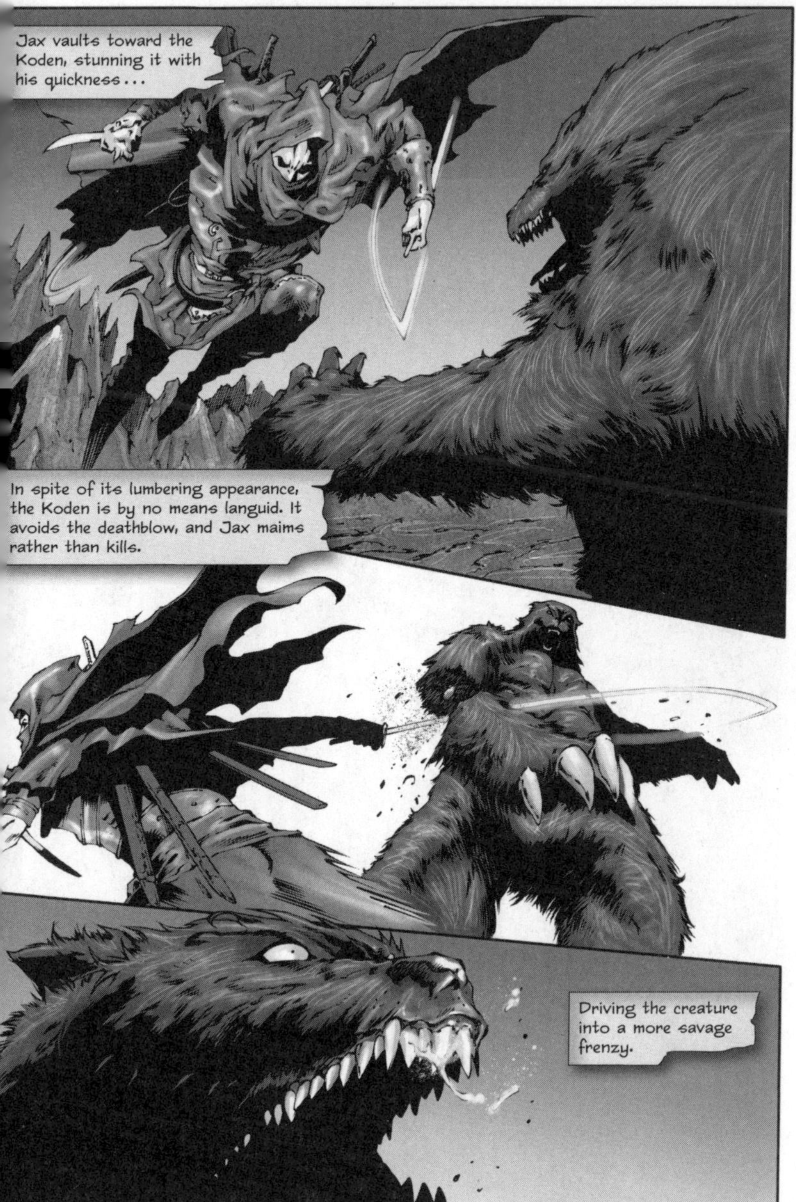
Jax vaults toward the Koden, stunning it with his quickness...
In spite of its lumbering appearance, the Koden is by no means languid. It avoids the deathblow, and Jax maims rather than kills.
Driving the creature into a more savage frenzy.

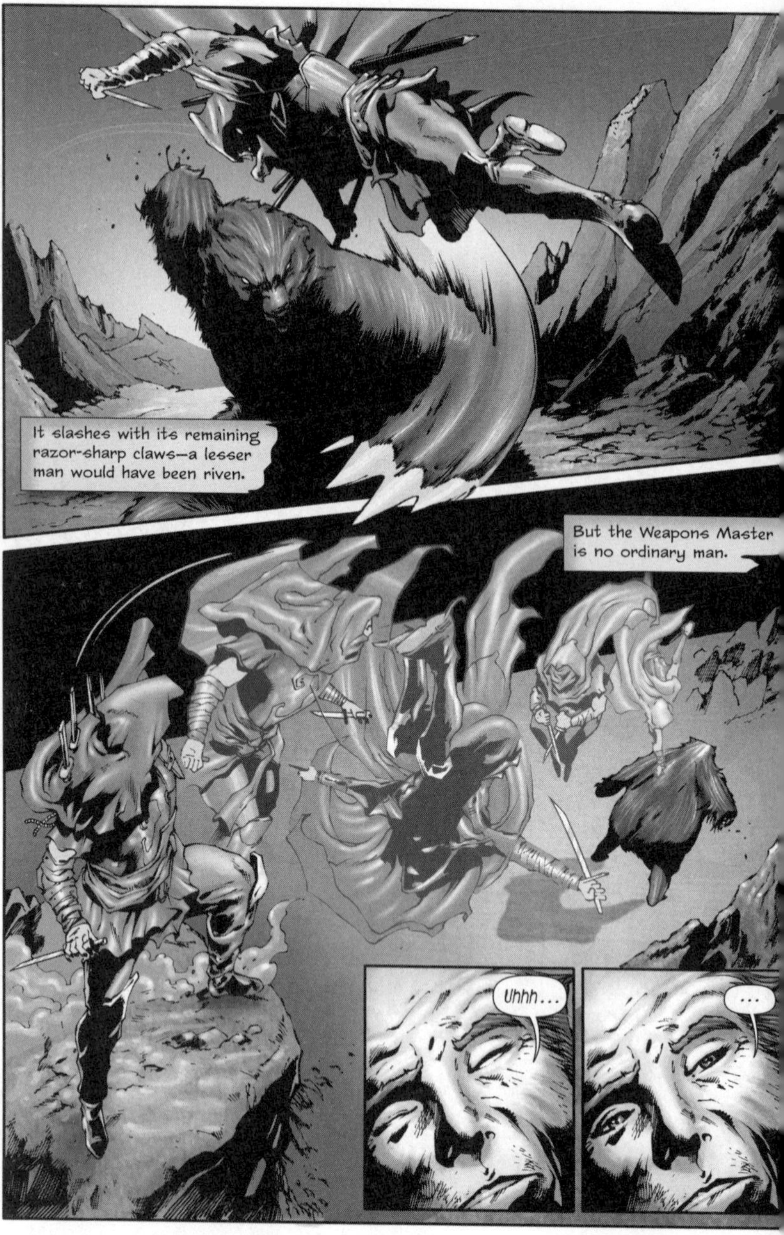
It slashes with its remaining razor-sharp claws—a lesser man would have been riven.
But the Weapons Master is no ordinary man.
Uhhh...
...

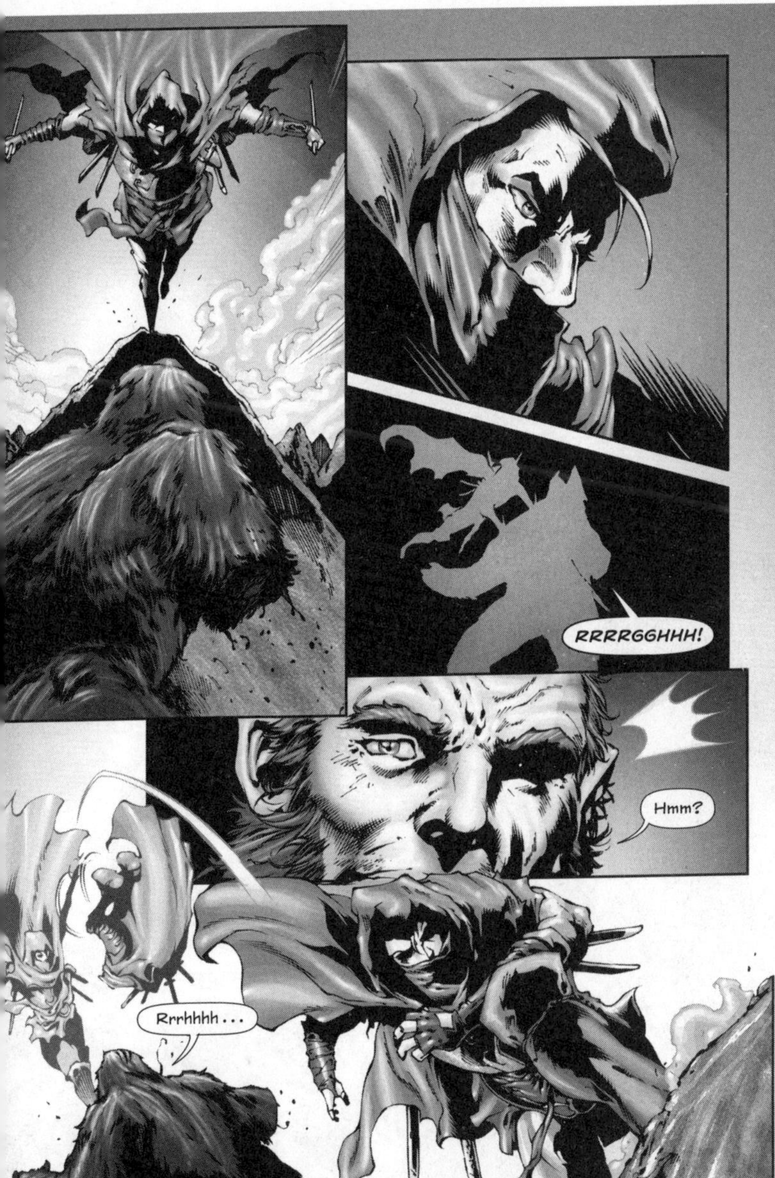
RRRRGGHHH!
Hmm?
Rrhhhh . . .

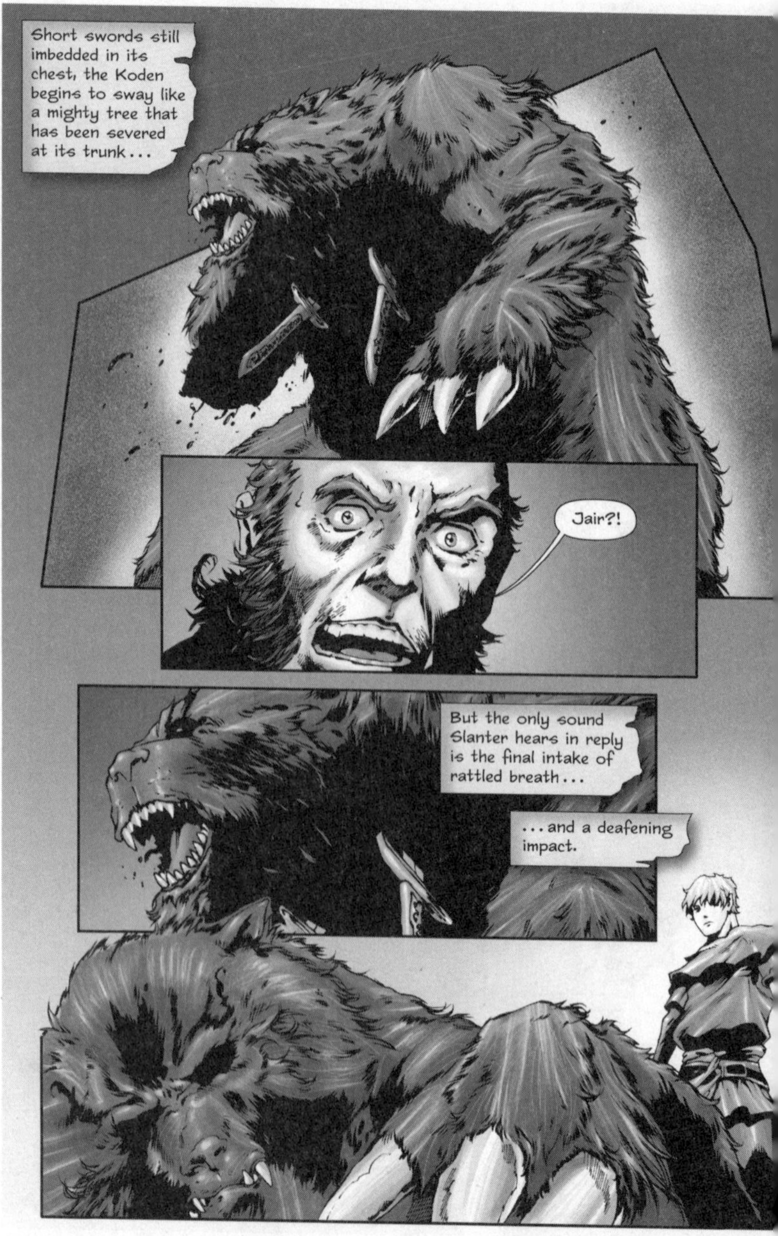
Short swords still imbedded in its chest, the Koden begins to sway like a mighty tree that has been severed at its trunk...
Jair?!
But the only sound Slanter hears in reply is the final intake of rattled breath...
...and a deafening impact.

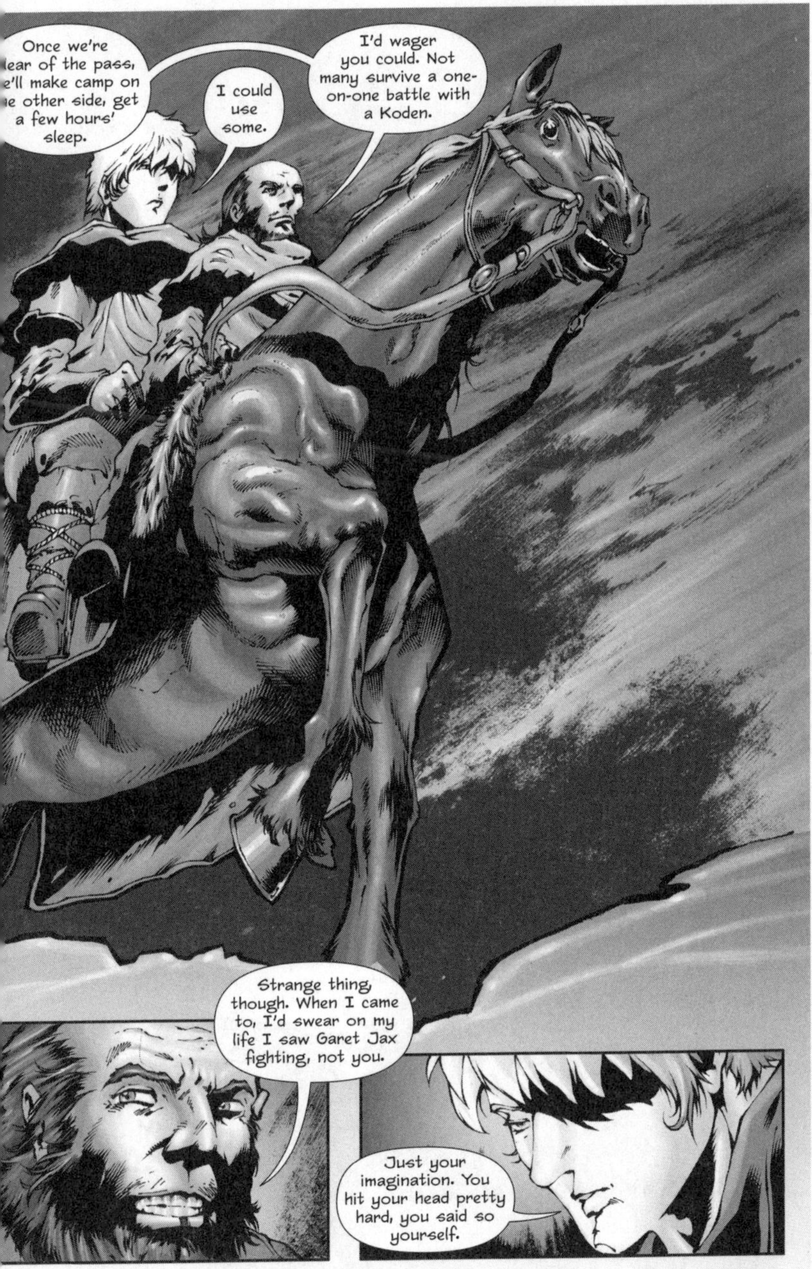
Once we're lear of the pass, e'll make camp on e other side, get a few hours' sleep.
I could use some.
I'd wager you could. Not many survive a one-on-one battle with a Koden.
Strange thing, though. When I came to, I'd swear on my life I saw Garet Jax fighting, not you.
Just your imagination. You hit your head pretty hard, you said so yourself.

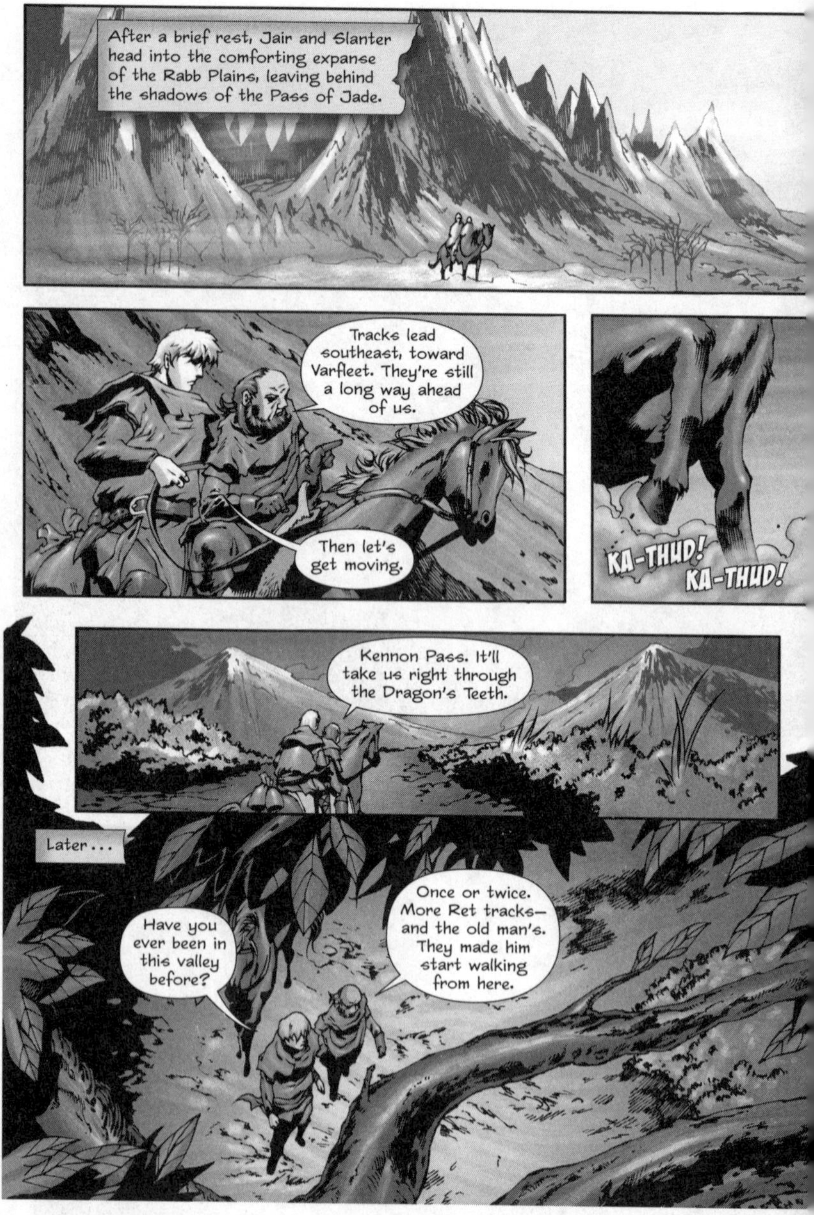
After a brief rest, Jair and Slanter head into the comforting expanse of the Rabb Plains, leaving behind the shadows of the Pass of Jade.
Tracks lead southeast, toward Varfleet. They're still a long way ahead of us.
Then let's get moving.
KA-THUD! KA-THUD!
Kennon Pass. It'll take us right through the Dragon's Teeth.
Later...
Have you ever been in this valley before?
Once or twice. More Ret tracks— and the old man's. They made him start walking from here.

SNIFF!
SNIFF!

Smoke—
that direction.
Let's go on foot.
Horses make too
much noise.

We're close,
don't make a
sound until
I tell you.

All right.

ꓚꓯꓱ ꓞꓲꓶꓴꓹ
ꓚꓯꓞꓲꓴ ꓶꓴꓬ ꓬꓳꓓ
ꓴꓴ ꓷꓬꓯꓕ

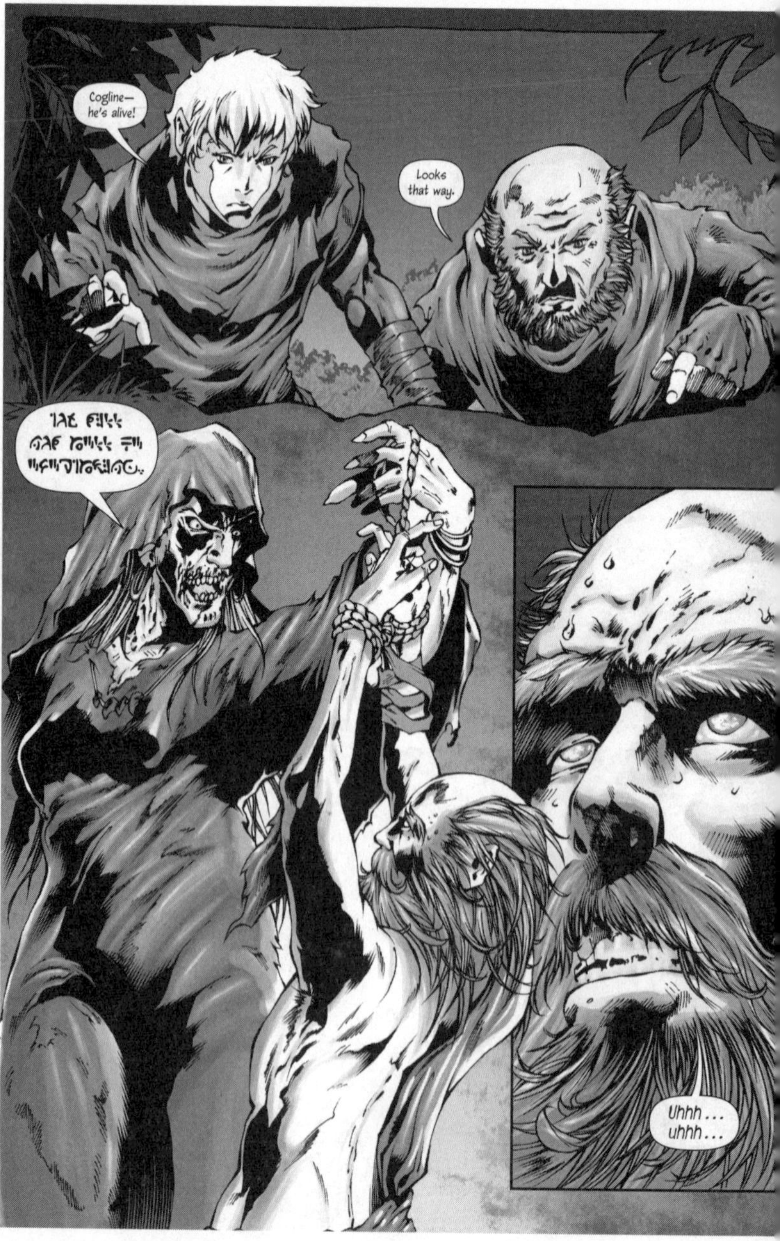
Cogline—
he's alive!
Looks
that way.
Uhhh...
uhhh...

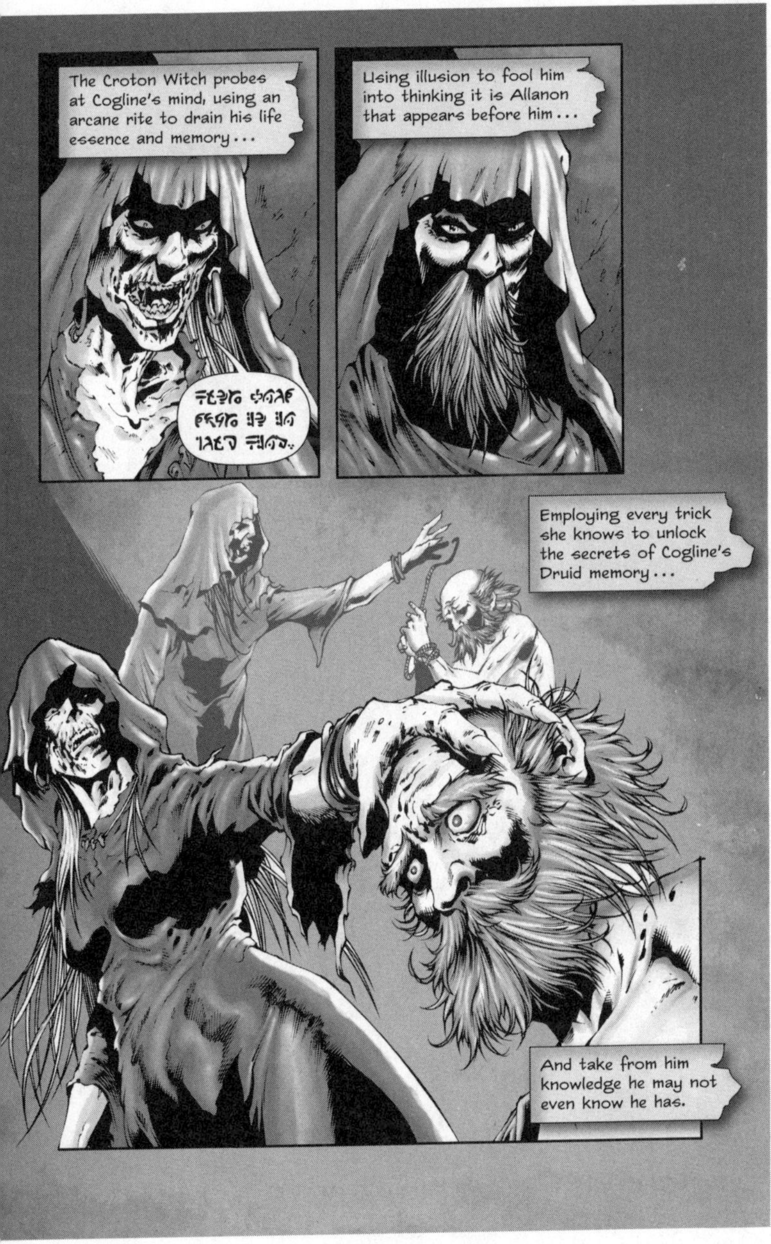
The Croton Witch probes at Cogline's mind, using an arcane rite to drain his life essence and memory . . .
Using illusion to fool him into thinking it is Allanon that appears before him . . .
Employing every trick she knows to unlock the secrets of Cogline's Druid memory . . .
And take from him knowledge he may not even know he has.

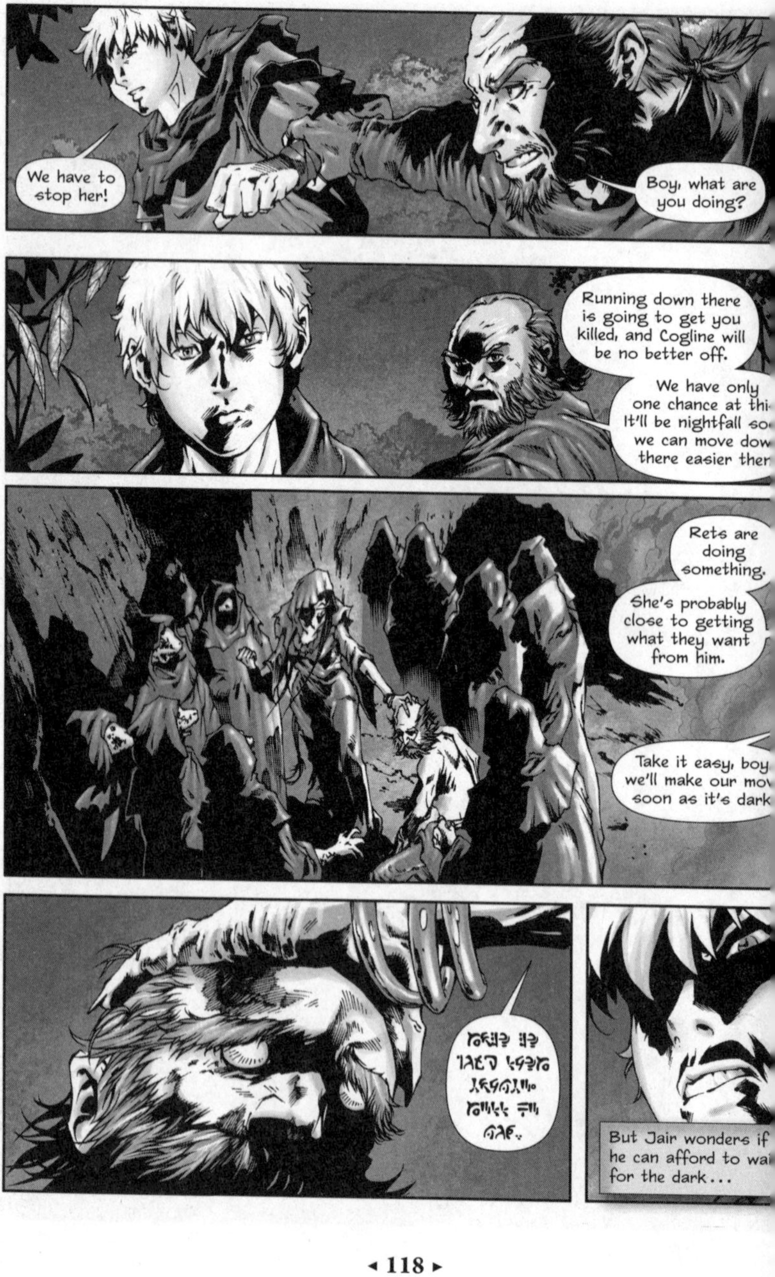
We have to stop her!
Boy, what are you doing?
Running down there is going to get you killed, and Cogline will be no better off.
We have only one chance at thi It'll be nightfall so we can move dow there easier ther
Rets are doing something.
She's probably close to getting what they want from him.
Take it easy, boy we'll make our mov soon as it's dark
But Jair wonders if he can afford to wa for the dark...

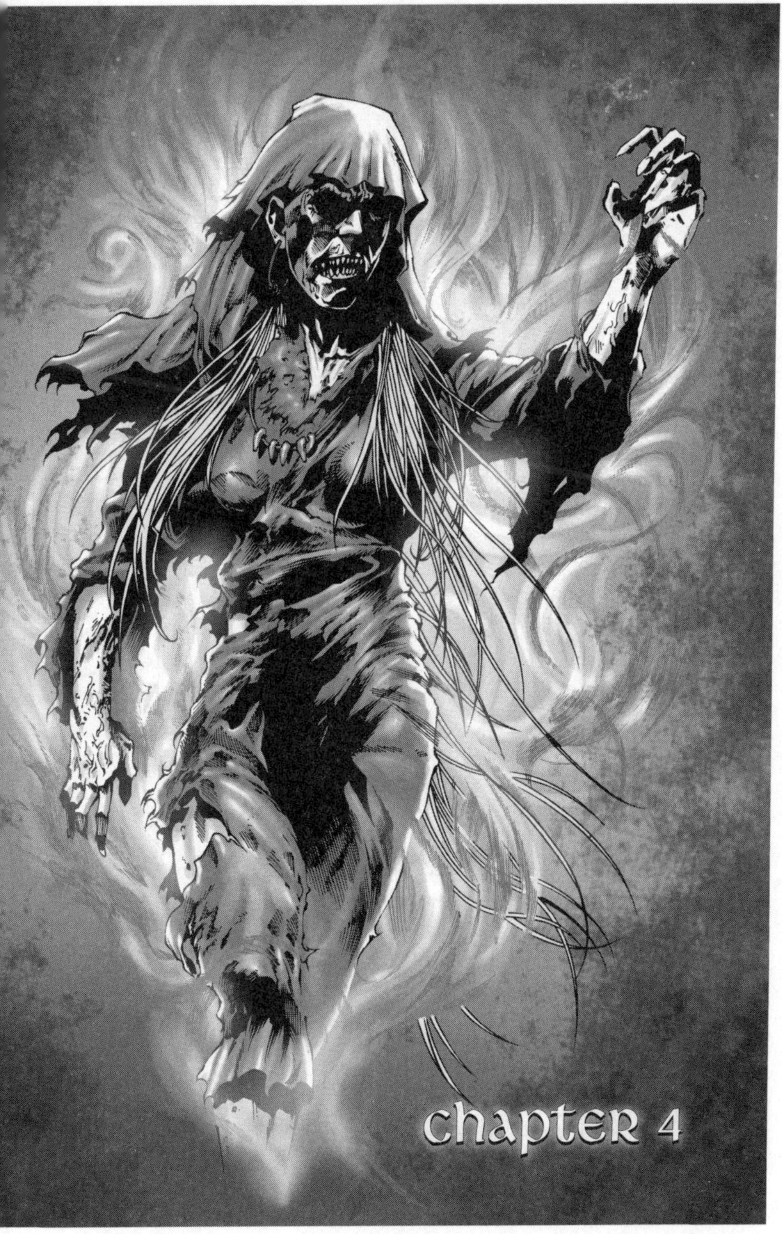
chapter 4

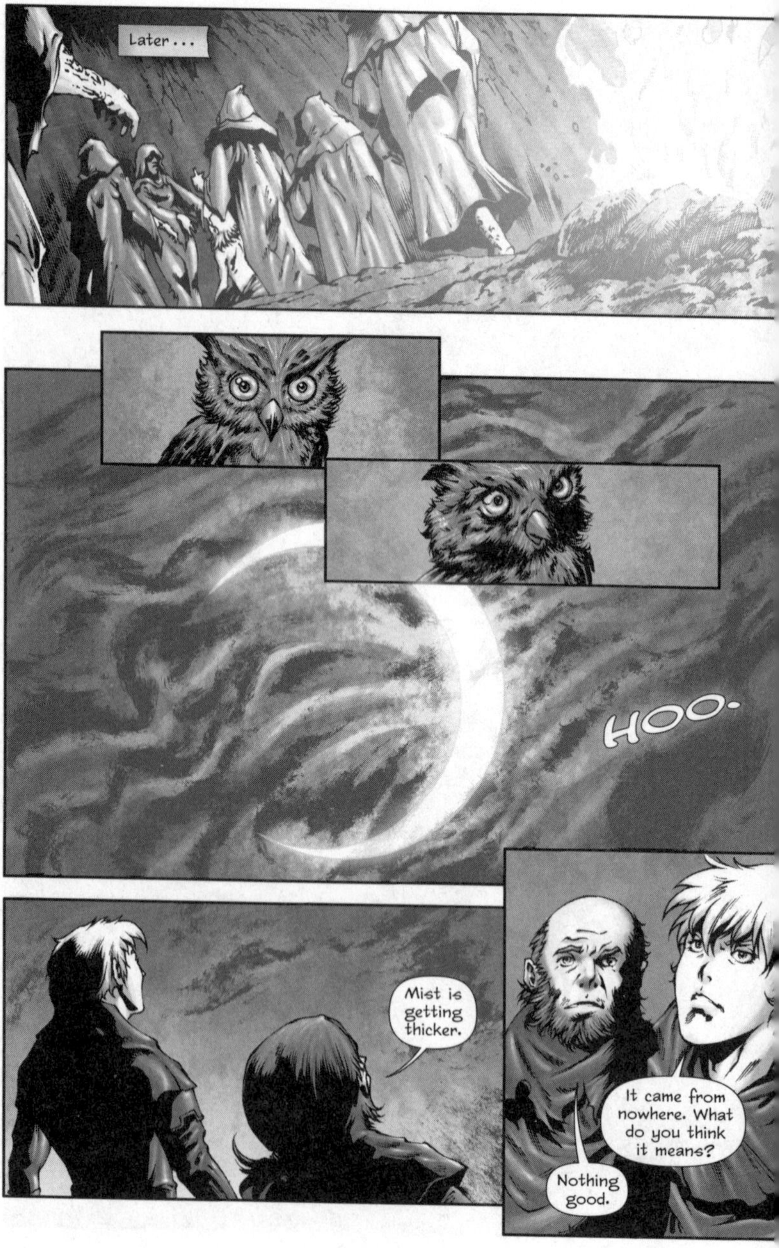
Later . . .
HOO-
Mist is getting thicker.
It came from nowhere. What do you think it means?
Nothing good.

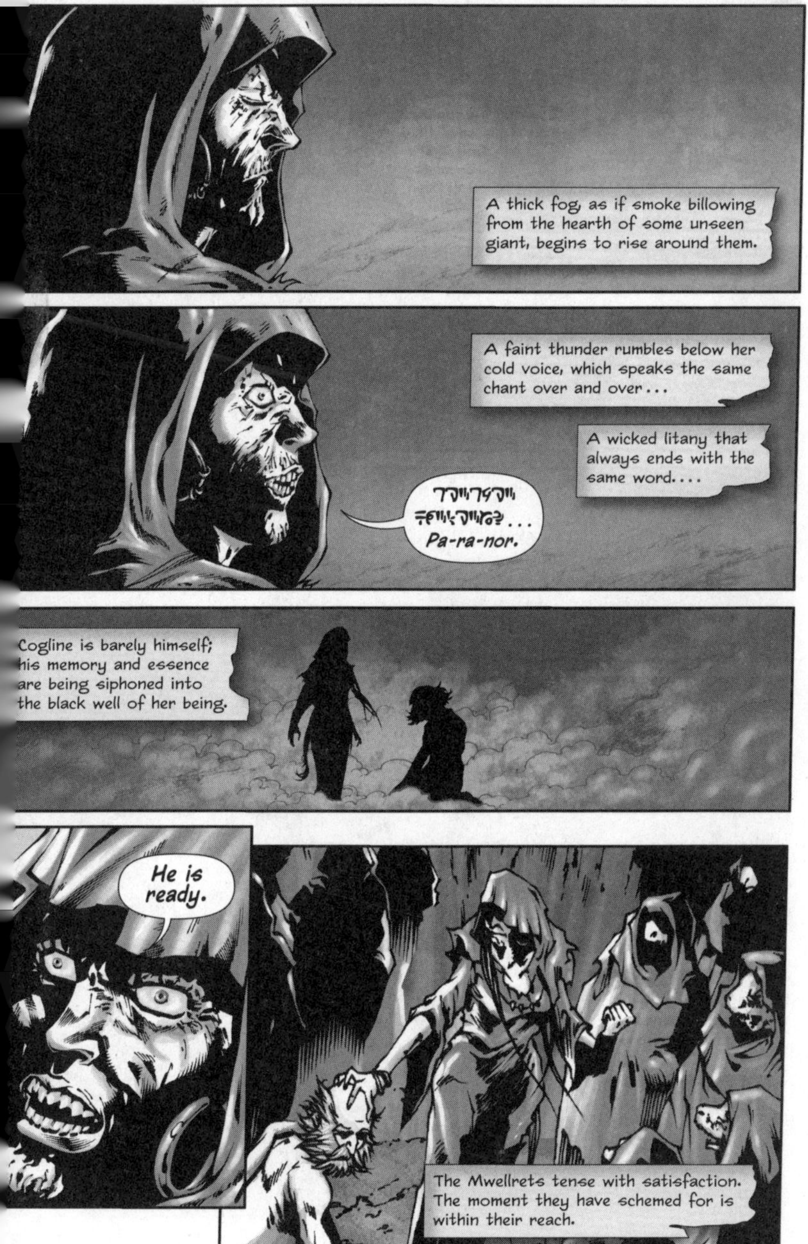
A thick fog, as if smoke billowing from the hearth of some unseen giant, begins to rise around them.
A faint thunder rumbles below her cold voice, which speaks the same chant over and over...
A wicked litany that always ends with the same word....
... Pa-ra-nor.
Cogline is barely himself; his memory and essence are being siphoned into the black well of her being.
He is ready.
The Mwellrets tense with satisfaction. The moment they have schemed for is within their reach.

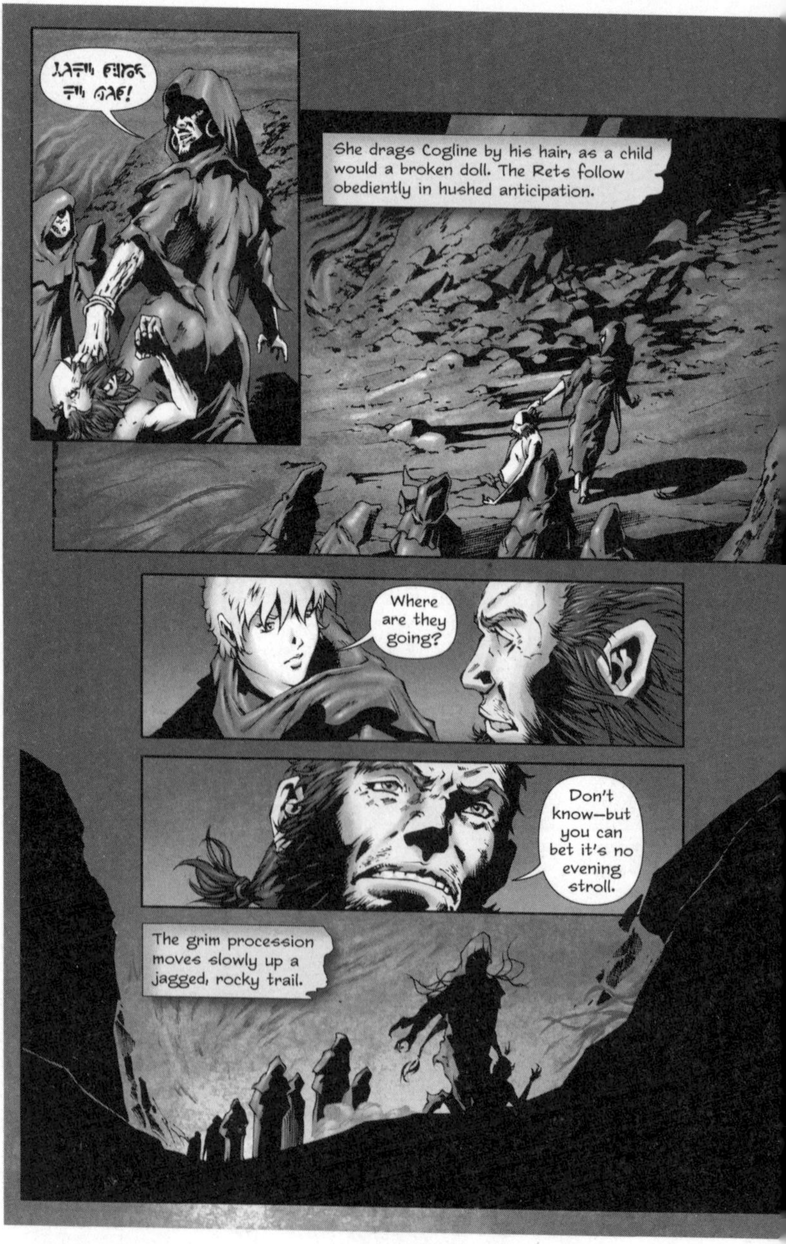
She drags Cogline by his hair, as a child would a broken doll. The Rets follow obediently in hushed anticipation.
Where are they going?
Don't know—but you can bet it's no evening stroll.
The grim procession moves slowly up a jagged, rocky trail.

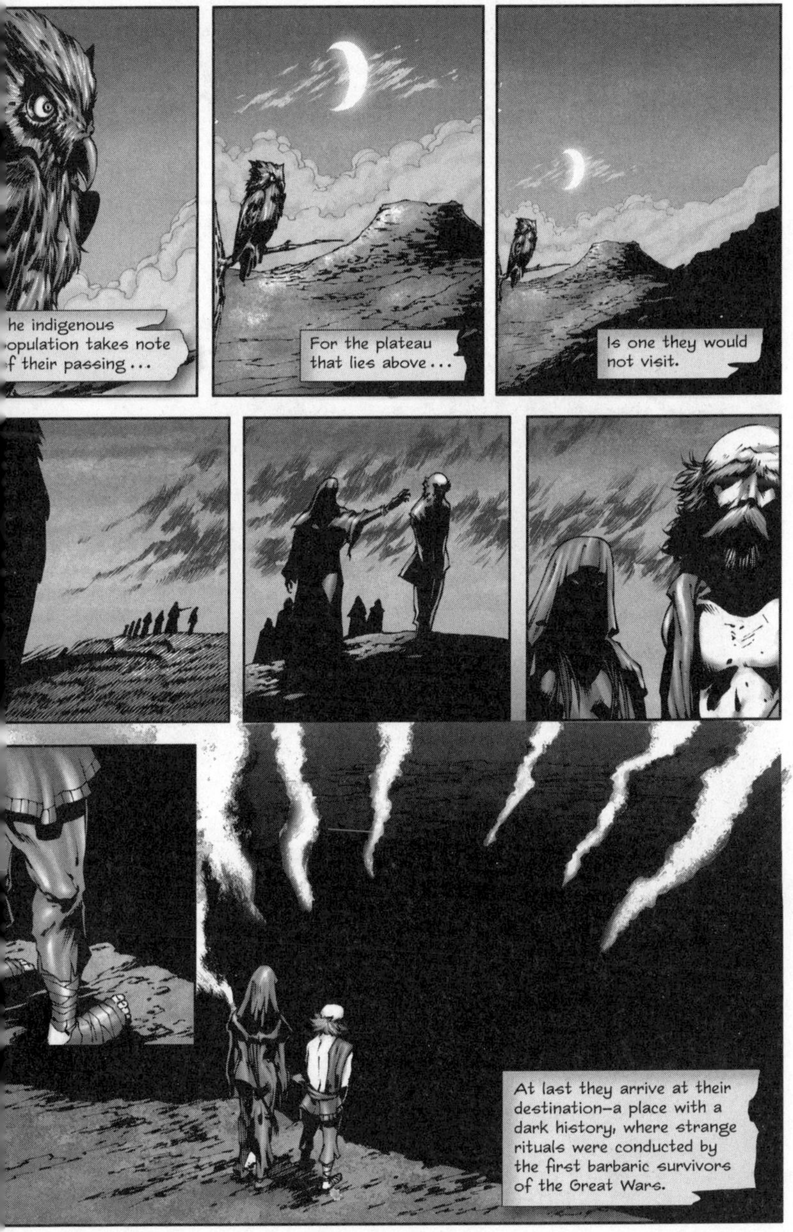
he indigenous
opulation takes note
f their passing . . .
For the plateau
that lies above . . .
Is one they would
not visit.
At last they arrive at their destination—a place with a dark history, where strange rituals were conducted by the first barbaric survivors of the Great Wars.

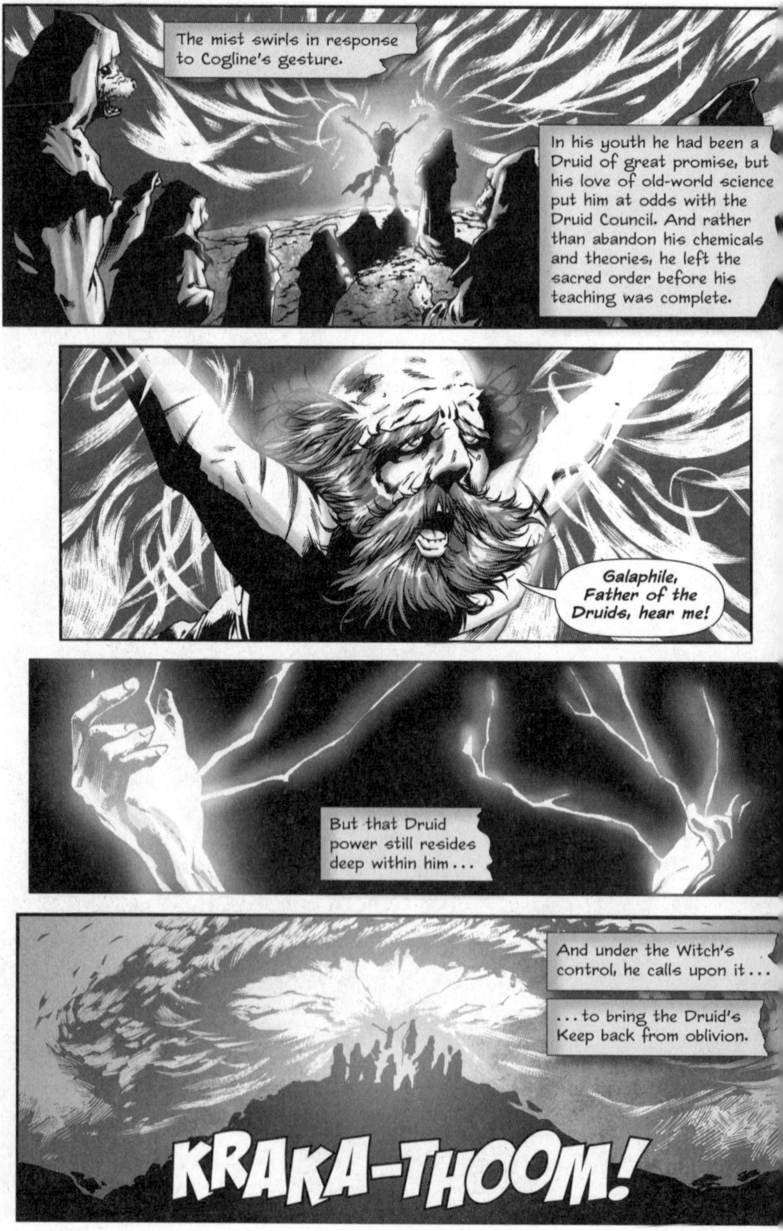
The mist swirls in response to Cogline's gesture.
In his youth he had been a Druid of great promise, but his love of old-world science put him at odds with the Druid Council. And rather than abandon his chemicals and theories, he left the sacred order before his teaching was complete.
Galaphile, Father of the Druids, hear me!
But that Druid power still resides deep within him...
And under the Witch's control, he calls upon it...
...to bring the Druid's Keep back from oblivion.
KRAKA-THOOM!

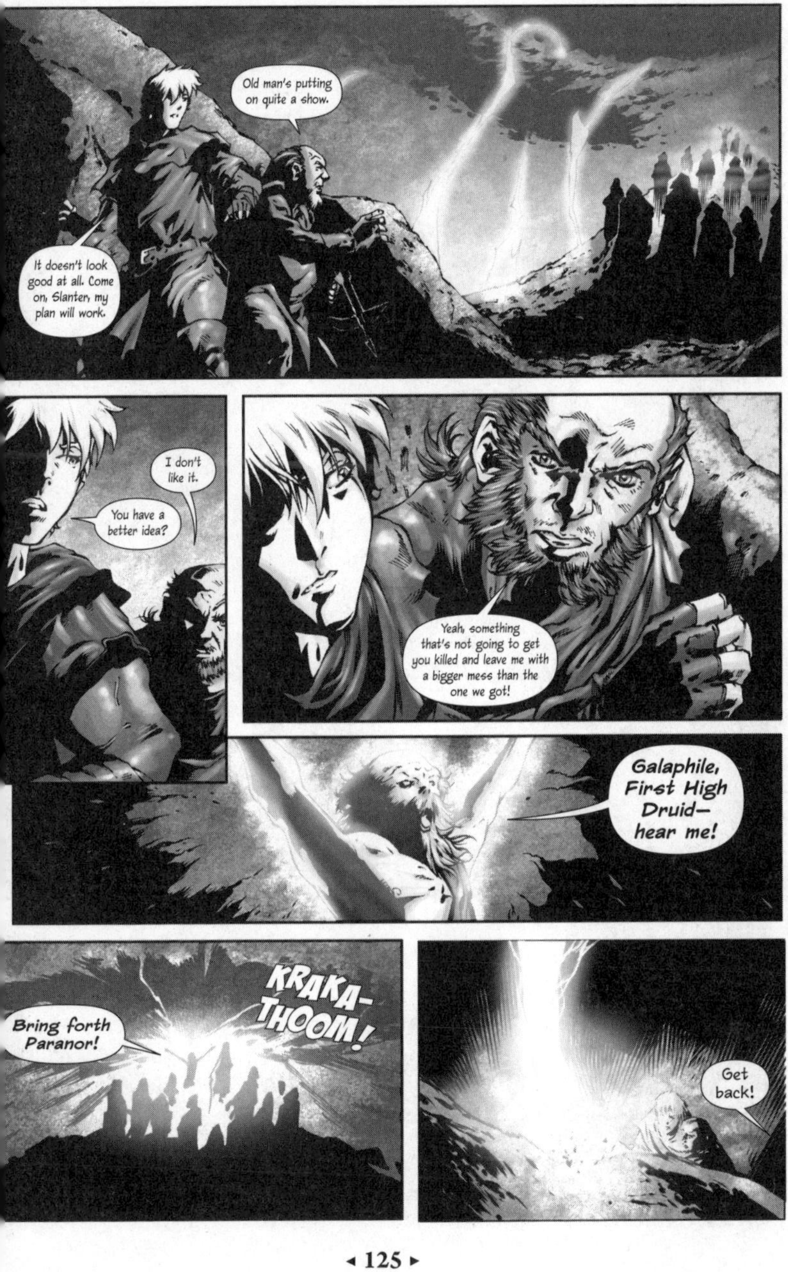
Old man's putting on quite a show.
It doesn't look good at all. Come on, Slanter, my plan will work.
I don't like it.
You have a better idea?
Yeah, something that's not going to get you killed and leave me with a bigger mess than the one we got!
Galaphile, First High Druid— hear me!
Bring forth Paranor!
KRAKA-THOOM!
Get back!

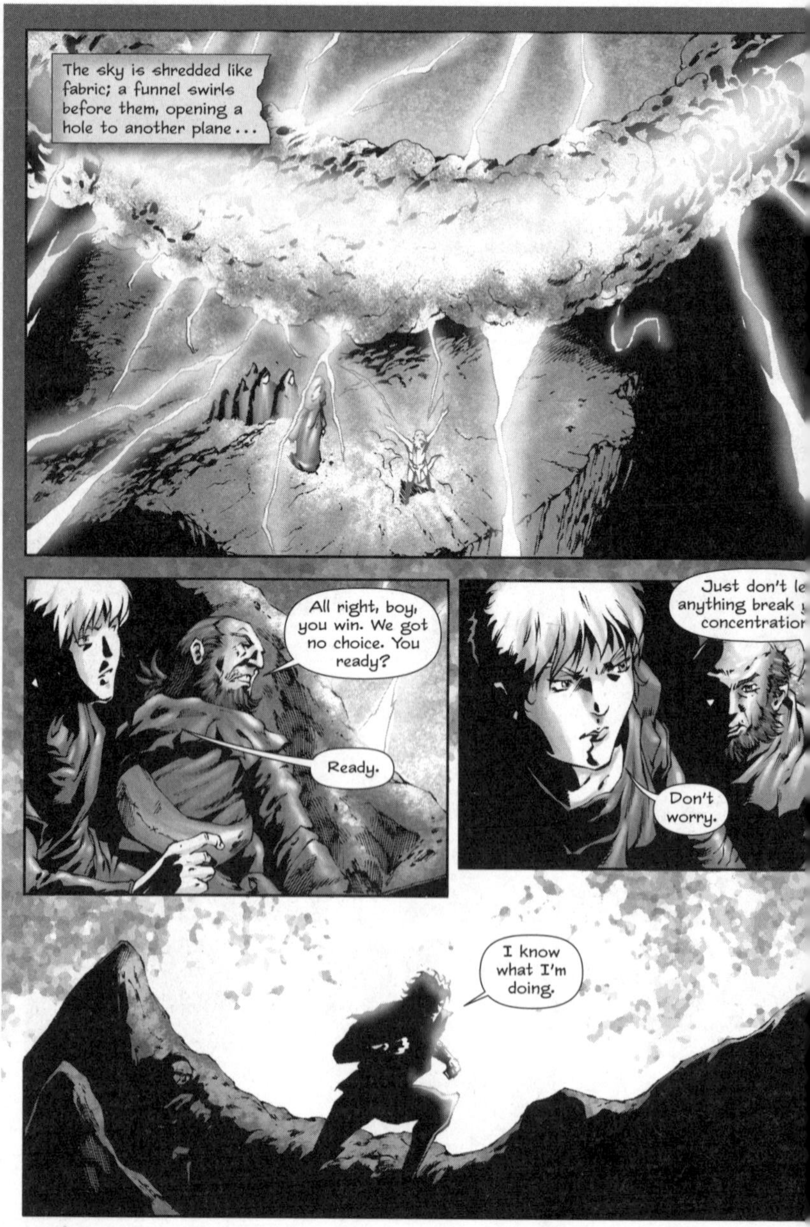
The sky is shredded like fabric; a funnel swirls before them, opening a hole to another plane . . .
All right, boy, you win. We got no choice. You ready?
Ready.
Just don't le anything break concentratio
Don't worry.
I know what I'm doing.

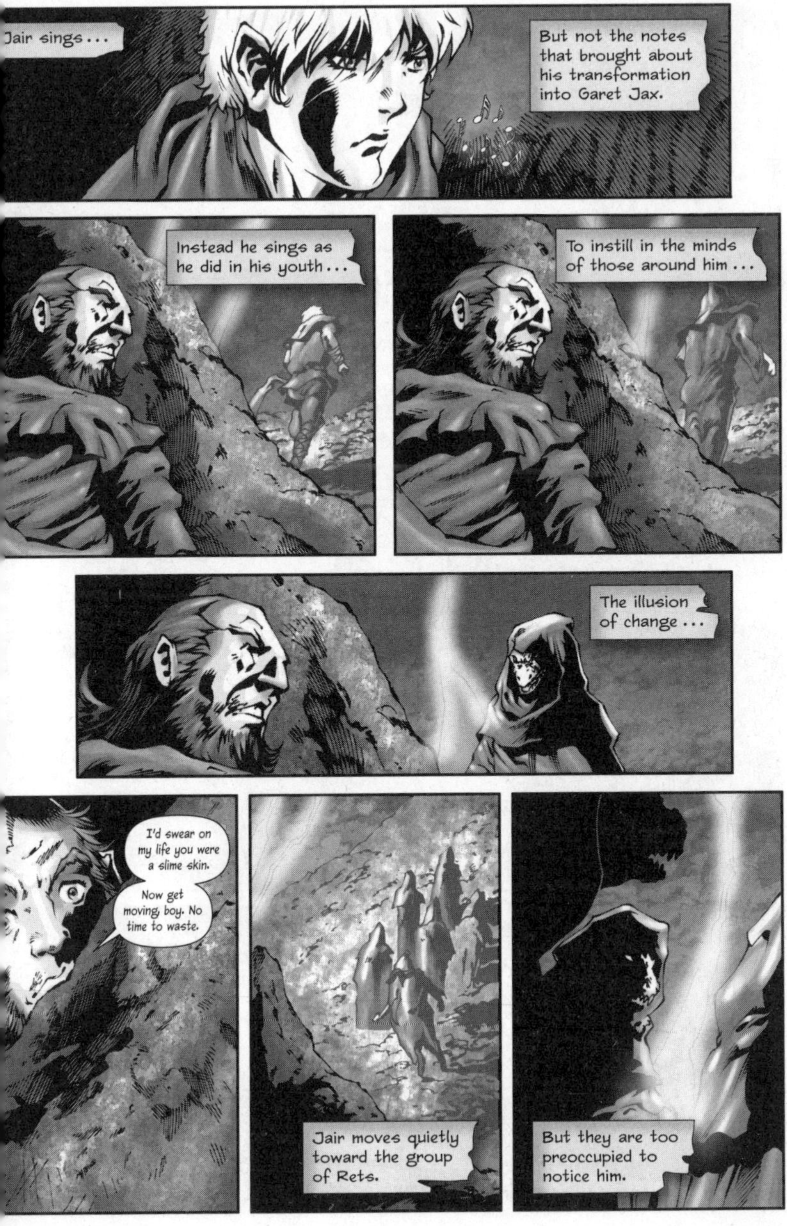
Jair sings . . .
But not the notes that brought about his transformation into Garet Jax.
Instead he sings as he did in his youth . . .
To instill in the minds of those around him . . .
The illusion of change . . .
I'd swear on my life you were a slime skin.
Now get moving, boy. No time to waste.
Jair moves quietly toward the group of Rets.
But they are too preoccupied to notice him.

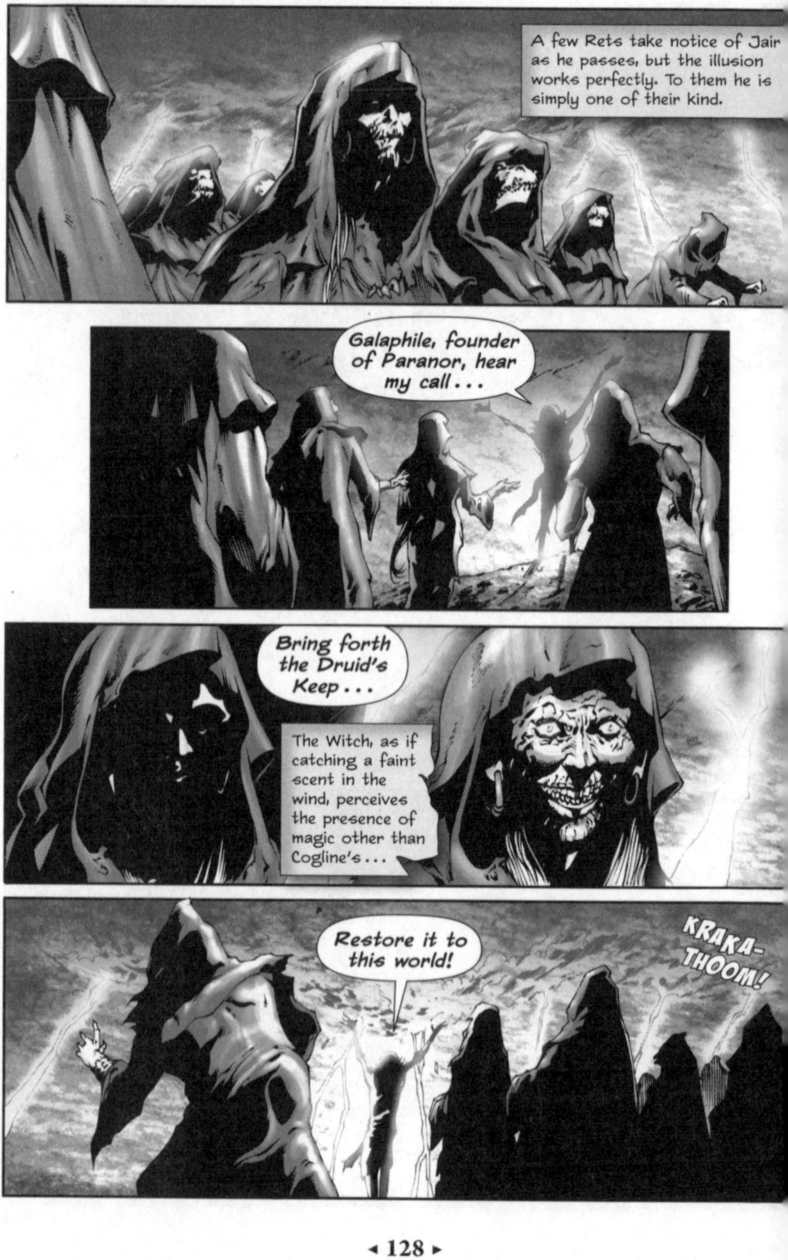
A few Rets take notice of Jair as he passes, but the illusion works perfectly. To them he is simply one of their kind.
Galaphile, founder of Paranor, hear my call . . .
Bring forth the Druid's Keep . . .
The Witch, as if catching a faint scent in the wind, perceives the presence of magic other than Cogline's . . .
Restore it to this world!
KRAKA-THOOM!

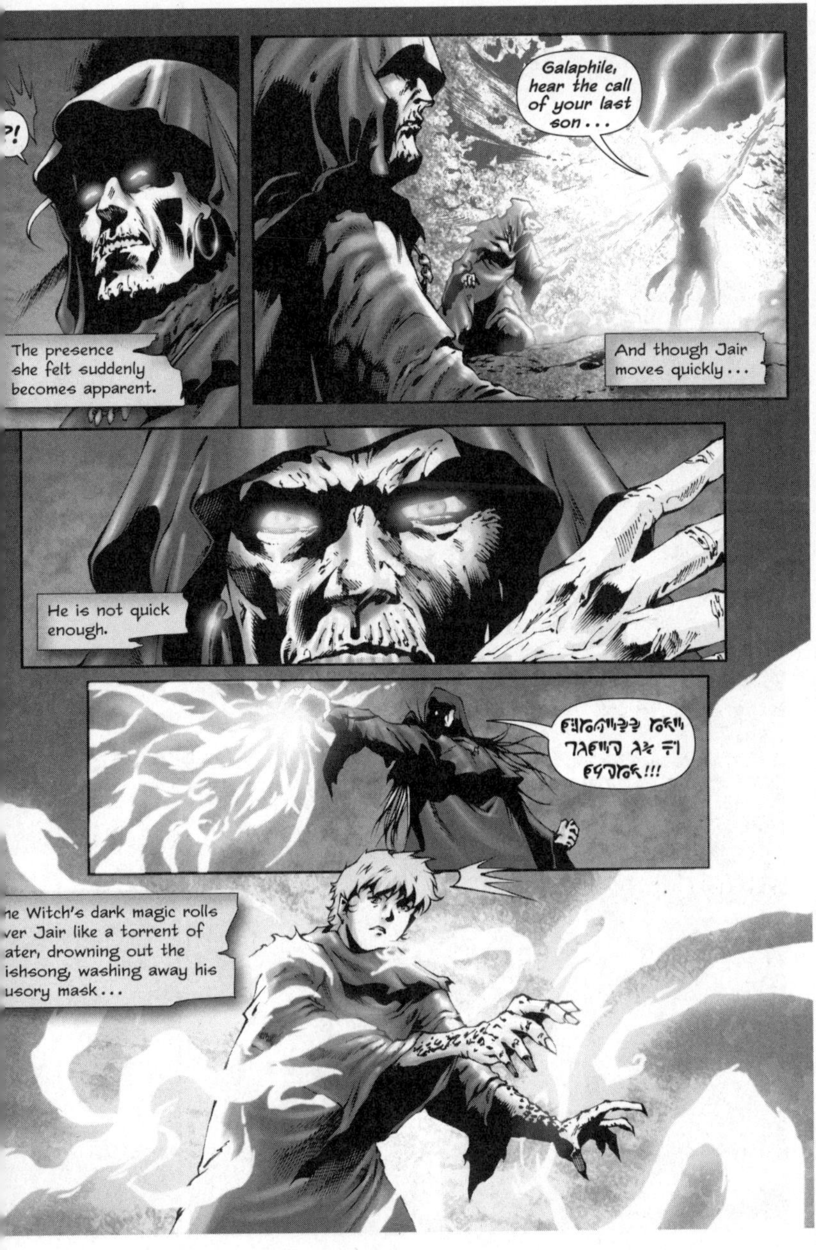
?!
The presence she felt suddenly becomes apparent.
Galaphile, hear the call of your last son . . .
And though Jair moves quickly . . .
He is not quick enough.
ne Witch's dark magic rolls ver Jair like a torrent of ater, drowning out the ishsong, washing away his usory mask . . .

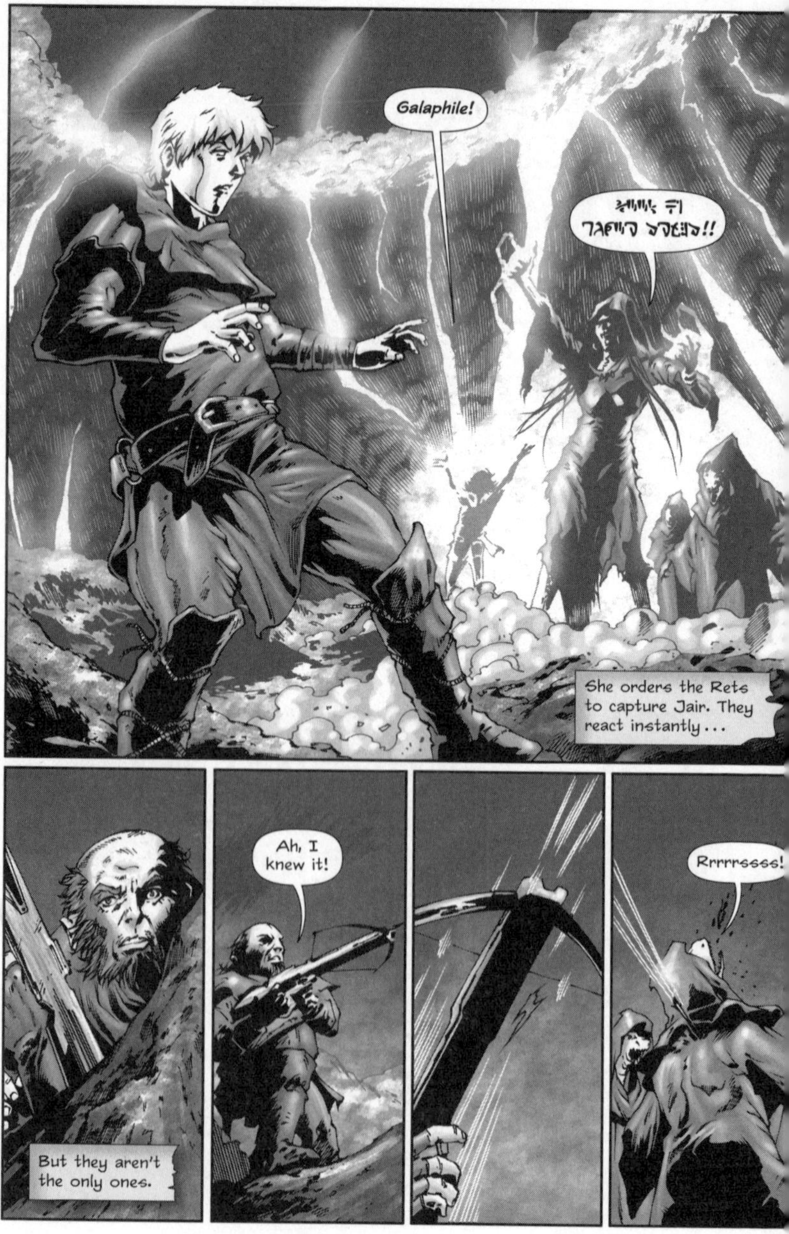
Galaphile!
She orders the Rets to capture Jair. They react instantly...
But they aren't the only ones.
Ah, I knew it!
Rrrrrssss!

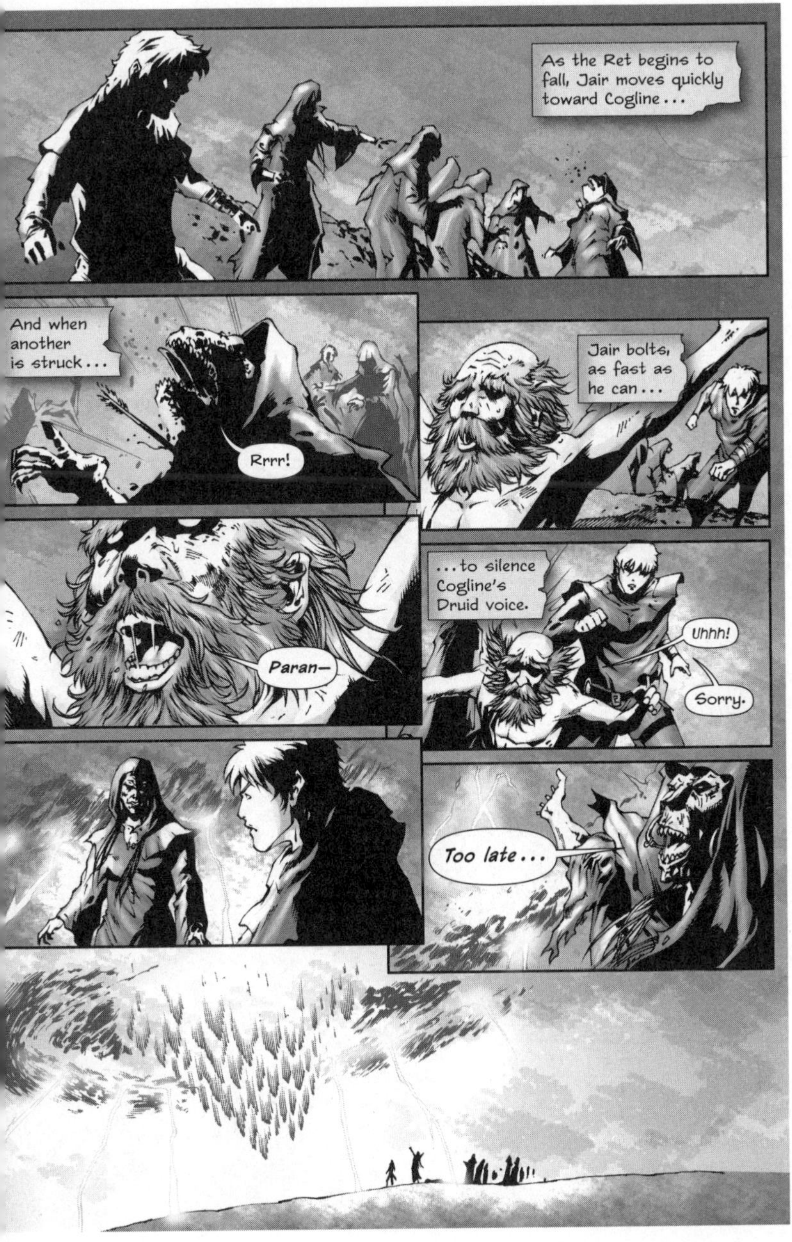
As the Ret begins to fall, Jair moves quickly toward Cogline . . .
And when another is struck . . .
Rrrr!
Jair bolts, as fast as he can . . .
Paran—
. . . to silence Cogline's Druid voice.
Uhhh!
Sorry.
Too late . . .

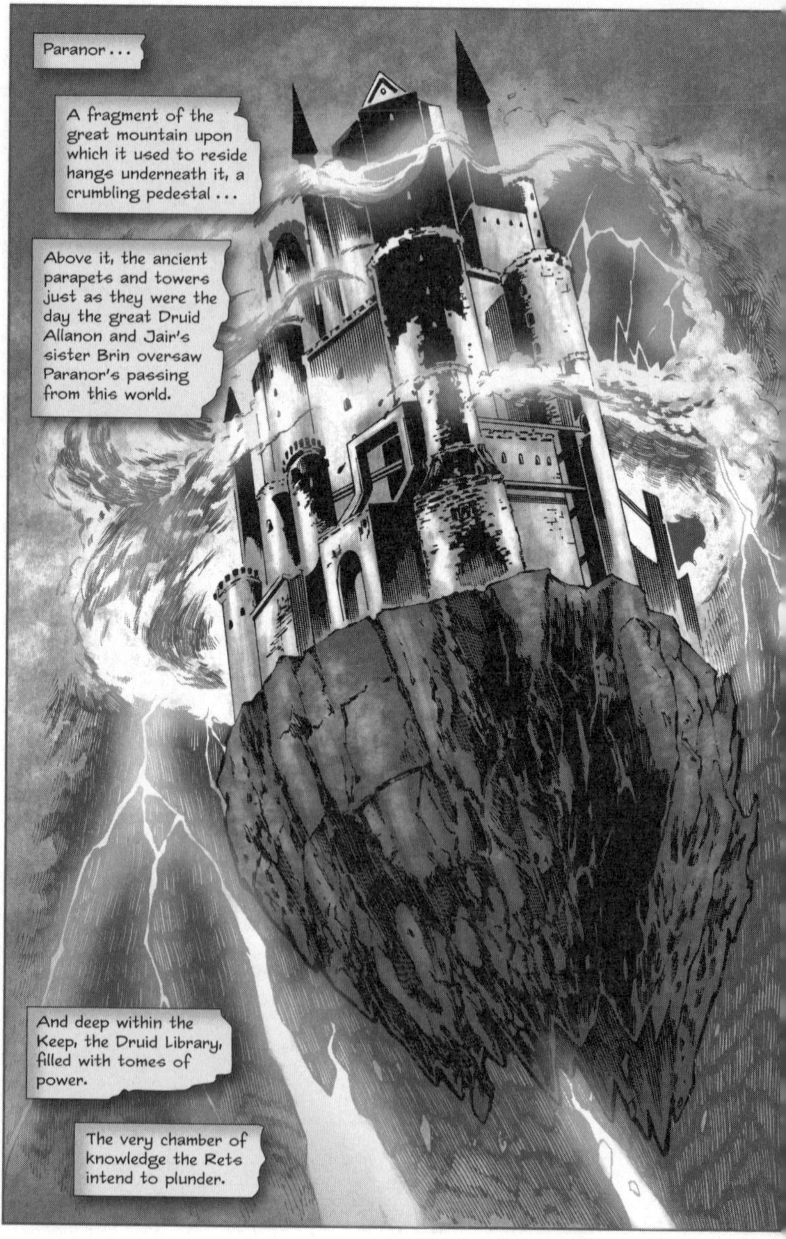
Paranor...
A fragment of the great mountain upon which it used to reside hangs underneath it, a crumbling pedestal...
Above it, the ancient parapets and towers just as they were the day the great Druid Allanon and Jair's sister Brin oversaw Paranor's passing from this world.
And deep within the Keep, the Druid Library, filled with tomes of power.
The very chamber of knowledge the Rets intend to plunder.

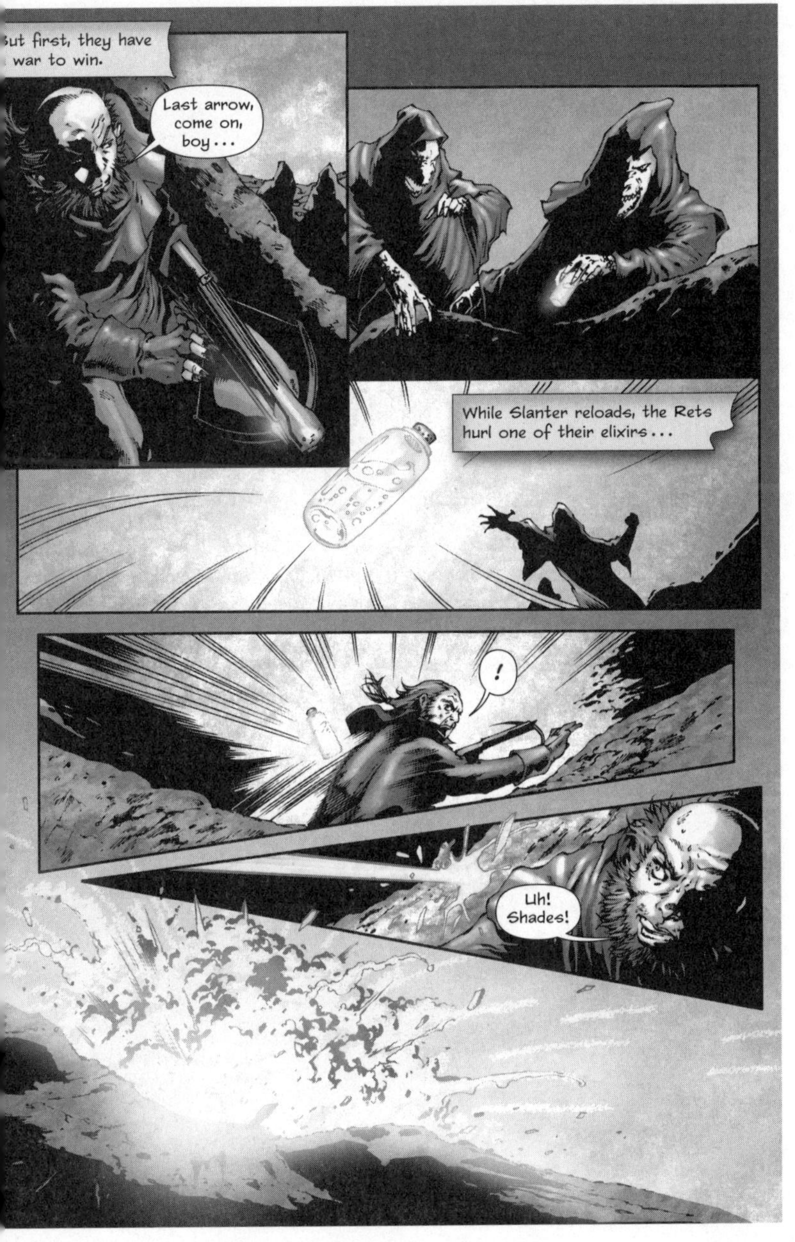
But first, they have a war to win.
Last arrow, come on, boy...
While Slanter reloads, the Rets hurl one of their elixirs...
!
Uh! Shades!

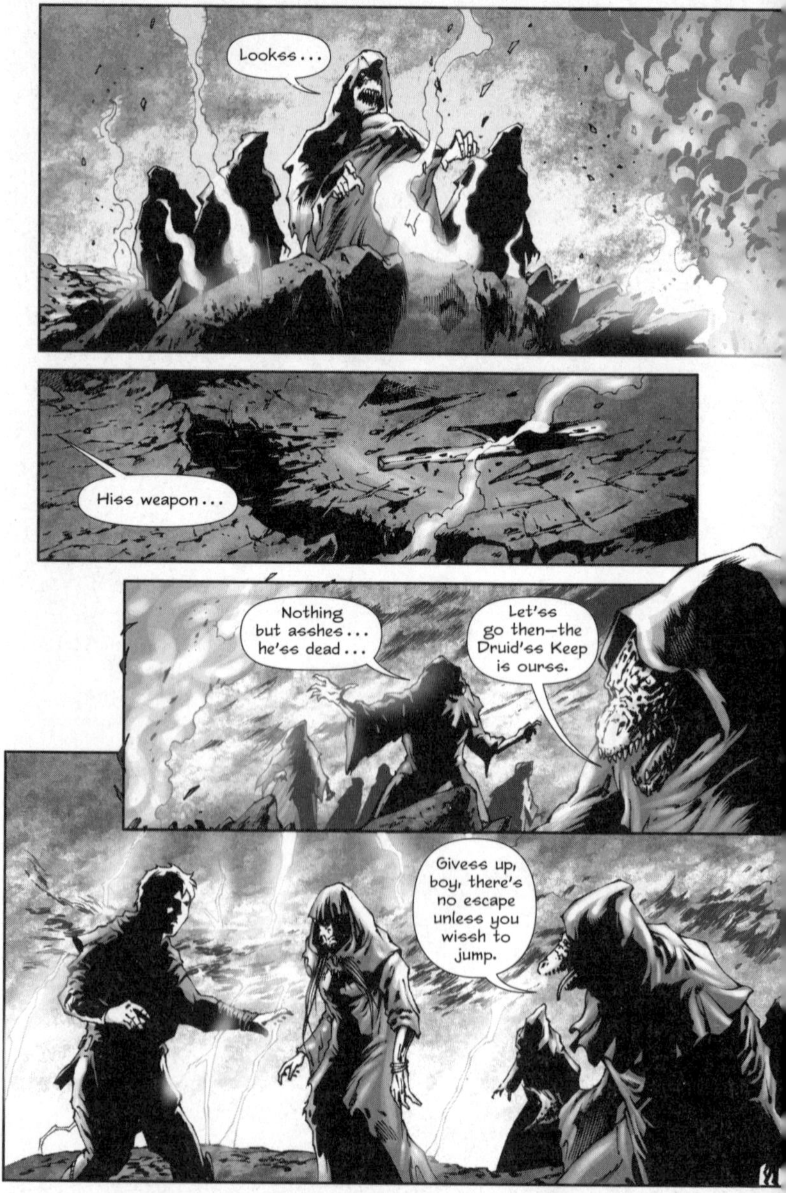
Lookss...
Hiss weapon...
Nothing but asshes... he'ss dead...
Let'ss go then—the Druid'ss Keep is ourss.
Givess up, boy, there's no escape unless you wissh to jump.

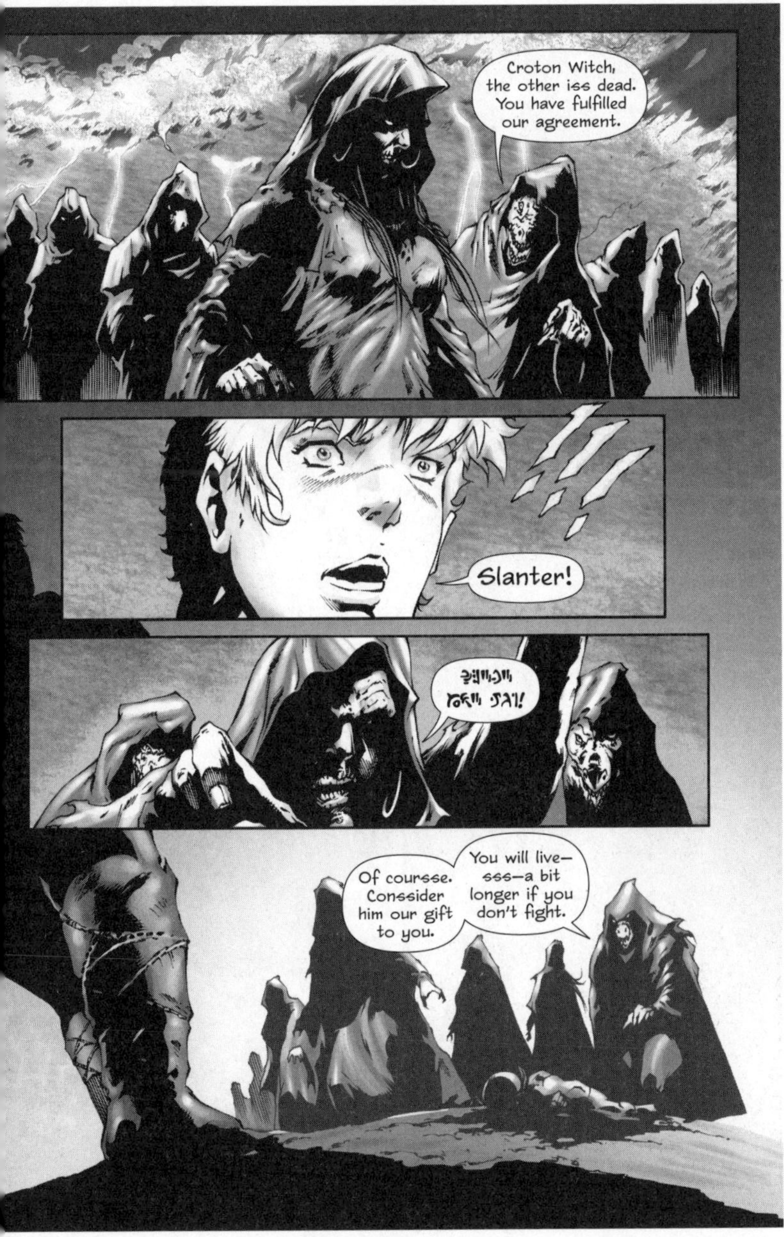
Croton Witch, the other iss dead. You have fulfilled our agreement.
Slanter!
Of coursse. Conssider him our gift to you.
You will live—sss—a bit longer if you don't fight.

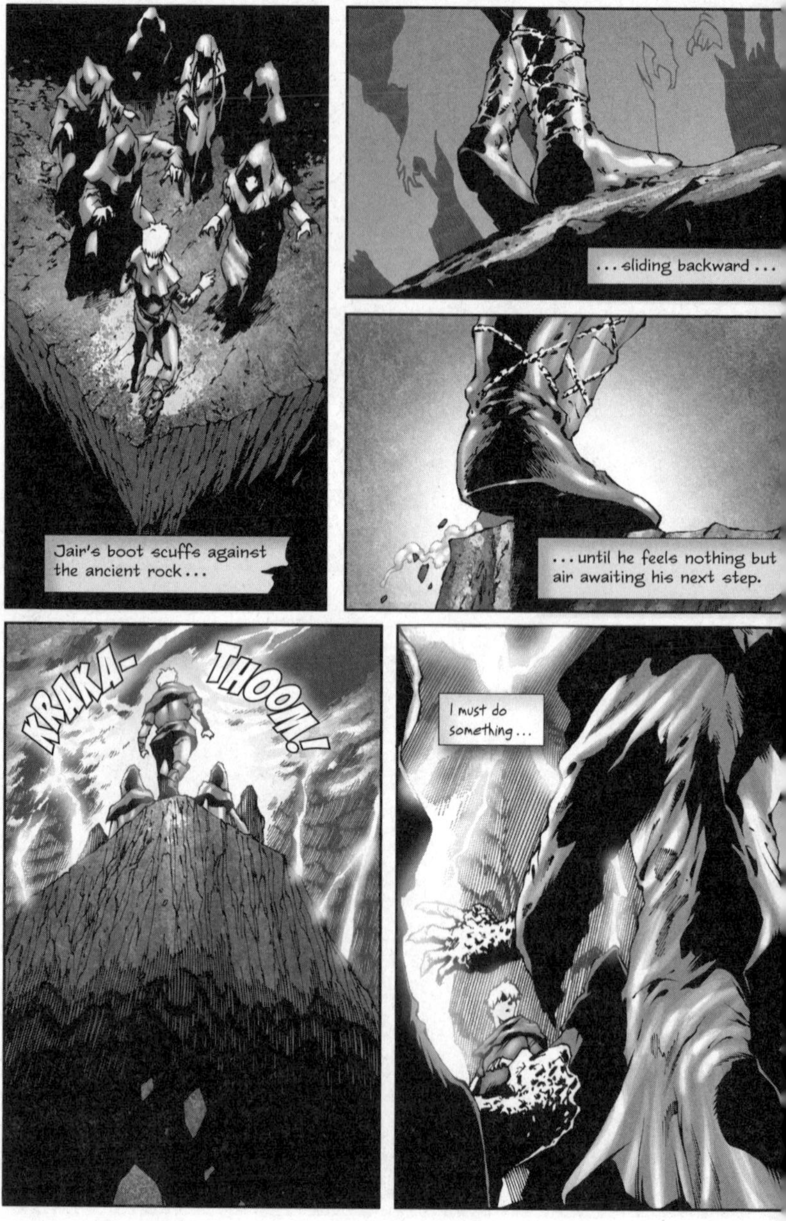
Jair's boot scuffs against the ancient rock...
...sliding backward...
...until he feels nothing but air awaiting his next step.
KRAKA-
THOOM!
I must do something...

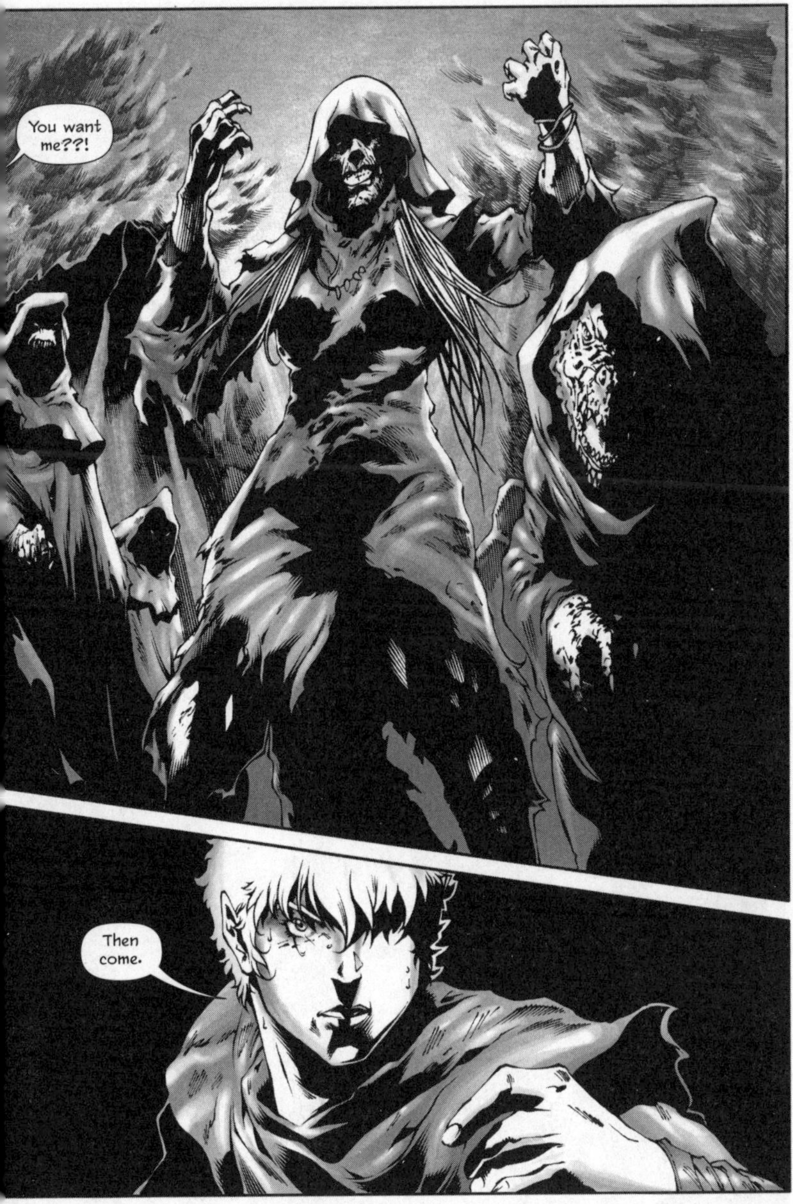
You want me??!
Then come.

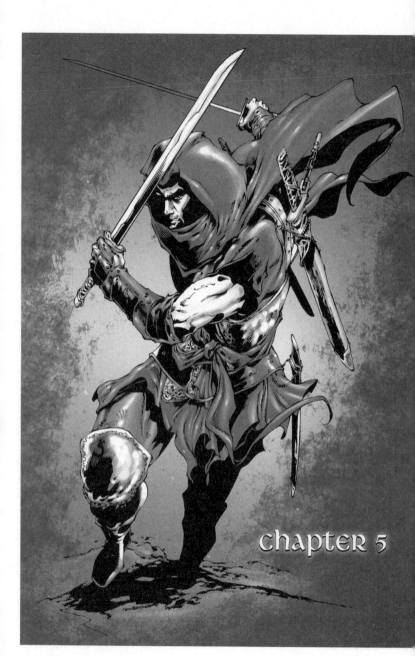

chapter 5

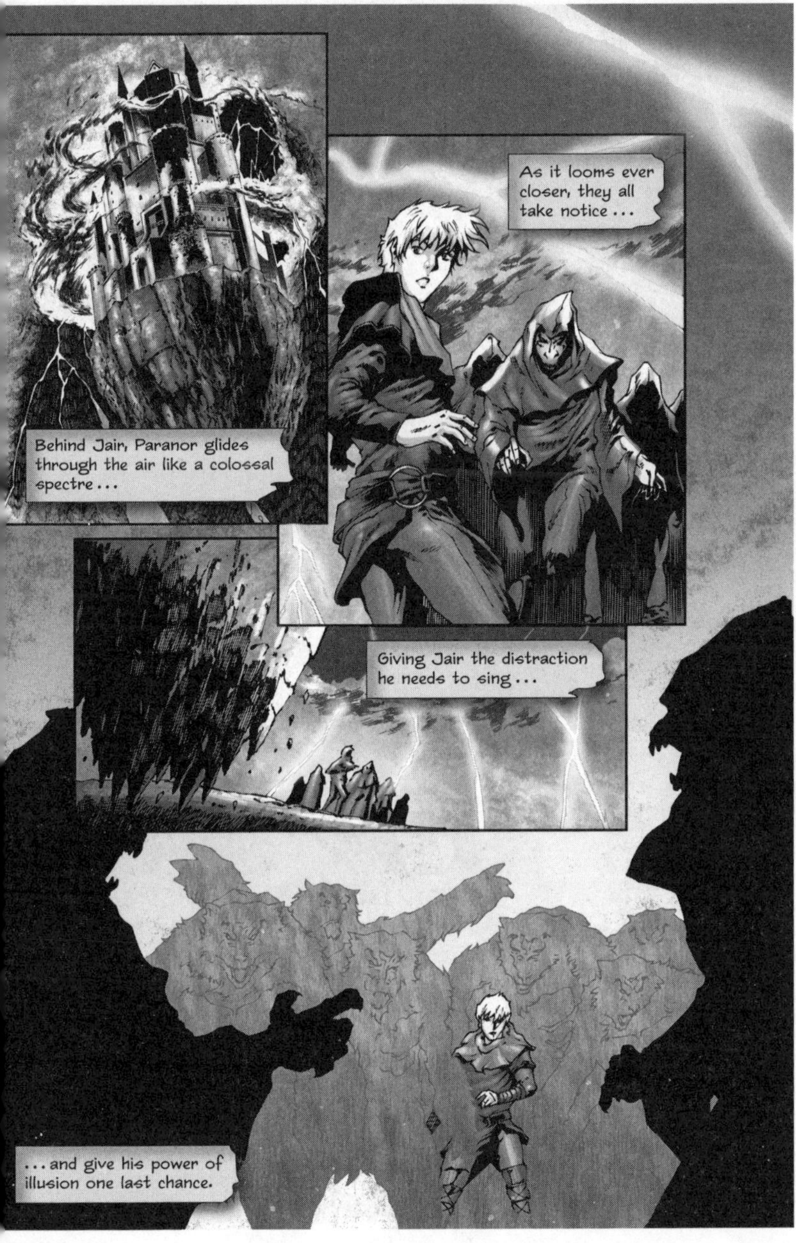
Behind Jair, Paranor glides through the air like a colossal spectre . . .
As it looms ever closer, they all take notice . . .
Giving Jair the distraction he needs to sing . . .
. . . and give his power of illusion one last chance.

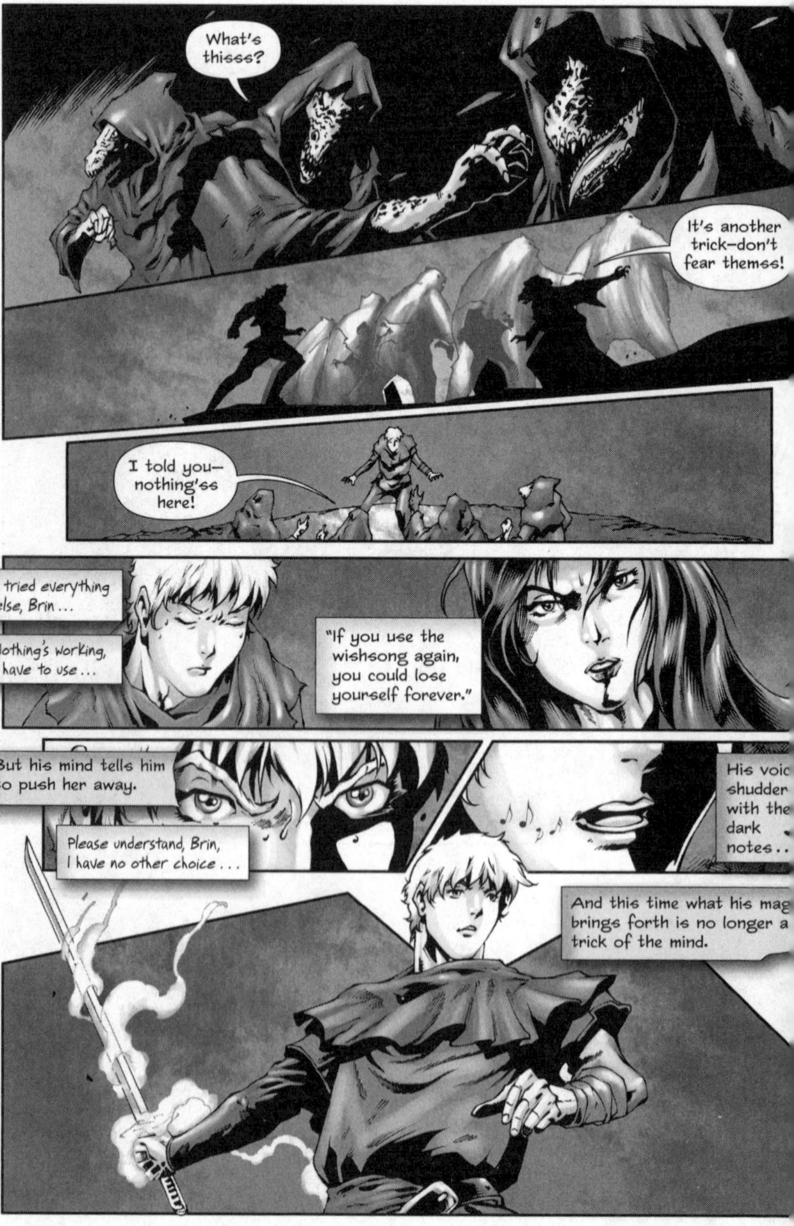
What's thisss?
It's another trick—don't fear themss!
I told you— nothing'ss here!
I tried everything else, Brin...
Nothing's working, I have to use...
"If you use the wishsong again, you could lose yourself forever."
But his mind tells him to push her away.
Please understand, Brin, I have no other choice...
His voic shudder with the dark notes..
And this time what his mag brings forth is no longer a trick of the mind.

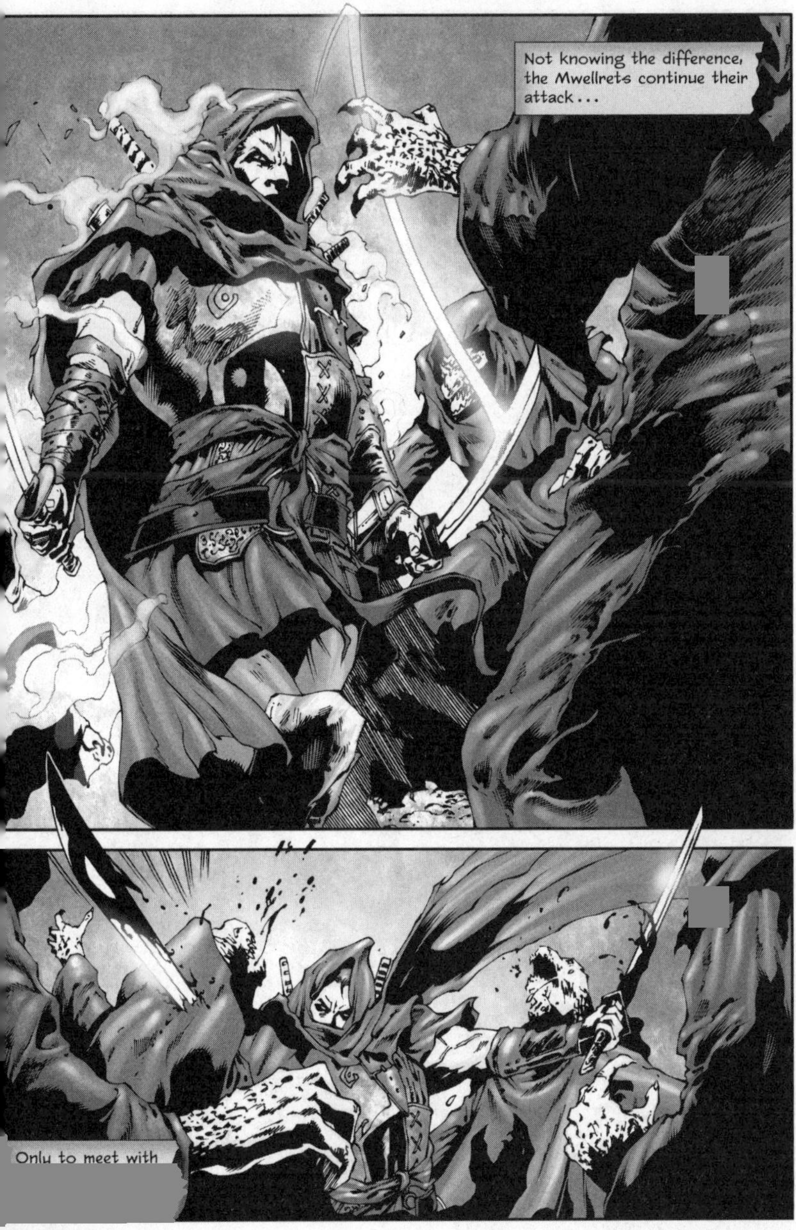
Not knowing the difference, the Mwellrets continue their attack...
Only to meet with

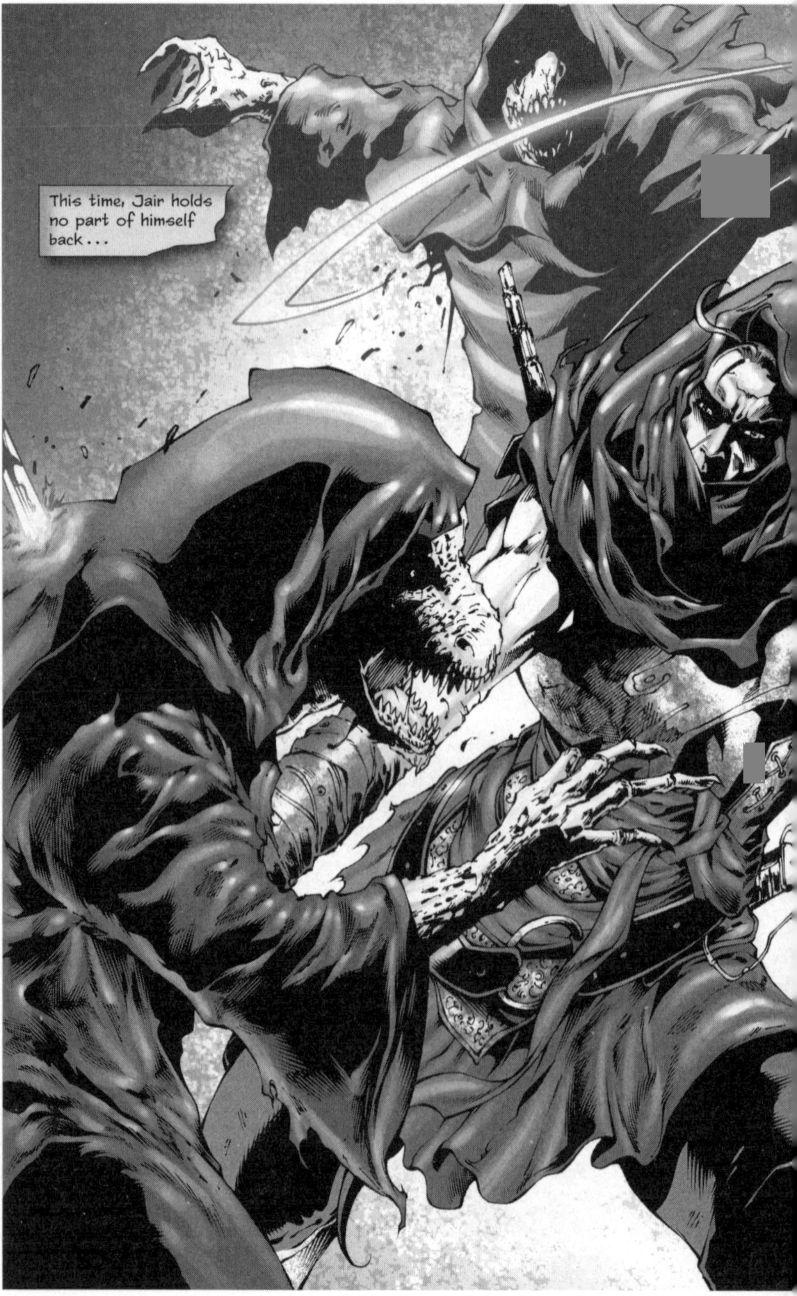
This time, Jair holds no part of himself back...

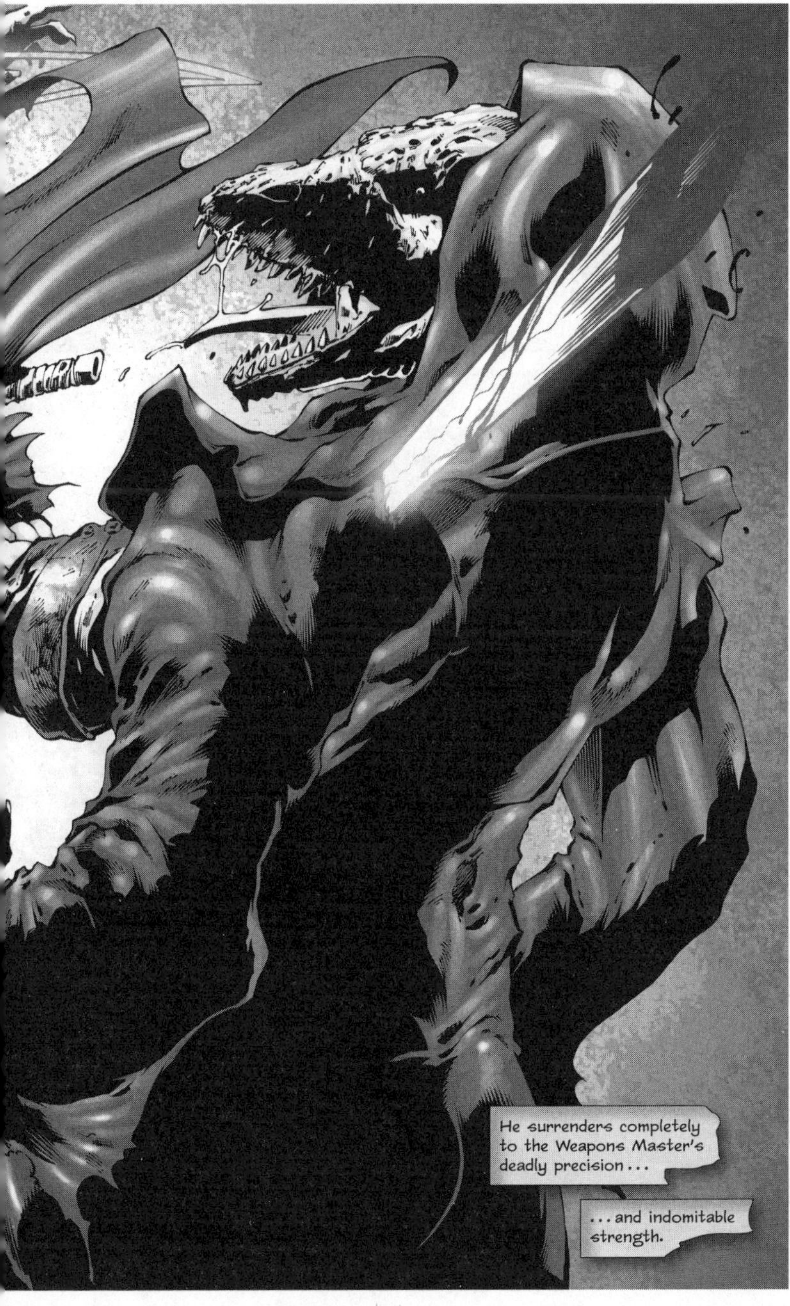
He surrenders completely to the Weapons Master's deadly precision...
...and indomitable strength.

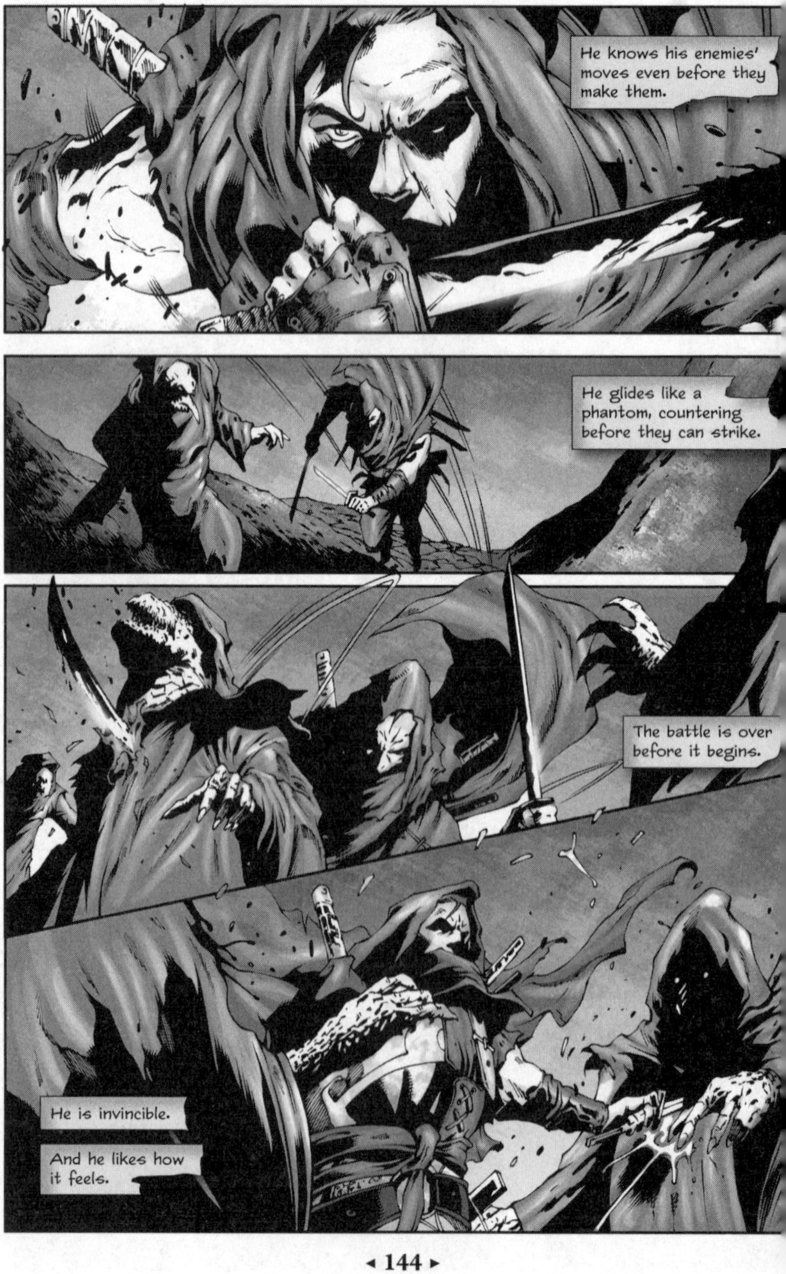
He knows his enemies' moves even before they make them.
He glides like a phantom, countering before they can strike.
The battle is over before it begins.
He is invincible.
And he likes how it feels.

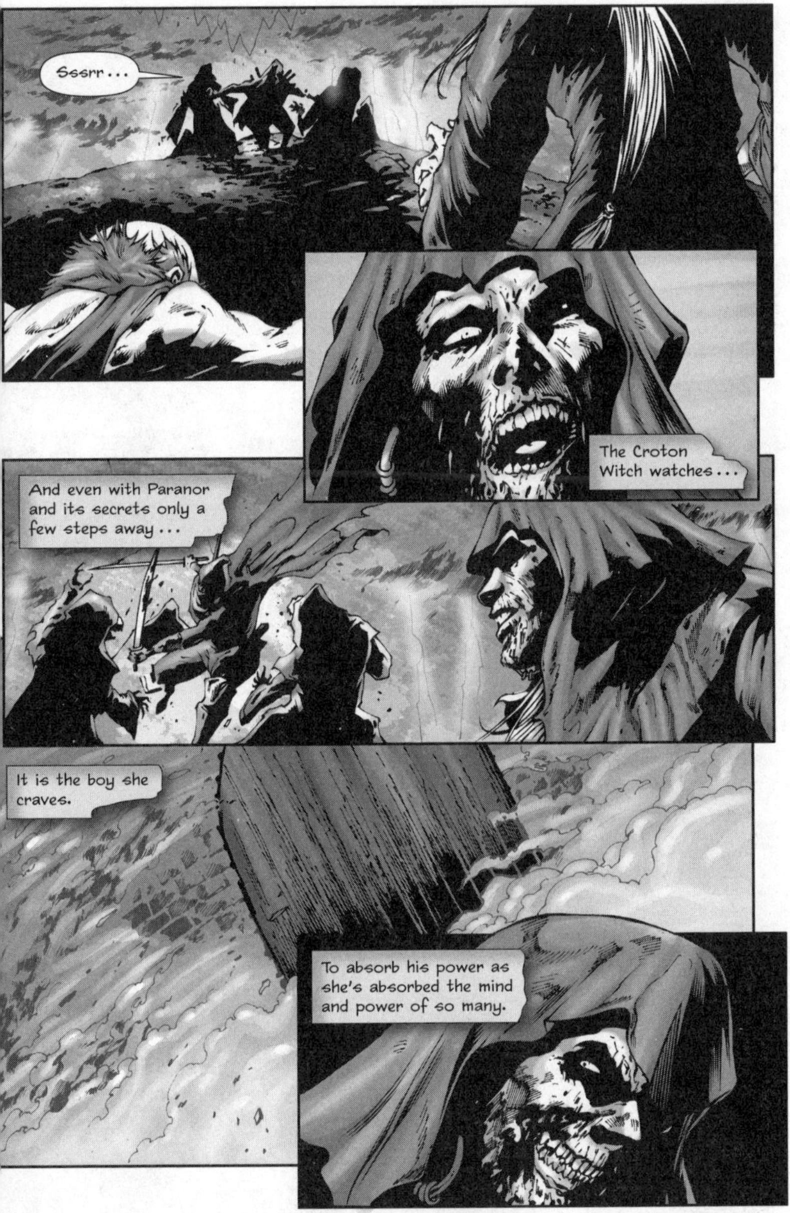
Sssrr...
The Croton Witch watches...
And even with Paranor and its secrets only a few steps away...
It is the boy she craves.
To absorb his power as she's absorbed the mind and power of so many.

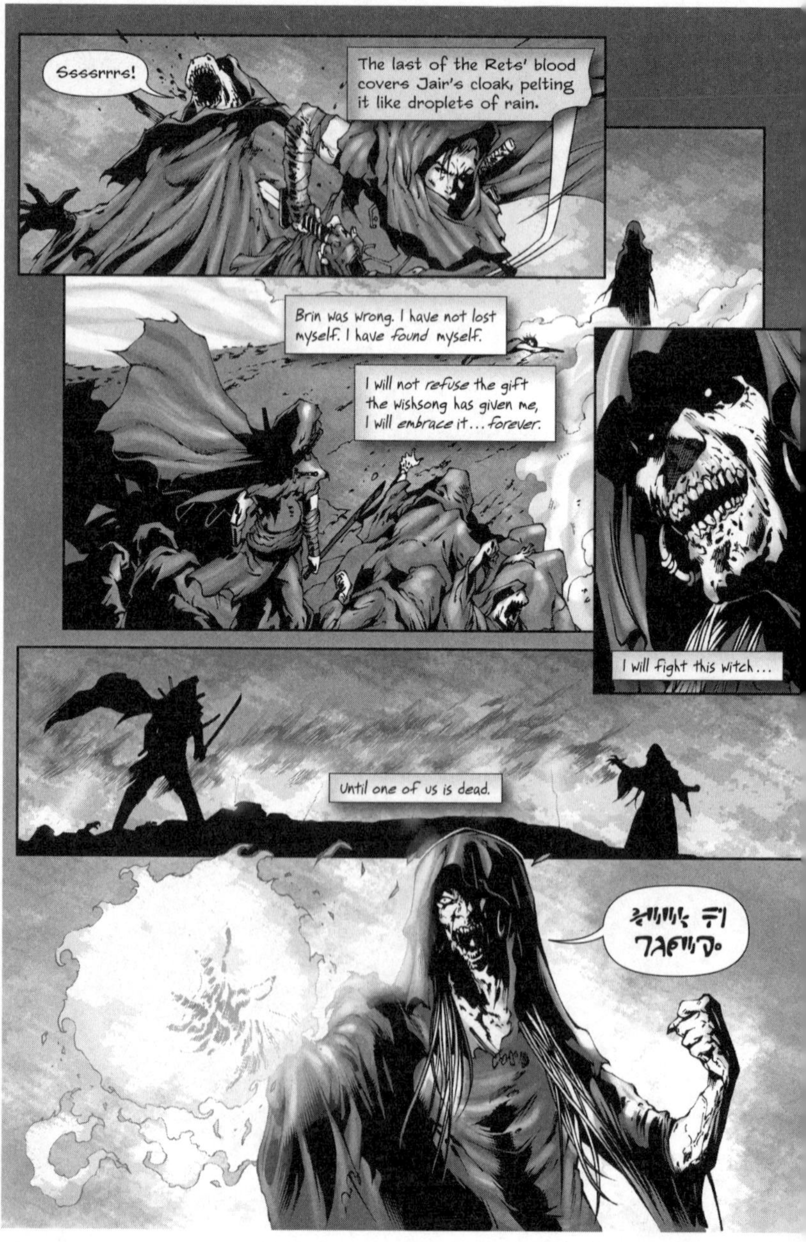
Ssssrrrs!
The last of the Rets' blood covers Jair's cloak, pelting it like droplets of rain.
Brin was wrong. I have not lost myself. I have found myself.
I will not refuse the gift the wishsong has given me, I will embrace it... forever.
I will fight this witch...
Until one of us is dead.

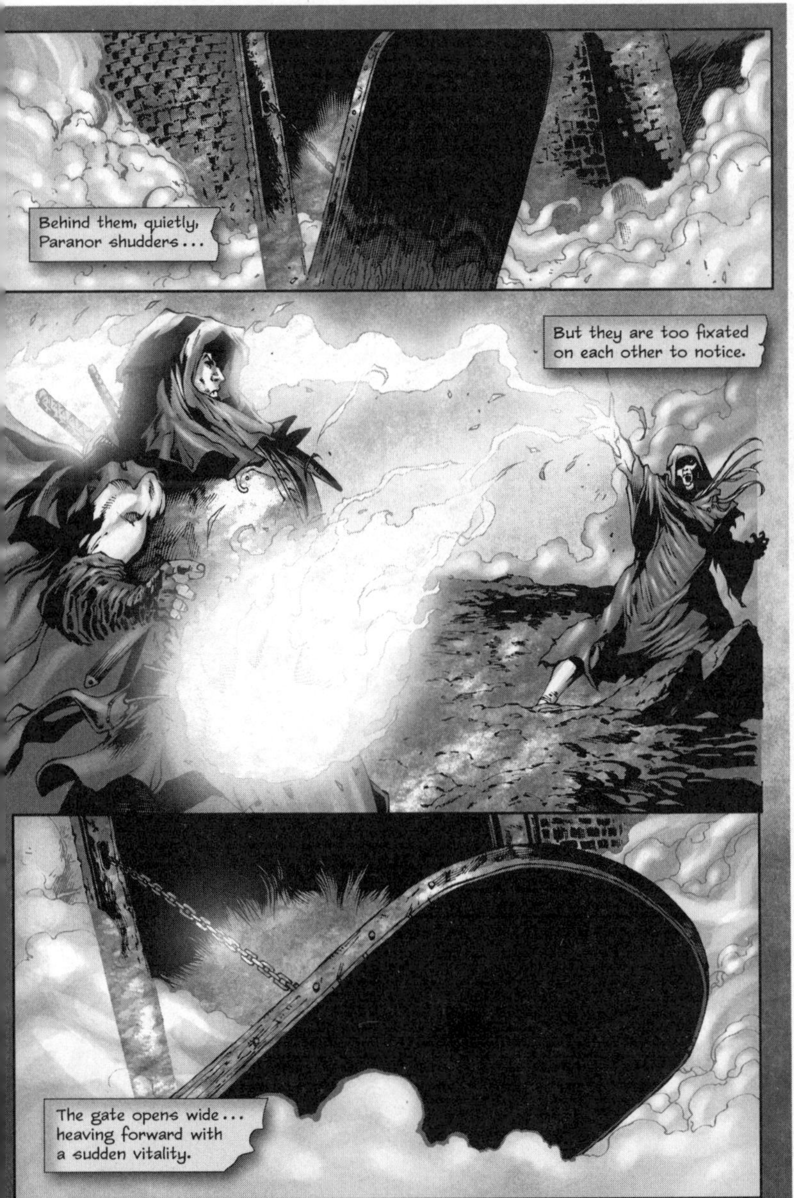
Behind them, quietly,
Paranor shudders...
But they are too fixated
on each other to notice.
The gate opens wide...
heaving forward with
a sudden vitality.

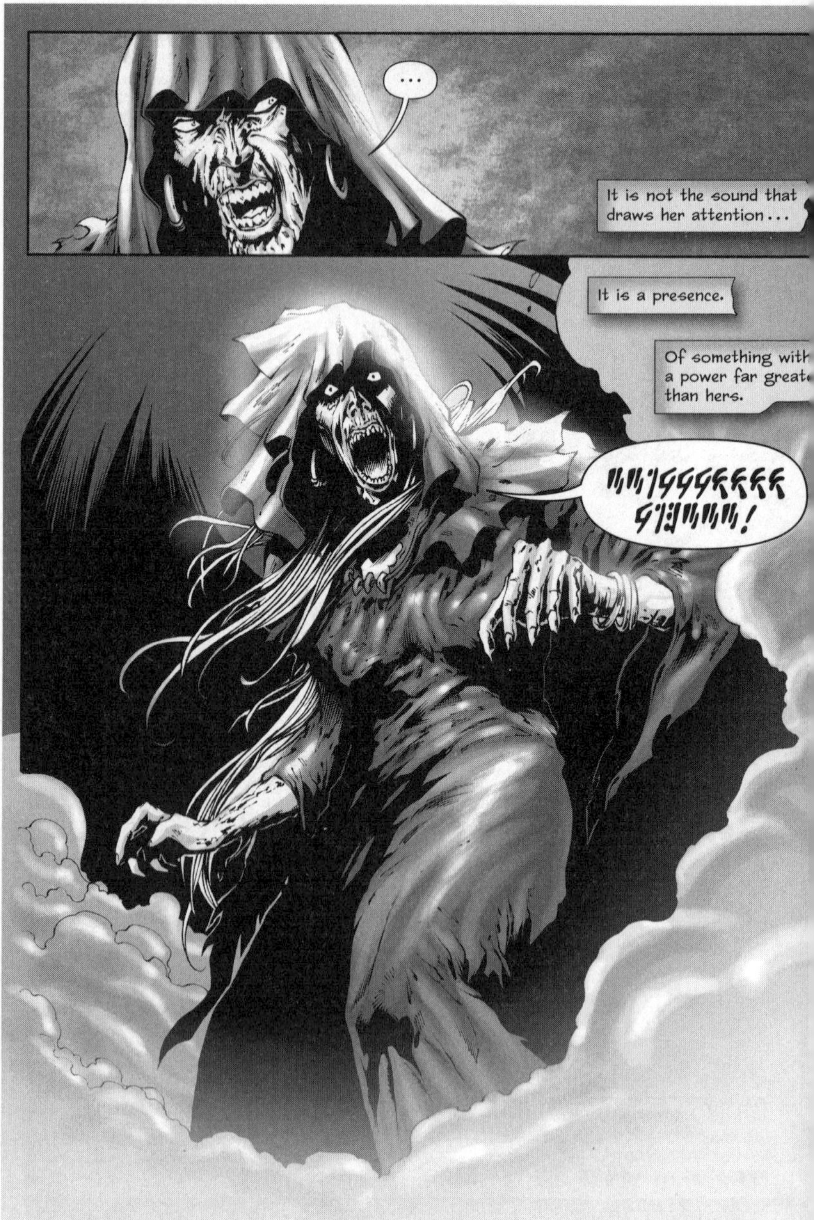
...
It is not the sound that draws her attention...
It is a presence.
Of something with a power far greate than hers.

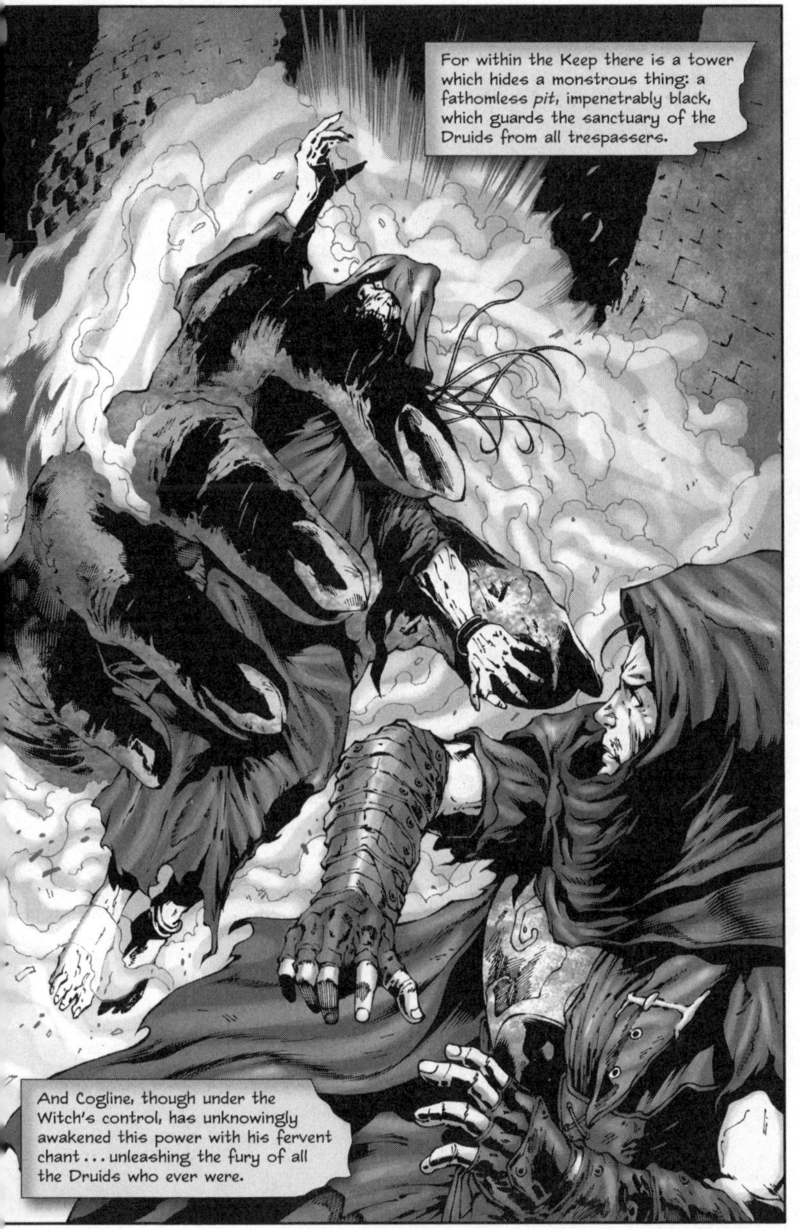
For within the Keep there is a tower which hides a monstrous thing: a fathomless *pit*, impenetrably black, which guards the sanctuary of the Druids from all trespassers.
And Cogline, though under the Witch's control, has unknowingly awakened this power with his fervent chant . . . unleashing the fury of all the Druids who ever were.

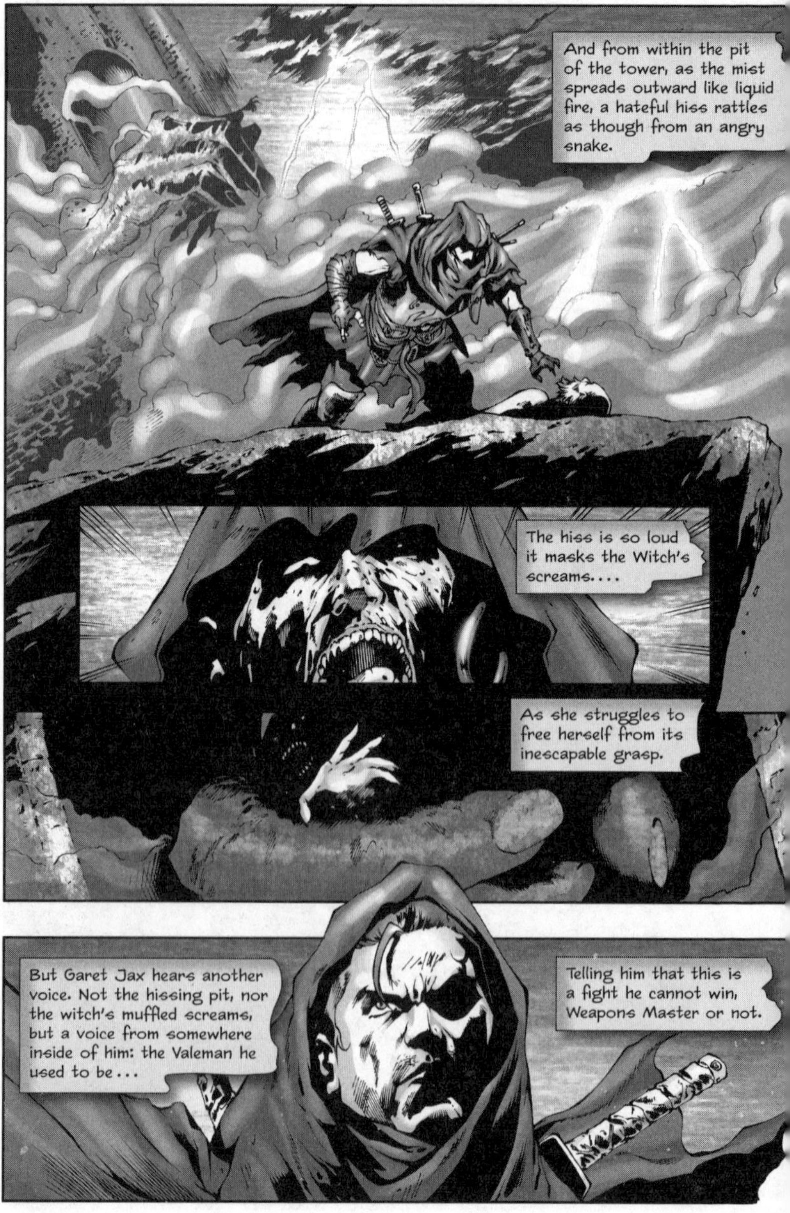
And from within the pit of the tower, as the mist spreads outward like liquid fire, a hateful hiss rattles as though from an angry snake.
The hiss is so loud it masks the Witch's screams....
As she struggles to free herself from its inescapable grasp.
But Garet Jax hears another voice. Not the hissing pit, nor the witch's muffled screams, but a voice from somewhere inside of him: the Valeman he used to be...
Telling him that this is a fight he cannot win, Weapons Master or not.

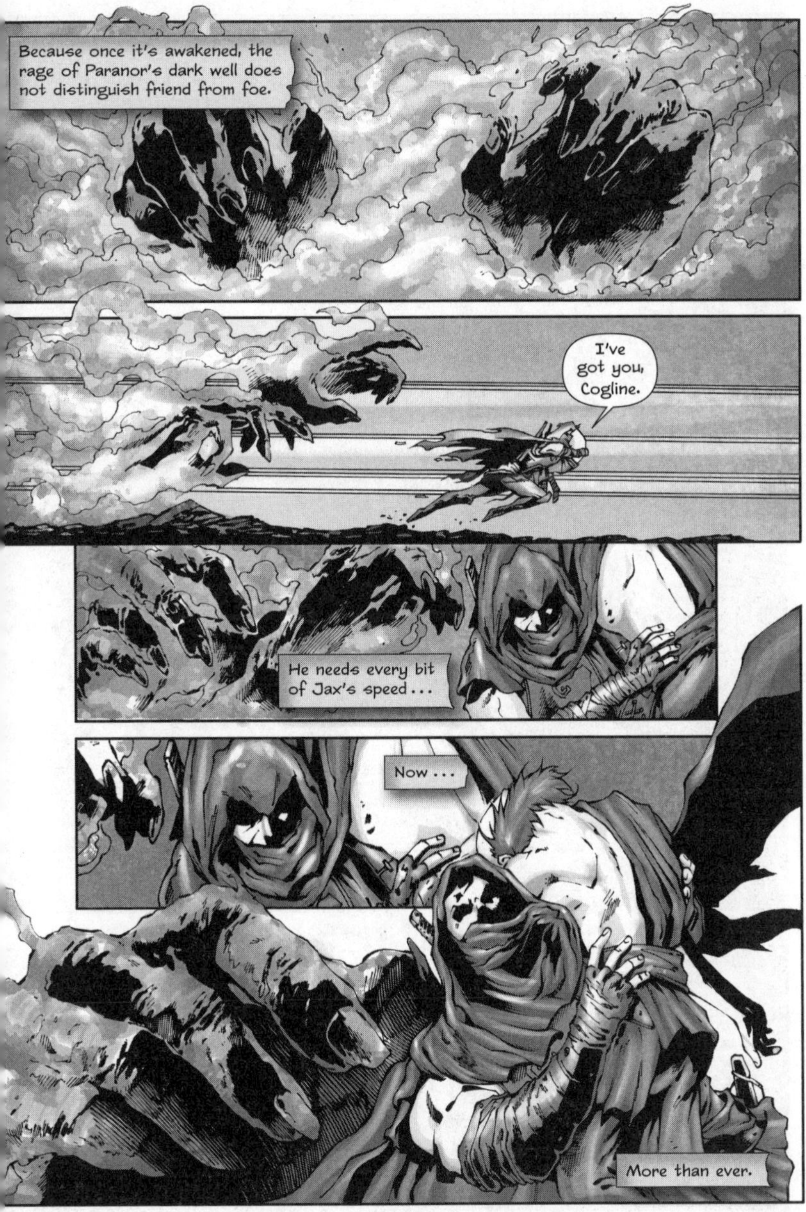
Because once it's awakened, the rage of Paranor's dark well does not distinguish friend from foe.
I've got you, Cogline.
He needs every bit of Jax's speed...
Now...
More than ever.

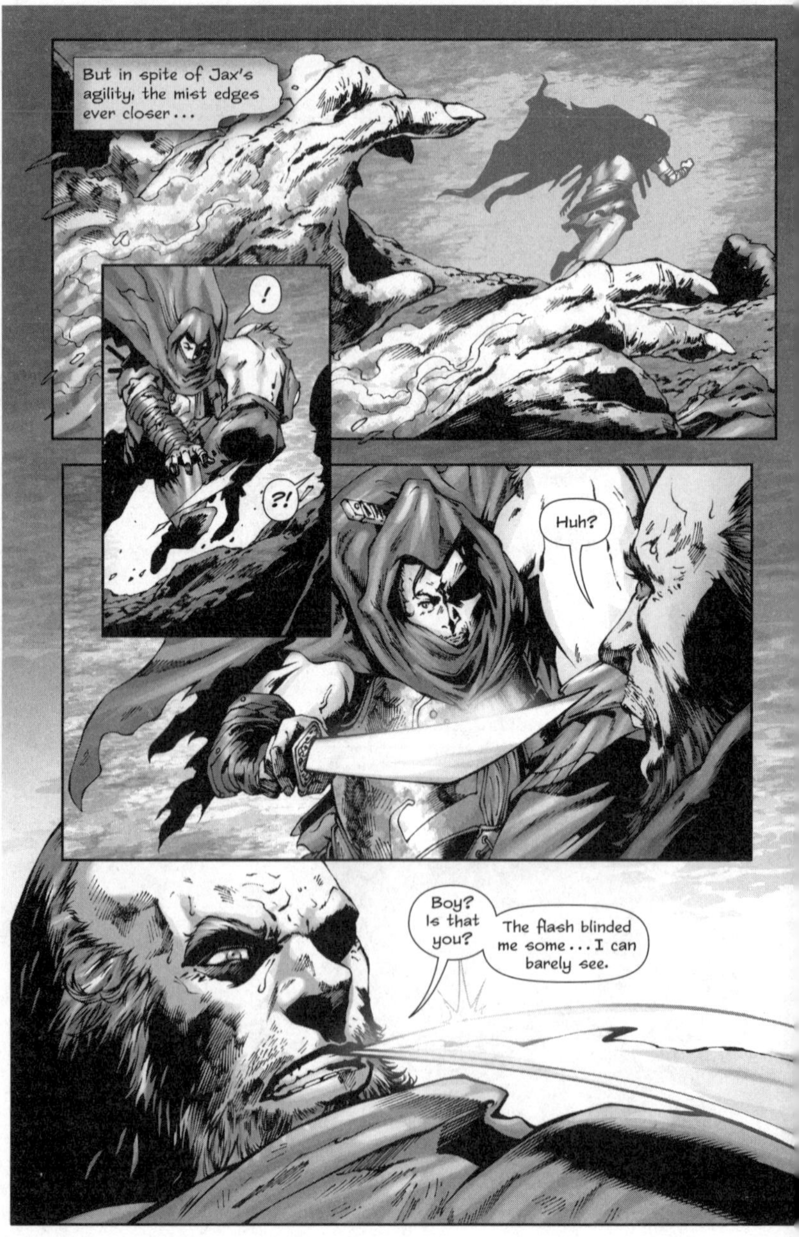
But in spite of Jax's agility, the mist edges ever closer...
!
?!
Huh?
Boy? Is that you?
The flash blinded me some... I can barely see.

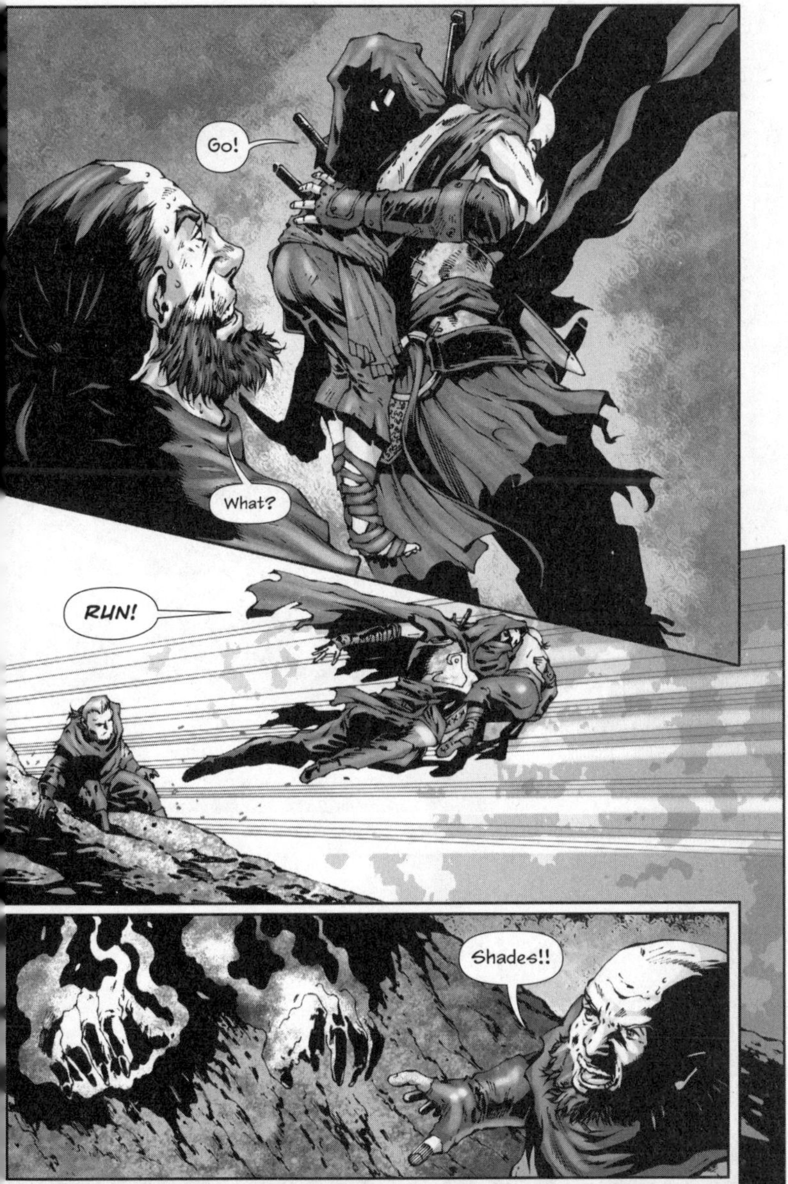
Go!
What?
RUN!
Shades!!

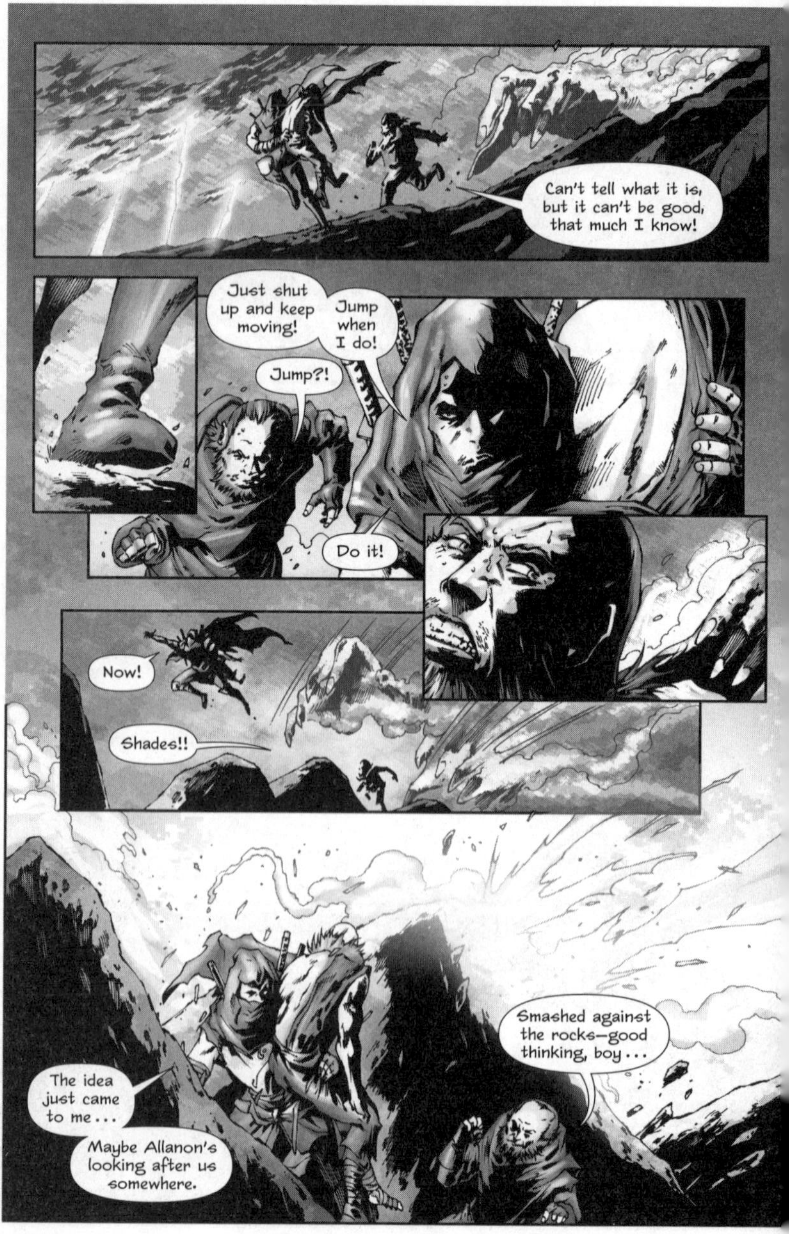
Can't tell what it is, but it can't be good, that much I know!
Just shut up and keep moving!
Jump when I do!
Jump?!
Do it!
Now!
Shades!!
Smashed against the rocks—good thinking, boy . . .
The idea just came to me . . .
Maybe Allanon's looking after us somewhere.

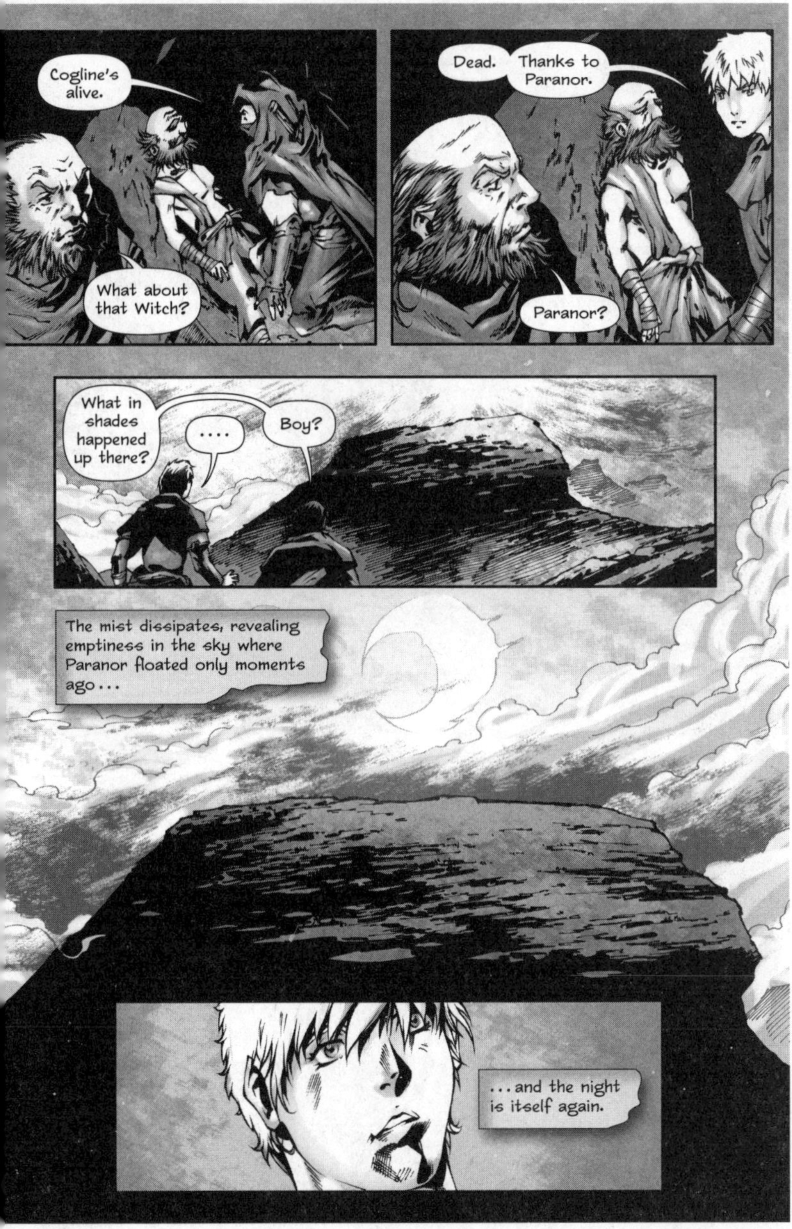
Cogline's alive.
What about that Witch?
Dead.
Thanks to Paranor.
Paranor?
What in shades happened up there?
....
Boy?
The mist dissipates, revealing emptiness in the sky where Paranor floated only moments ago...
...and the night is itself again.

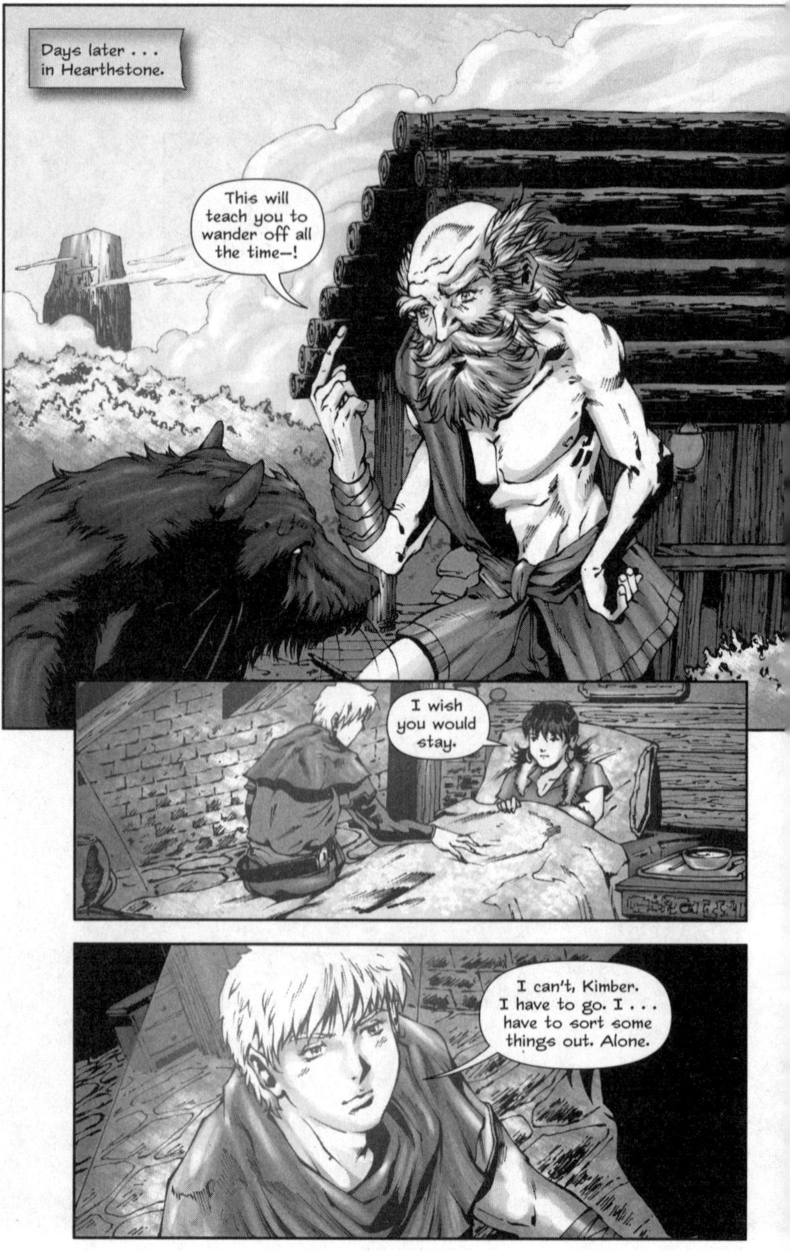
Days later . . . in Hearthstone.
This will teach you to wander off all the time—!
I wish you would stay.
I can't, Kimber. I have to go. I . . . have to sort some things out. Alone.

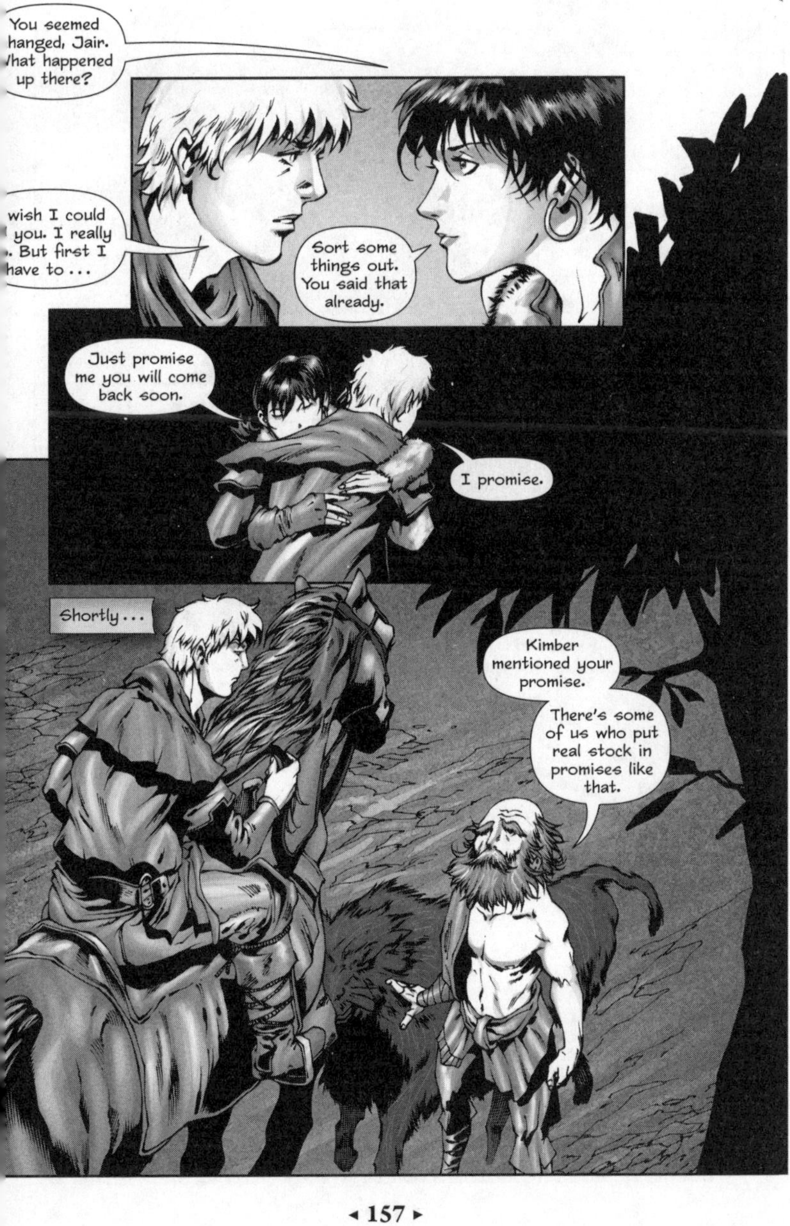
You seemed hanged, Jair. hat happened up there?
wish I could you. I really . But first I have to . . .
Sort some things out. You said that already.
Just promise me you will come back soon.
I promise.
Shortly . . .
Kimber mentioned your promise.
There's some of us who put real stock in promises like that.

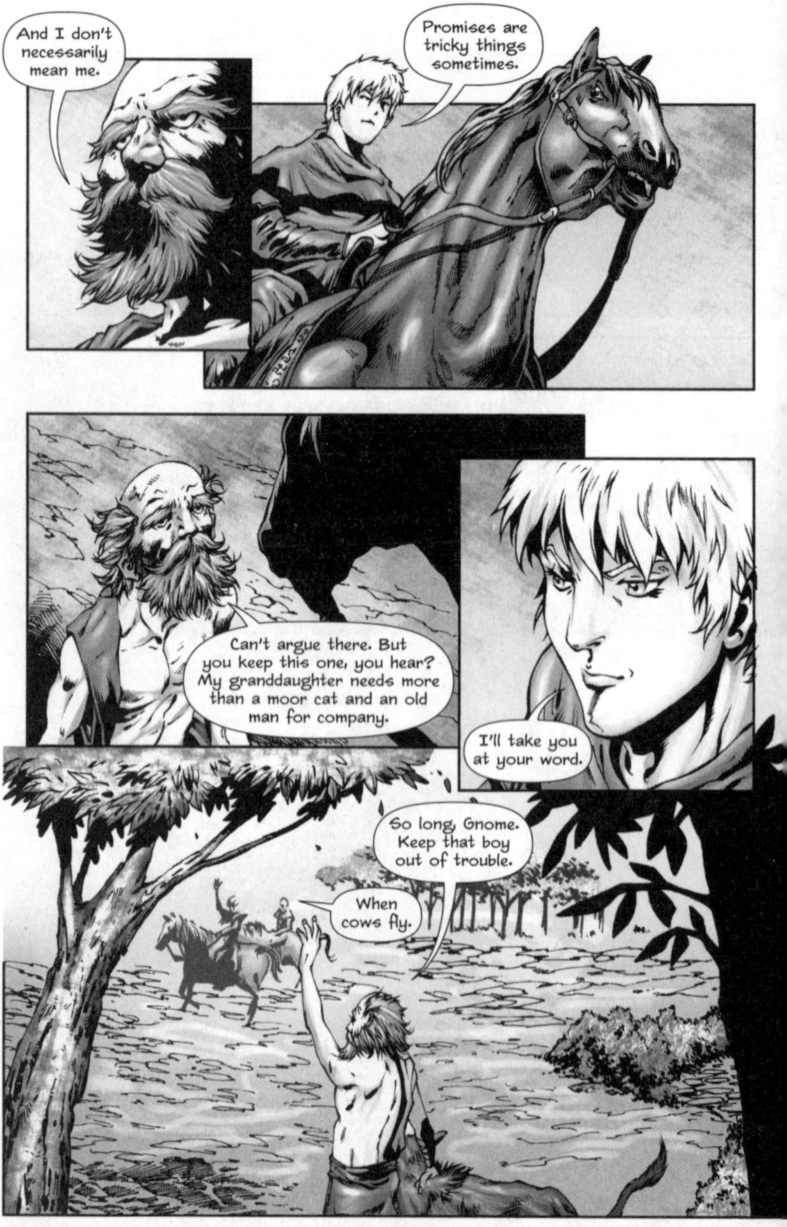
And I don't necessarily mean me.
Promises are tricky things sometimes.
Can't argue there. But you keep this one, you hear? My granddaughter needs more than a moor cat and an old man for company.
I'll take you at your word.
So long, Gnome. Keep that boy out of trouble.
When cows fly.

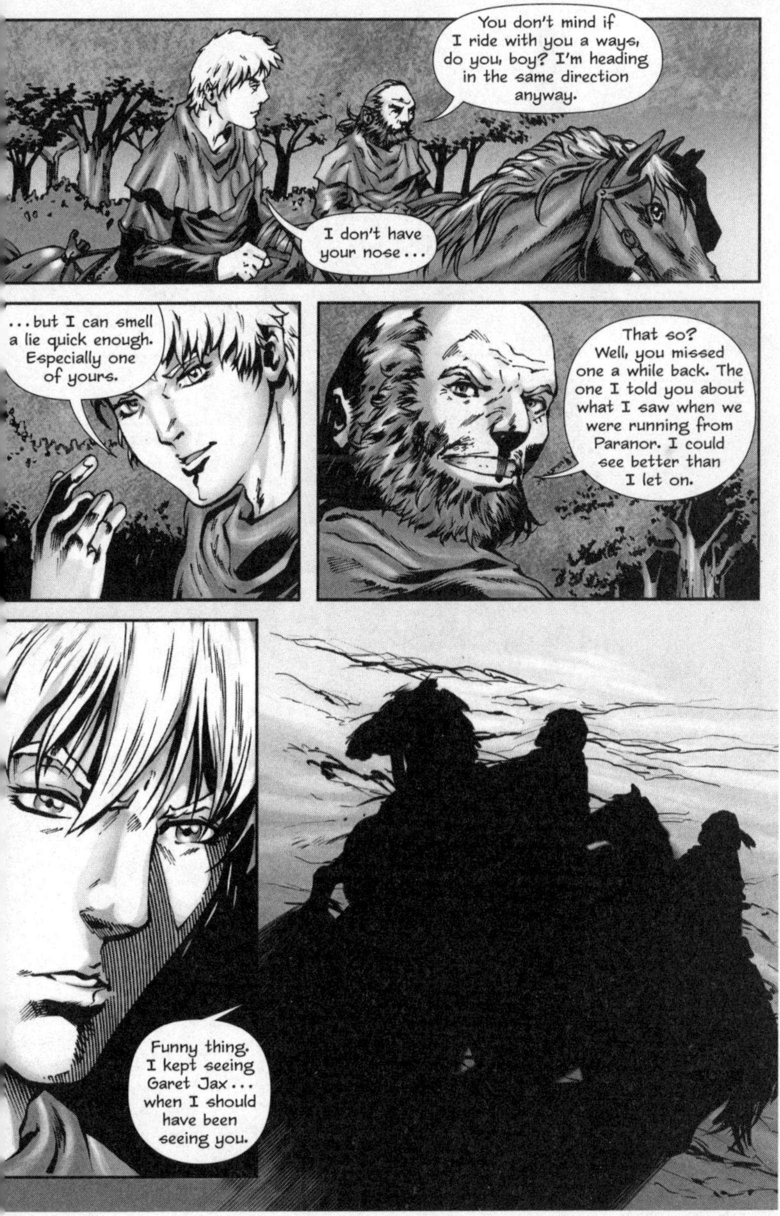
You don't mind if I ride with you a ways, do you, boy? I'm heading in the same direction anyway.
I don't have your nose...
...but I can smell a lie quick enough. Especially one of yours.
That so? Well, you missed one a while back. The one I told you about what I saw when we were running from Paranor. I could see better than I let on.
Funny thing. I kept seeing Garet Jax... when I should have been seeing you.

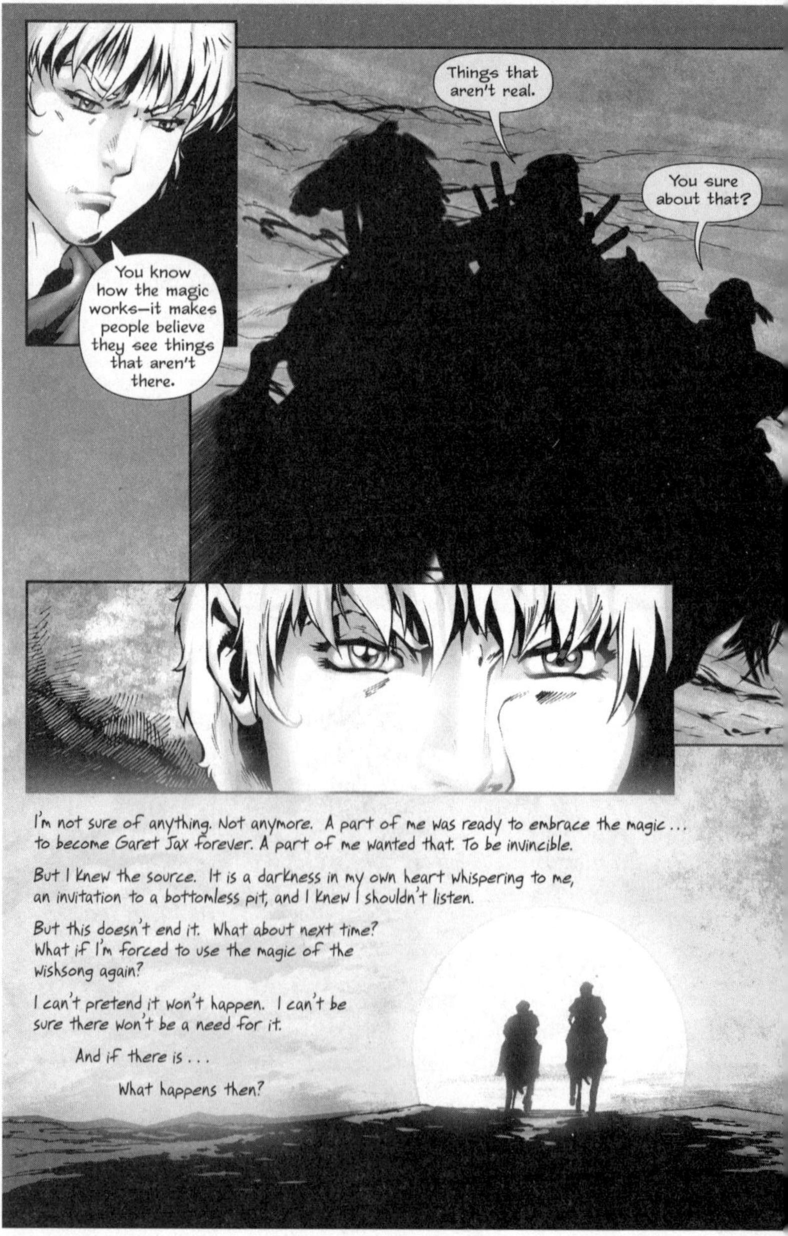
Things that aren't real.
You sure about that?
You know how the magic works—it makes people believe they see things that aren't there.
I'm not sure of anything. Not anymore. A part of me was ready to embrace the magic ... to become Garet Jax forever. A part of me wanted that. To be invincible.
But I knew the source. It is a darkness in my own heart whispering to me, an invitation to a bottomless pit, and I knew I shouldn't listen.
But this doesn't end it. What about next time? What if I'm forced to use the magic of the wishsong again?
I can't pretend it won't happen. I can't be sure there won't be a need for it.
And if there is ...
What happens then?

about the creators

TERRY BROOKS is the *New York Times* bestselling author of more than twenty-five books, including the Genesis of Shannara novels *Armageddon's Children* and *The Elves of Cintra*; *The Sword of Shannara*; the nonfiction book *Sometimes the Magic Works: Lessons from a Writing Life*; and many more, including *Wishsong of Shannara*, which forms the basis for this graphic novel. His novels *Running with the Demon* and *A Knight of the Word* were selected by the *Rocky Mountain News* as two of the best science fiction/fantasy novels of the twentieth century. The author was a practicing attorney for many years but now writes full-time. He lives with his wife, Judine, in the Pacific Northwest. Visit the world of Shannara online at **www.terrybrooks.net** and at **www.orbitbooks.net**

ROBERT PLACE NAPTON has been writing comic books and graphic novels since the 1990s; among his titles are *Deity* and *Saint Angel*. His current works include *Battlestar Galactica Origins: Adama*, based on the Sci-Fi Channel television series, and the pirate adventure series *Blackbeard*, both from Dynamite Entertainment, as well as the historical epic *Rostam* from Hyperwerks Comics. His upcoming works include an original graphic novel entitled *Sage: A Fantasy Documentary* and his first prose novel, *Creatures of the Dust*. He lives with his wife, Anna, (and two cats and a turtle) in Pasadena, California.

EDWIN HUANG DAVID is a comic book artist, digital graphic designer, and painter. He has worked with Alex Ross on *Battle of the Planets* for Top Cow and is currently working on an original series titled *ShadowChasers*. Visit his website at **www.edwindavidart.com**

the making of
dark wraith of shannara

In the Beginning

Dark Wraith of Shannara was the work of many hands over many months. The participants communicated across the distance between two continents, four states, and who knows how many time zones. Yet a shared dedication to bringing this adventure to life resulted in a book that author, adapter, editor, inker, and toner are all proud to call their own.

The book began with a story by Terry Brooks. As Terry describes it:

"The approach to creating the graphic novel was simple. I was to come up with a new story set in the Shannara world centered around the characters from , and Jair Ohmsford in particular. My concerns about having to write and draw the story were quickly resolved. Stick figures and dialogue consisting of exclamations were the limit of my very rudimentary skills, and we all knew that wasn't going to cut it. So writer Robert Napton and artist Edwin David were brought aboard to do the heavy lifting."

Terry's detailed story outline went to adapter Robert Place Napton for the next step. Robert was selected for the project partly because he was a longtime reader of the Shannara stories.

"The first question I get about this project is if I was a fan of Terry's before taking on the assignment, and the answer is absolutely yes: Terry's writing had a big impact on me. So naturally the second question I get is if I was daunted or intimidated to adapt one of his stories, and I have to say honestly the answer is no. There's a statement people use which I always thought was a cliché, and it goes something like 'Everything I've ever done has prepared me for this.' But in all honesty that's how I felt about *Dark Wraith*. I really felt I could bring all my experience as a comic book and graphic novel writer to bear."

Robert had a unique take on the outline provided by Terry Brooks. "I was excited to learn that the story would be a direct sequel to the first Shannara trilogy, focusing on the characters introduced in the novel *Wishsong of Shannara*. I also thought that the story worked perfectly with the form we were planning on using: black, white, and gray art. Terry himself commented once on the influence of the film *The Seven Samurai* on *Wishsong*'s storyline, and that really inspired my own thinking in terms of what *Dark Wraith* should look like—I wanted the art to have that beautiful Kurasawa-inspired black-and-white poetry that explored not only a world but the nature of humanity in that world. To me that's what Kurasawa's work is about, and it's what Terry's work is about. It's about us. The us we would like to be."

Creating the Overall Look

"My first consideration was the chapter breaks Terry had created in the outline," Robert explains. "My first notion was to have no chapter breaks at all—I wanted the story to play out in a more cinematic nature, harking back to *The Seven Samurai* experience I wanted to re-create. But upon reflection, I wanted to honor the story's novelistic roots, so I proposed five chapter breaks where I thought they would make most sense in a graphic novel, and Terry agreed.

"Once that was settled, I began the job of adding the necessary details to springboard *Dark Wraith*'s plot into 160 pages of graphic novel. Terry's outline was dense, rich with detail, and I wished at times I had more than 160 pages to adapt the story. I revisited a manga I hadn't looked at for years, the brilliant classic *Lone Wolf and Cub*, for its astonishing and very Eastern panel pacing. But *Lone Wolf* has twenty-eight volumes of three hundred pages each or some such, so a bit more real estate than we had to play with. You'll notice the inspirations I drew from before the project started were both Eastern and Western, playing to Edwin's strengths as an artist and perfectly matching the theme and feel of Terry's story. With these influences acting upon me, I felt it was important to write the plot by breaking down the shots panel by panel and describing the story and action to Edwin, but leaving the dialogue for later."

Next Step: Artist Edwin David

Edwin David, who lives in the Philippines, relied on the Internet to keep in touch with Robert Napton in California, Terry Brooks in Seattle, and editor Betsy Mitchell in New York City. Bad weather in the Pacific affected communications and sometimes meant a slowdown in the process!

"It was daunting to be able to work with Terry Brooks," Edwin says. "To be given the chance to design the characters was really exhilarating, yet nerve-racking at the same time. But he's a really open-minded guy, and gave support to the designs we gave him." The Croton Witch, just as one example, was a new character to the Shannara world, and Terry gave Edwin carte blanche to bring her to visual life. Edwin's first concept drawings of her were a little too "over the top" for Terry (see Artist's Sketchbook section), but, adds Edwin, "a few adjustments were made and the designs were finally approved.

"As for the level of comfort in our working relationship," Edwin said, "as the book slowly progressed from the early sketches to the layouts, the level of trust grew so that the final layouts could be drawn roughly, as if Mr. Brooks already had a feel for what was going on even without the details."

Here is an example of a very detailed page layout submitted by Edwin early in the process.

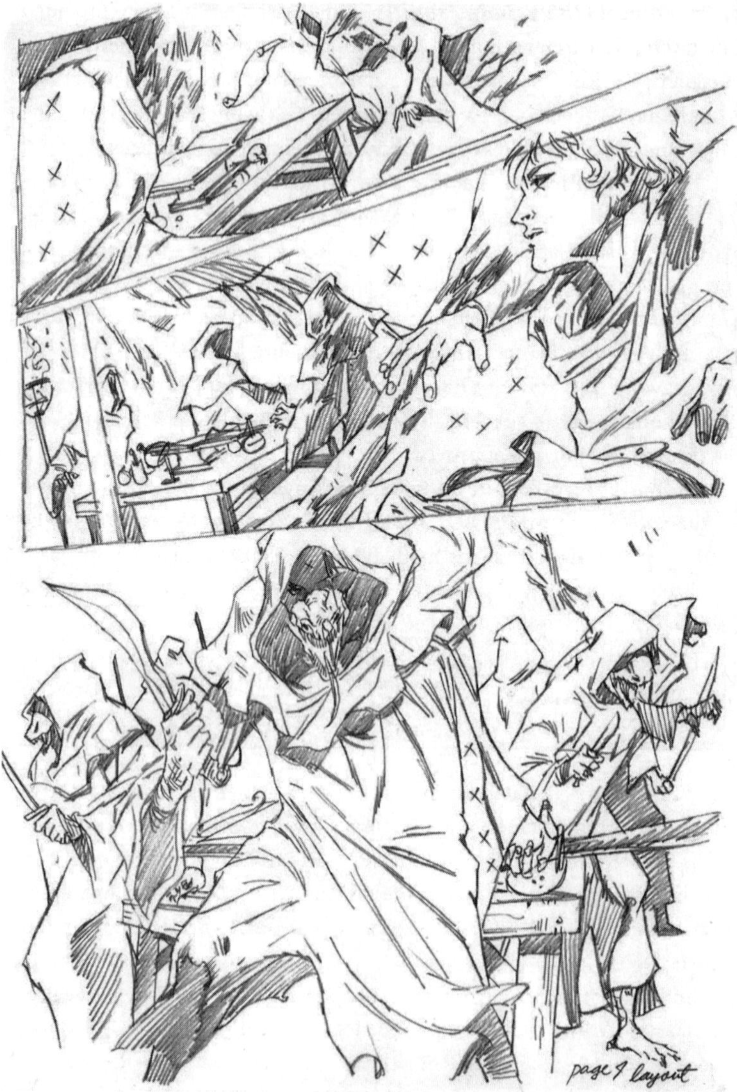
page 4 layout

And here is an example of the way the later sketches were provided, after Terry, Robert, and Edwin had established a comfortable working relationship.

"Edwin was fantastic at interpreting my panel descriptions and in every case improving upon them with his great artistic and compositional skills," says Robert Napton. "Though I can't draw , I would sketch my ideas for the panels before I would write out the plot. These sketches were of such quality that my wife referred to them as potato heads, or 'taters' for short, to give you an idea of how well I can draw. Still, as bad as they were, I found it was important to consider the physicality of the panels on a page in order to suggest the best flow of panels and beats for Edwin. Of course, every step of the way, Terry would comment on the plot (the written version, not the taters—I never let those out of the house) and the subsequent page layouts that resulted. I really wanted sweeping wide shots to show the vistas that Terry so vividly describes in the novels. One of the joys of reading Shannara, in my opinion, is the amazing richness of detail and beauty Terry sees in the natural world and how he brings that to life in his prose. I really wanted the shots to convey that same majesty and poetry and respect and affection that I think Terry has for nature.

"The same goes for the action sequences. An amazing passage in is the description of Allanon's battle to the death—it is the written equivalent of a great film director staging an amazing battle scene. So I took a big cue from that scene, along with a healthy dash of Kurasawa and *Lone Wolf and Cub*, and then tried to give Edwin as many ideas as I could before he'd cut loose and make the action sequences his own with his amazing artwork, taking what I had written to the next level with his great artist's eye. I'll never forget when I got all the early pages from Edwin of the first time Jair becomes Jax and the subsequent battle with the Rets. It was something special.

"Having Terry approve everything every step of the way was a great safety net," Robert concludes. "I knew if we strayed from his vision of Shannara Terry would let us know, and he did. He was our guide and he always urged us to explore ideas, even if they differed from his. Since this is the first-ever Shannara graphic novel, I felt it would be impossible to please all the fans out there, but if we pleased Terry and he gave us the thumbs up, then there was nothing more we needed to do."

The Script

Plot and artwork took almost a year, with inker Dennis Crisostomo and toner Brian Buccellato contributing their work after Edwin David finished the pencils. After all 160 pages of art were completed, Robert Napton began writing the dialogue. For him, Robert says, "This is where I would really get a chance to have some fun—because other than Terry no writer had ever brought these characters to life, and I had the chance to play in his sandbox. A character that really stands out for me is Slanter. I enjoyed finding his voice, and hopefully I brought something a little different to it rather than just emulating the exact rhythm of his character in *Wishsong*. I tried to move everyone a bit forward in time, in terms of personality and temperament. These aren't the exact same characters from *Wishsong* and the novella "Indomitable"—people change and grow, so I tried to reflect that in the characters' attitudes and voices.

"As with the plot, I'd submit the script to Terry and he'd give me notes. There were changes here and there, but Terry approved and encouraged the direction I was taking. The third act presented the biggest challenges. Because the Croton Witch was a brand-new character, her personality wasn't as defined—there wasn't a novel or short story to draw upon for her motivations and persona. I had an idea of her being mute, but then I thought she should talk, but only in a demonic tongue not understandable to the reader. I felt this would make her more mysterious and scary, and Terry agreed with this notion. But because she was undefined, I tried a few ideas that didn't work as well. I had the idea of her being more of a temptress for Jair—trying to lure him into the darkness—but it really didn't fit Terry's vision of the character, so I rewrote these scenes more than any other in the book to strike the right chord for our new villainous Witch. Similarly, Jair's final scene took a few passes, and Terry himself took to the keyboard and did the final pass, ending it on a note that left me, and hopefully the reader, wondering about the future and ready for more."

As the project drew to a close, Terry Brooks had nothing but praise for his collaborators: "Their considerable talents are evident in every panel of the book. My job was to supervise and approve the work, and it turned out to be much easier than I had expected. Both Robert and Edwin knew the Shannara world and pretty much got it right on the first try."

ARtist's sketchbook

Terry Brooks and Edwin David worked closely to come up with the correct visual representation of each character. Terry's notes to Edwin appear under each concept sketch.

'CROTON WITCH'

TOMO

The Croton Witch, first concept sketch

Terry Brooks: "She's human, so she wouldn't have a tail, or long twisted limbs, or claws. She would be more like a crone. She's cunning, conniving, but not insane. Think Cruella De Ville."

The Croton Witch, revised concept sketch

'ALLANON'

TOMO

Allanon, first concept sketch

Terry Brooks: "Allanon wears a plain, hooded robe, much like a monk's, with no belt or objects hanging off of it. He should not look as menacing as you portray him in this sketch. He can look serious but also somewhat vulnerable."

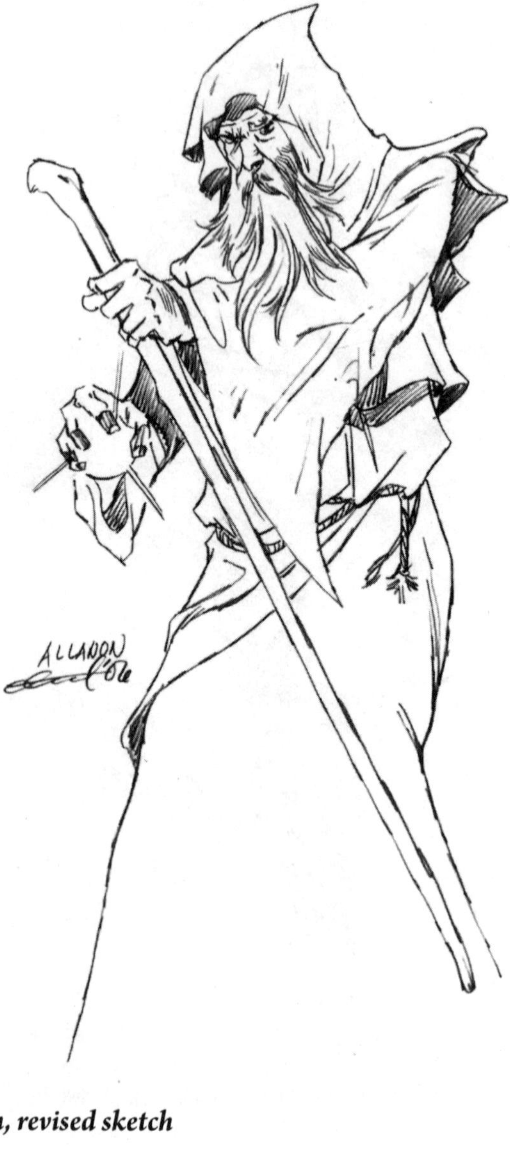
ALLANON

Allanon, revised sketch

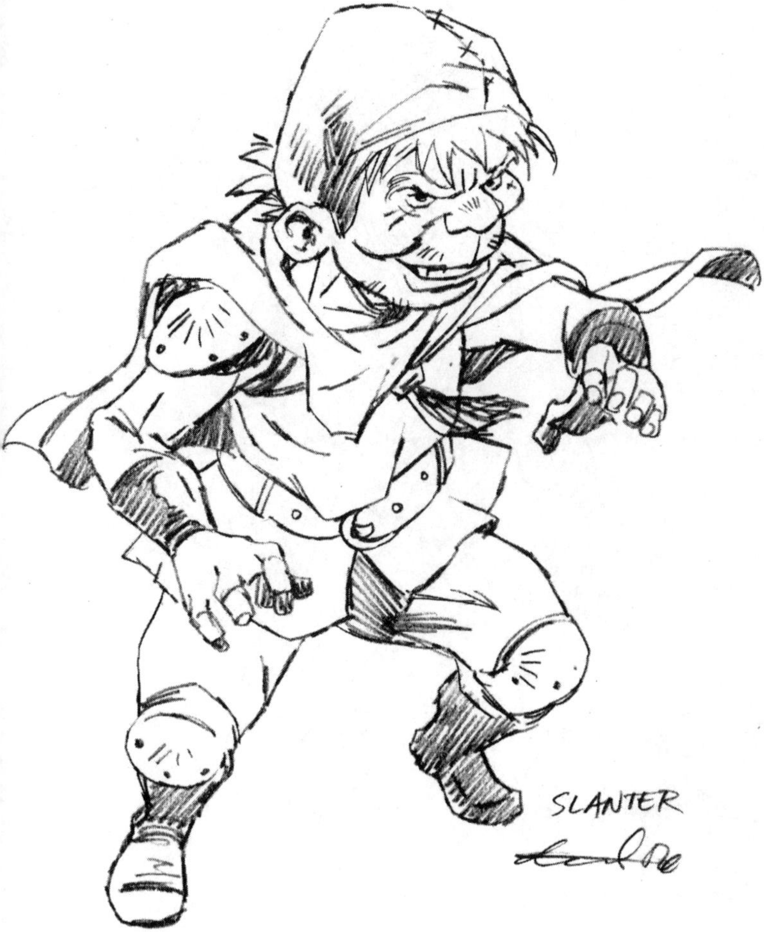
SLANTER

Slanter, first concept sketch

Terry Brooks: “Slanter’s cunning is good, but I think he should look a little harder. He is a tough cookie, not an imp.”

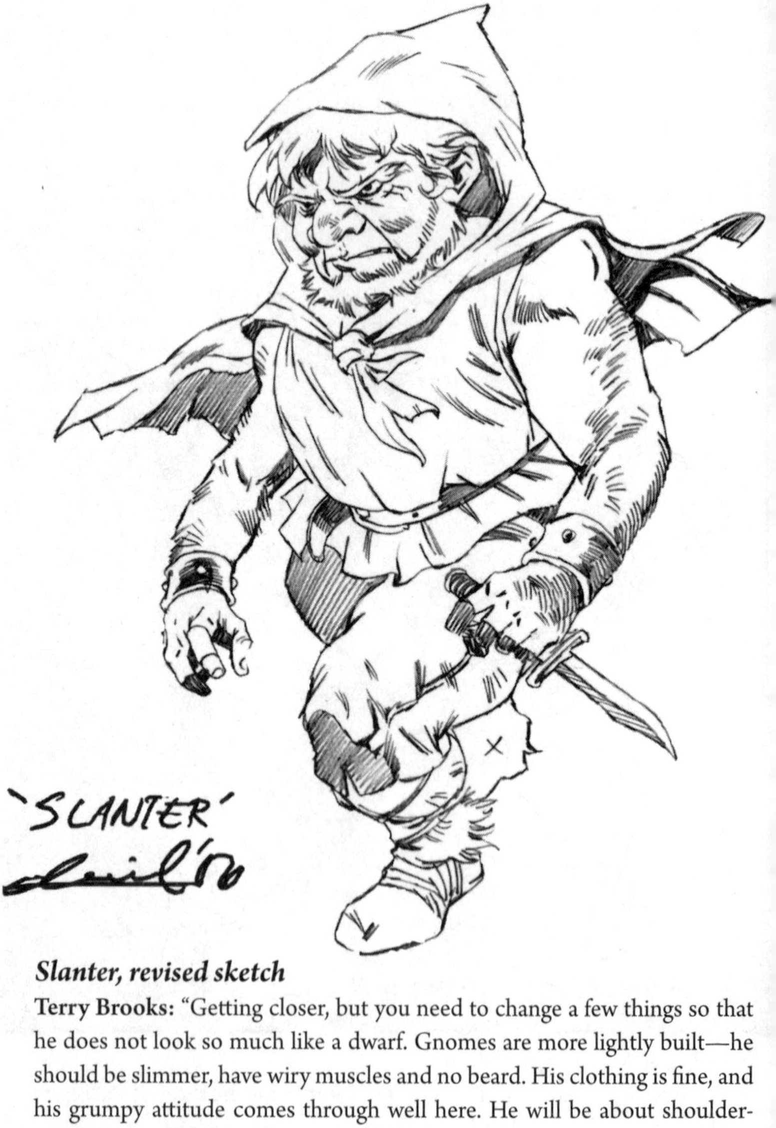
'SLANTER'

Slanter, revised sketch

Terry Brooks: "Getting closer, but you need to change a few things so that he does not look so much like a dwarf. Gnomes are more lightly built—he should be slimmer, have wiry muscles and no beard. His clothing is fine, and his grumpy attitude comes through well here. He will be about shoulder-height to the human characters in the story."

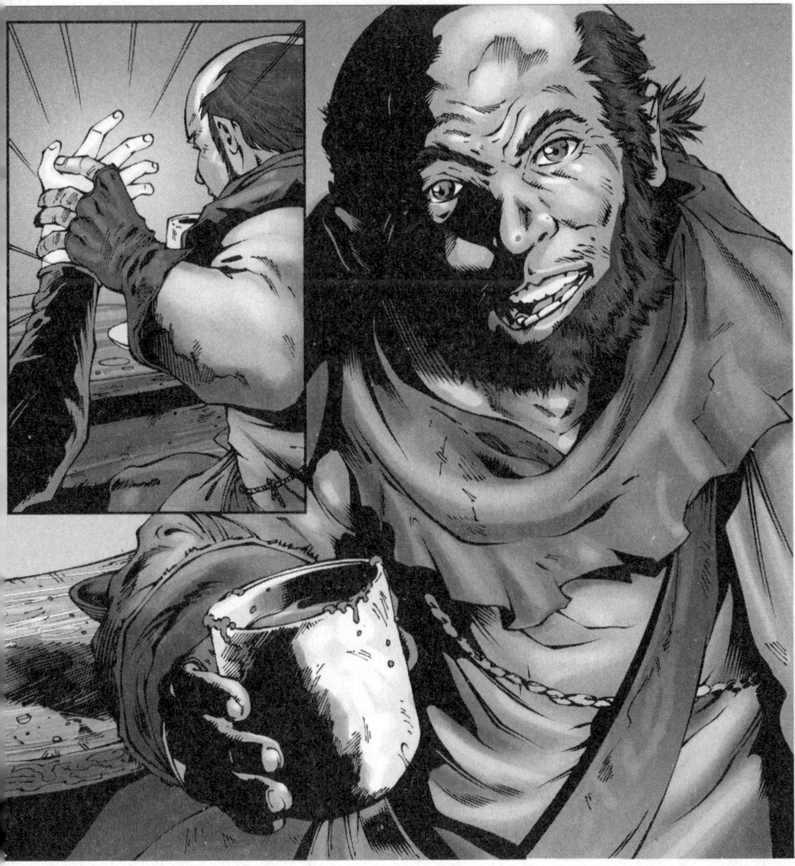

Slanter, final sketch

penciling, inking, toning

Three talented artists contributed to the final look of *Dark Wraith of Shannara*. Here are two examples of how each page in the book passed through three stages.

GARET JAX, THE WEAPONS MASTER
Pencils by Edwin David

Inks by Dennis Crisostomo

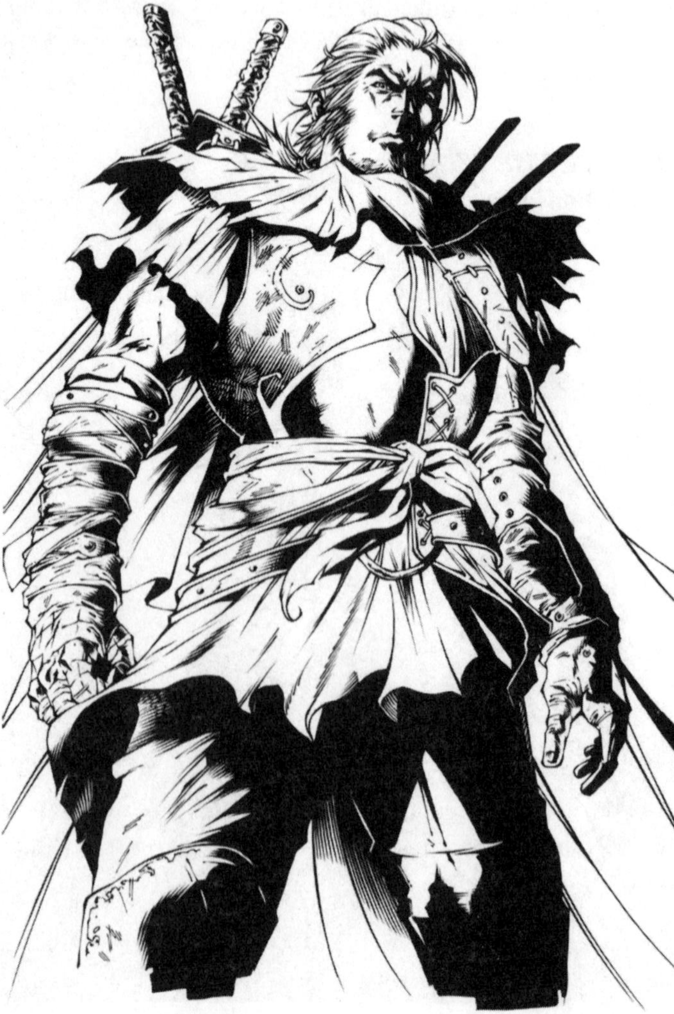

Tones by Brian Buccellato

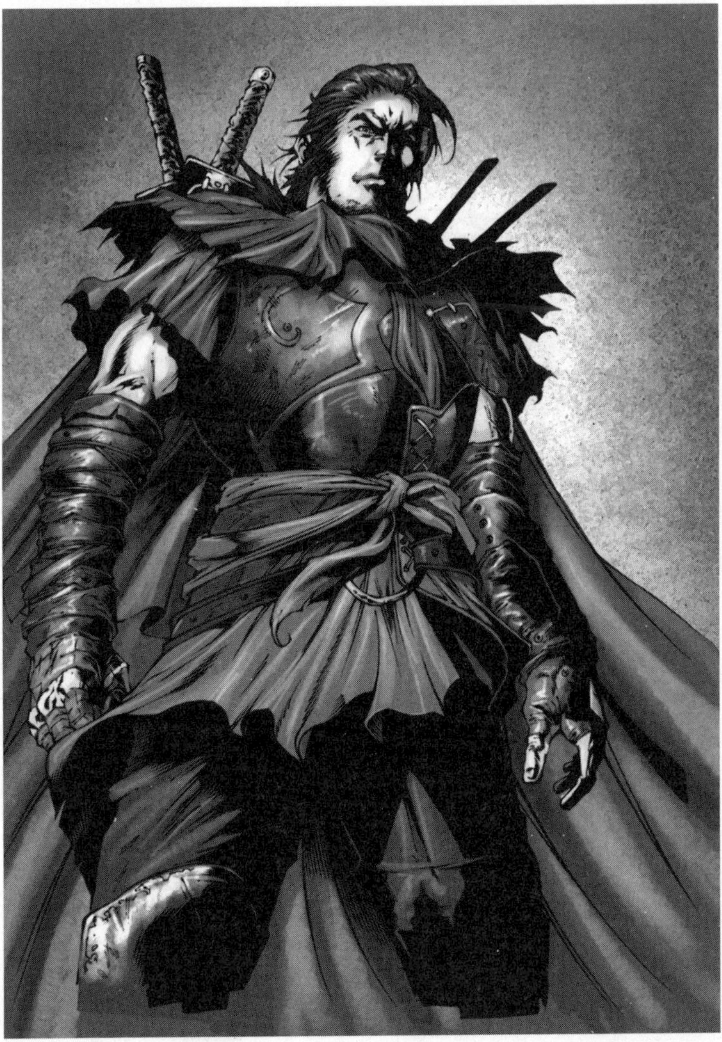

JAIR OHMSFORD STEALS THE ILDATCH
Pencils by Edwin David

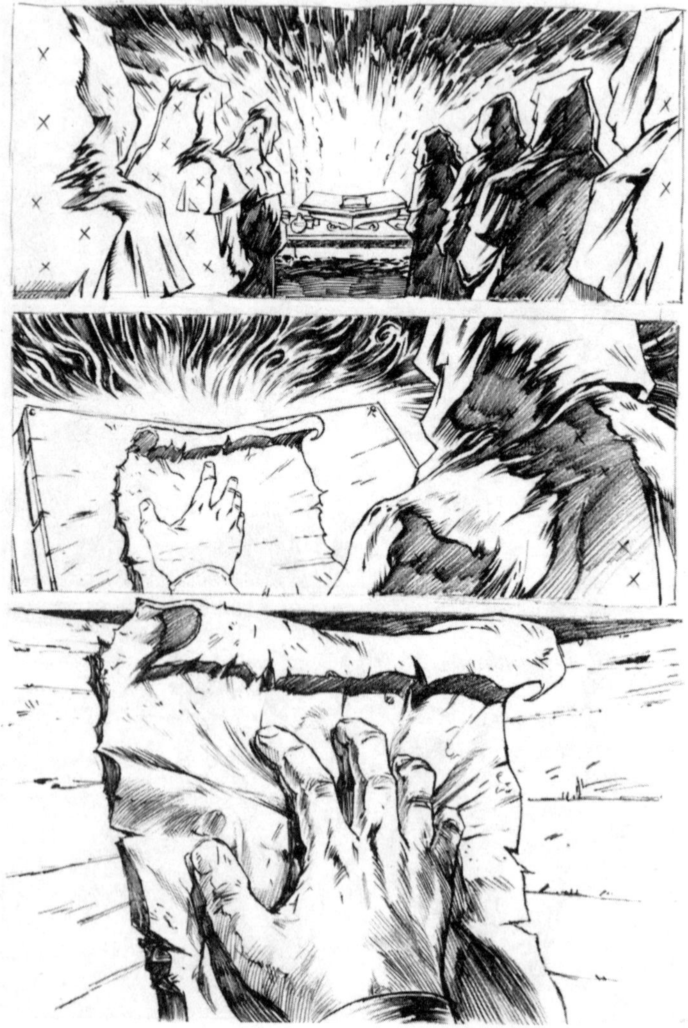

Inks by Dennis Crisostomo

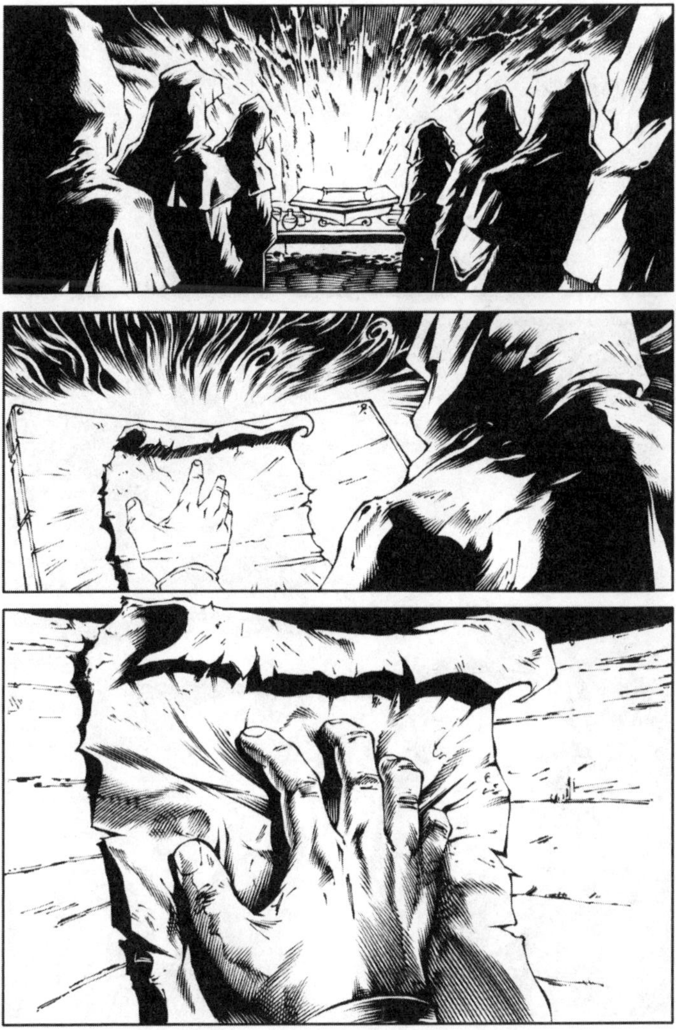

Tones by Brian Buccellato

(Note how the toning process results in a "special effects" feel in the magical glow around the Ildatch.)

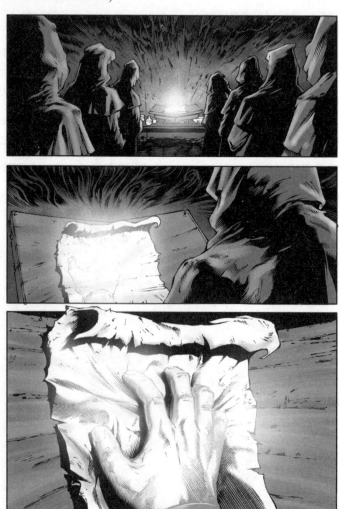

AN EXCERPT FROM

The Wishsong of Shannara

BY TERRY BROOKS

If you haven't discovered the magic and adventure
contained within the world of Shannara,
begin now!

Here is the first chapter of
The Wishsong of Shannara by Terry Brooks,
also published by Orbit.

I

a CHANGE OF SEASONS WAS upon the Four Lands as late summer faded slowly into autumn. Gone were the long, still days of midyear where sweltering heat slowed the pace of life and there was a sense of having time enough for anything. Though summer's warmth lingered, the days had begun to shorten, the humid air to dry, and the memory of life's immediacy to reawaken. The signs of transition were all about. In the forests of Shady Vale, the leaves had already begun to turn.

Brin Ohmsford paused by the flowerbeds that bordered the front walkway of her home, losing herself momentarily in the crimson foliage of the old maple that shaded the yard beyond. It was a massive thing, its trunk broad and gnarled. Brin smiled. That old tree was the source of many childhood memories for her. Impulsively, she stepped off the walkway and moved over to the aged tree.

She was a tall girl—taller than her parents or her brother Jair, nearly as tall as Rone Leah—and although there was a delicate look to her slim body, she was as fit as any of them. Jair would argue the point of course, but that was only because Jair found it hard enough as it was to accept his role as the youngest. A girl, after all, was just a girl.

Her fingers touched the roughened trunk of the maple softly, caressing, and she stared upward into the tangle of limbs overhead. Long, black hair fell away from her face and there was no mistaking whose child she was. Twenty years ago, Eretria had looked exactly as her daughter looked now, from dusky skin and black eyes to soft, delicate features. All that Brin lacked was her mother's fire. Jair had gotten that. Brin had her father's temperament, cool, self-assured, and disciplined. In comparing his children one time—a time occasioned by one of Jair's more reprehensible misadventures—Wil Ohmsford had remarked rather ruefully that the difference between the two was that Jair was apt to do anything, while Brin was also apt to do it, but only after thinking it through first. Brin still wasn't sure who had come out on the short end of that reprimand.

Her hands slipped back to her sides. She remembered the time she had used the wishsong on the old tree. She had still been a child, experimenting with the Elven magic. It had been midsummer and she had used the wishsong to turn the tree's summer green to autumn crimson; in her child's mind, it seemed perfectly all right to do so, since red was a far prettier color than green. Her father had been furious; it had taken almost three years for the tree to come back again after the shock to its system. That had been the last time either she or Jair had used the magic when their parents were about.

"Brin, come help me with the rest of the packing, please."

It was her mother calling. She gave the old maple a final pat and turned toward the house.

Her father had never fully trusted the Elven magic. A little more than twenty years earlier he had used the Elfstones given him by the Druid Allanon in his efforts to protect the Elven Chosen Amberle Elessedil in her quest for the Bloodfire. Use of the Elven magic had changed him; he had known it even then, though not known how. It was only after Brin was born, and later Jair, that it became apparent what had been done. It was not Wil Ohmsford who would manifest the change the magic had wrought; it was his children. They were the ones who would carry within them the visible effects of the magic—they, and perhaps generations of Ohmsfords to come, although there was no way of ascertaining yet that they would carry within them the magic of the wishsong.

Brin had named it the wishsong. Wish for it, sing for it, and it was yours. That was how it had seemed to her when she had first discovered that she possessed the power. She learned early that she could affect the behavior of living things with her song. She could change that old maple's leaves. She could soothe an angry dog. She could bring a wild bird to light on her wrist. She could make herself a part of any living thing—or make it a part of her. She wasn't sure how she did it; it simply happened. She would sing, the music and the words coming as they always did, unplanned, unrehearsed—as if it were the most natural thing in the world. She was always aware of what she was singing, yet at the same time heedless, her mind caught up in feelings of indescribable sensation. They would sweep through her, drawing her in, making her somehow new again, and the wish would come to pass.

It was the gift of the Elven magic—or its curse. The latter was how her father had viewed it when he had discovered she possessed it. Brin knew that, deep inside, he was frightened of what the Elfstones could do and what he had felt them do to him. After Brin had caused the family dog to chase its tail until it nearly dropped and had wilted an entire garden of vegetables, her father had been quick to reassert his decision that the Elfstones would never be used again by anyone. He had hidden them, telling no one where they could be found, and hidden they had remained ever since. At least, that was what her father thought. She was not altogether certain. One time, not too many months earlier, when there was mention of the hidden Elfstones, Brin had caught Jair smiling rather smugly. He would not admit to anything, of course, but she knew how difficult it was to keep anything hidden from her brother, and she suspected he had found the hiding place.

Rone Leah met her at the front door, tall and rangy, rust brown hair loose about his shoulders and tied back with a broad headband. Mischievous gray eyes narrowed appraisingly. "How about lending a hand, huh? I'm doing all the work and I'm not even a member of the family, for cat's sake!"

"As much time as you spend here, you ought to be," she chided. "What's left to be done?"

"Just these cases to be carried out—that should finish it." A gathering of leather trunks and smaller bags stood stacked in the entry. Rone picked up the largest. "I think your mother wants you in the bedroom."

He disappeared down the walkway and Brin moved through her home toward the back bedrooms. Her parents were getting ready to depart on their annual fall pilgrimage to the outlying communities south of Shady Vale, a journey that would keep them gone from their home for better than two weeks. Few Healers possessed the skills of Wil Ohmsford, and not one could be found within five hundred miles of the Vale. So twice a year, in the spring and fall, her father traveled down to the outlying villages, lending his services where they were needed. Eretria always accompanied him, a skilled aide to her husband by now, trained nearly as thoroughly as he in the care of the sick and injured. It was a journey they need not have made—would not, in fact, had they been less conscientious than they were. Others would not have gone. But Brin's parents were governed by a strong sense of duty. Healing was the profession to which both had dedicated their lives, and they did not take their commitment to it lightly.

While they were gone on these trips of mercy, Brin was left to watch over Jair. On this occasion, Rone Leah had traveled down from the highlands to watch over them both.

Brin's mother looked up from the last of her packing and smiled as Brin entered the bedroom. Long black hair fell loosely about her shoulders, and she brushed it back from a face that looked barely older than Brin's.

"Have you seen your brother? We're almost ready to leave."

Brin shook her head. "I thought he was with father. Can I help you with anything?"

Eretria nodded, took Brin by the shoulders, and pulled her down next to her on the bed. "I want you to promise me something, Brin. I don't want you to use the wishsong while your father and I are gone—you or your brother."

Brin smiled. "I hardly use it at all anymore." Her dark eyes searched her mother's dusky face.

"I know. But Jair does, even if he thinks I don't know about it. In any case, while we are gone, your father and I don't want either of you using it even a single time. Do you understand?"

Brin hesitated. Her father understood that the Elven magic was a part of his children, but he did not accept that it was either a good or necessary part. You are intelligent, talented people just as you are, he would tell them. You have no need of tricks and artifices to advance yourselves. Be who and what you can without the song. Eretria had echoed that advice, although she seemed to recognize more readily than he that they were likely to ignore it when discretion suggested that they could.

In Jair's case, unfortunately, discretion seldom entered into the picture. Jair was both impulsive and distressingly headstrong; when it came to use of the wishsong, he was inclined to do exactly as he pleased—as long as he could safely get away with it.

Still, the Elven magic worked differently with Jair . . .

"Brin?"

Her thoughts scattered. "Mother, I don't see what difference it makes if Jair wants to play around with the wishsong. It's just a toy."

Eretria shook her head. "Even a toy can be dangerous if used unwisely. Besides, you ought to know enough of the Elven magic by now to appreciate the fact that it is never harmless. Now listen to me. You and your brother are both grown beyond the age when you need your mother and father looking over your shoulder. But a little advice is still necessary now and then. I don't want you using the magic while we're gone. It draws attention where it's not needed. Promise me that you won't use it—and that you will keep Jair from using it as well."

Brin nodded slowly. "It's because of the rumors of the black walkers, isn't it?" She had heard the stories. They talked about it all the time down at the inn these days. Black walkers—soundless, faceless things born of the dark magic, appearing out of nowhere. Some said it was the Warlock Lord and his minions come back again. "Is that what this is all about?"

"Yes." Her mother smiled at Brin's perceptiveness. "Now promise me."

Brin smiled back. "I promise."

Nevertheless, she thought it all a lot of nonsense.

The packing and loading took another thirty minutes, and then her parents were ready to depart. Jair reappeared, back from the inn where he had gone to secure a special sweet as a parting gift for his mother who was fond of such things, and good-byes were exchanged.

"Remember your promise, Brin," her mother whispered as she kissed her on the cheek and hugged her close.

Then the elder Ohmsfords were aboard the wagon in which they would make their journey and moving slowly up the dusty roadway.

Brin watched them until they were out of sight.

Brin, Jair, and Rone Leah went hiking that afternoon in the forests of the Vale, and it was late in the day when at last they turned homeward. By then, the sun had begun to dip beneath the rim of the Vale and the forest shadows of midday to lengthen slowly into evening. It was an hour's walk to the hamlet, but both Ohmsfords and the highlander had come this way so often before that they could have navigated the forest trails even in blackest night. They proceeded at a leisurely pace, enjoying the close of what had been an altogether beautiful autumn day.

"Let's fish tomorrow," Rone suggested. He grinned at Brin. "With weather like this, it won't matter if we catch anything or not."

The oldest of the three, he led the way through the trees, the worn and battered scabbard bearing the Sword of Leah strapped crosswise to his back, a vague outline beneath his hunting cloak. Once carried by the heir-apparent to the throne of Leah, it had long since outlived that purpose and been replaced. But Rone had always admired the old blade, borne years earlier by his great-grandfather Menion Leah when he had gone in search of the Sword of Shannara. Since Rone admired the weapon so, his father had given it to him, a small symbol of his standing as a Prince of Leah—even if he were its youngest prince.

Brin looked over at him and frowned. "You seem to be forgetting something. Tomorrow is the day we set aside for the house repairs we promised father we would make while he was away. What about that?"

He shrugged cheerfully. "Another day for the repairs—they'll keep."

"I think we should do some exploring along the rim of the Vale," Jair Ohmsford interjected. He was lean and wiry and had his father's face with its Elven features—narrow eyes, slanted eyebrows, and ears pointed slightly beneath a thatch of unruly blond hair. "I think we should see if we can find any sign of the Mord Wraiths."

Rone laughed. "Now what do you know about the walkers, tiger?" It was his pet name for Jair.

"As much as you, I'd guess. We hear the same stories in the Vale that you hear in the highlands," the Valeman replied. "Black walkers,

Mord Wraiths—things that steal out of the dark. They talk about it down at the inn all the time."

Brin glanced at her brother reprovingly. "That's all they are, too—just stories."

Jair looked at Rone. "What do you think?"

To Brin's surprise, the highlander shrugged. "Maybe. Maybe not."

She was suddenly angry. "Rone, there have been stories like this ever since the Warlock Lord was destroyed, and none of them has ever contained a word of truth. Why would it be any different this time?"

"I don't know that it would. I just believe in being careful. Remember, they didn't believe the stories of the Skull Bearers in Shea Ohmsford's time either—until it was too late."

"That's why I think we ought to have a look around," Jair repeated.

"For what purpose exactly?" Brin pressed, her voice hardening. "On the chance that we might find something as dangerous as these things are supposed to be? What would you do then—call on the wishsong?"

Jair flushed. "If I had to, I would. I could use the magic . . ."

She cut him short. "The magic is nothing to play around with, Jair. How many times do I have to tell you that?"

"I just said that . . ."

"I know what you said. You think that the wishsong can do anything for you and you're sadly mistaken. You had better pay attention to what father says about not using the magic. Someday, it's going to get you into a lot of trouble."

Her brother stared at her. "What are you so angry about?"

She was angry, she realized, and it was serving no purpose. "I'm sorry," she apologized. "I made mother a promise that neither of us would use the wishsong while she and father were away on this trip. I suppose that's why it upsets me to hear you talking about tracking Mord Wraiths."

Now there was a hint of anger in Jair's blue eyes. "Who gave you the right to make a promise like that for me, Brin?"

"No one, I suppose, but mother . . ."

"Mother doesn't understand . . ."

"Hold on, for cat's sake!" Rone Leah held up his hands imploringly. "Arguments like this make me glad that I'm staying down at the inn and not up at the house with you two. Now let's forget all this and get back to the original subject. Do we go fishing tomorrow or not?"

"We go fishing," Jair voted.

"We go fishing," Brin agreed. "After we finish at least some of the repairs."

They walked in silence for a time, Brin still brooding over what she viewed as Jair's increasing infatuation with the uses of the wishsong. Her mother was right; Jair practiced using the magic whenever he got the chance. He saw less danger in its use than Brin did because it worked differently for him. For Brin, the wishsong altered appearance and behavior in fact, but for Jair it was only an illusion. When he used the magic, things only seemed to happen. That gave him greater latitude in its use and encouraged experimentation. He did it in secret, but he did it nevertheless. Even Brin wasn't entirely sure what he had learned to do with it.

Afternoon faded altogether and evening settled in. A full moon hung above the eastern horizon like a white beacon, and stars began to wink into view. With the coming of night, the air began to cool rapidly, and the smells of the forest turned crisp and heavy with the fragrance of drying leaves. All about rose the hum of insects and night birds.

"I think we should fish the Rappahalladran," Jair announced suddenly.

No one said anything for a moment. "I don't know," Rone answered finally. "We could fish the ponds in the Vale just as well."

Brin glanced over at the highlander quizzically. He sounded worried.

"Not for brook trout," Jair insisted. "Besides, I want to camp out in the Duln for a night or two."

"We could do that in the Vale."

"The Vale is practically the same as the backyard," Jair pointed out, growing a bit irritated. "At least the Duln has a few places we haven't explored before. What are you frightened about?"

"I'm not frightened of anything," the highlander replied defensively. "I just think . . . Look, why don't we talk about this later. Let me tell you what happened to me on the way out here. I almost managed to get myself lost. There was this wolfdog . . ."

Brin dropped back a pace as they talked, letting them walk on ahead. She was still puzzled by Rone's unexpected reluctance to make even a short camping trip into the Duln—a trip they had all made dozens of times before. Was there something beyond the Vale of which they need be frightened? She frowned, remembering the concern voiced by her mother. Now it was Rone as well. The highlander had not been as quick as she to discount as rumors those stories of the Mord Wraiths. In fact, he had been unusually restrained. Normally, Rone would have laughed such stories off as so much nonsense, just as she had done. Why hadn't he done so this time? It was possible, she realized, that he had some cause to believe it wasn't a laughing matter.

Half an hour passed, and the lights of the village began to appear through the forest trees. It was dark now, and they picked their way along the path with the aid of the moon's bright light. The trail dipped downward into the sheltered hollow where the village proper sat, broadening as it went from a footpath to a roadway. Houses appeared; from within, the sound of voices could be heard. Brin felt the first hint of weariness slip over her. It would be good to crawl into the comfort of her bed and give herself over to a good night's sleep.

They walked down through the center of Shady Vale, passing by the old inn that had been owned and managed by the Ohmsford family for so many generations past. The Ohmsfords still owned the establishment, but no longer lived there—not since the passing of Shea and Flick. Friends of the family managed the inn these days, sharing the earnings and expenses with Brin's parents. Her father had never really been comfortable living at the inn, Brin knew, feeling no real connection with its business, preferring his own life as a Healer to that of innkeeper. Only Jair showed any real interest in the happenings of the inn and that was because he liked to go down to listen to the tales carried to Shady Vale by travelers passing through— tales filled with adventure enough to satisfy the spirit of the restless Valeman.

The inn was busy this night, its broad double-doors flung open, the lights within falling over tables and a long bar crowded with travelers and village folk, laughing and joking and passing the cool autumn evening with a glass or two of ale. Rone grinned over his shoulder at Brin and shook his head. No one was anxious for this day to end.

Moments later, they reached the Ohmsford home, a stone and mortar cottage set back within the trees on a small knoll. They were halfway up the cobblestone walk that ran through a series of hedgerows and flowering plum to the front door when Brin brought them to a sudden halt.

There was a light in the window of the front room.

"Did either of you leave a lamp burning when we left this morning?" she asked quietly, already knowing the answer. Both shook their heads.

"Maybe someone stopped in for a visit," Rone suggested.

Brin looked at him. "The house was locked."

They stared at each other wordlessly for a moment, a vague sense of uneasiness starting to take hold. Jair, however, was feeling none of it.

"Well, let's go on in and see who's there," he declared and started forward.

Rone put a hand on his shoulder and pulled him back. "Just a moment, tiger. Let's not be too hasty."

Jair pulled free, glanced again at the light, then looked back at Rone. "Who do you think's waiting in there—one of the walkers?"

"Will you stop that nonsense!" Brin ordered sharply.

Jair smirked. "That's who you think it is, don't you? One of the walkers, come to steal us away!"

"Good of them to put a light on for us," Rone commented dryly.

They stared again at the light in the front window, undecided.

"Well, we can't just stand out here all night," Rone said finally. He reached back over his shoulder and pulled free the Sword of Leah. "Let's have a look. You two stay behind me. If anything happens, get back to the inn and bring some help." He hesitated. "Not that anything is going to happen."

They proceeded up the walk to the front door and stopped, listening. The house was silent. Brin handed Rone the key to the door and they stepped inside. The anteway was pitch black, save for a sliver of yellow light that snaked down the short hallway leading in. They hesitated a moment, then passed silently down the hall and stepped into the front room.

It was empty.

"Well, no Mord Wraiths here," Jair announced at once. "Nothing here except . . ."

He never finished. A huge shadow stepped into the light from the darkened drawing room beyond. It was a man over seven feet tall, cloaked all in black. A loose cowl was pulled back to reveal a lean, craggy face that was weathered and hard. Black beard and hair swept down from his face and head, coarse and shot through with streaks of gray. But it was the eyes that drew them, deep-set and penetrating from within the shadow of his great brow, seeming to see everything, even that which was hidden.

Rone Leah brought up the broadsword hurriedly, and the stranger's hand lifted from out of the robes.

"You won't need that."

The highlander hesitated, stared momentarily into the other's dark eyes, then dropped the sword blade downward again. Brin and Jair stood frozen in place, unable to turn and run or to speak.

"There is nothing to be frightened of," the stranger's deep voice rumbled.

None of the three felt particularly reassured by that, yet all relaxed slightly when the dark figure made no further move to approach. Brin glanced hurriedly at her brother and found Jair watching the stranger intently, as if puzzling something through. The stranger looked at the boy, then at Rone, then at her.

"Does not one of you know me?" he murmured softly.

There was momentary silence, and then suddenly Jair nodded.

"Allanon!" he exclaimed, excitement reflected in his face. "You're Allanon!"